VANCOUVER

The History of Canadian Cities

VANCOUVER

An Illustrated History

Patricia E. Roy

James Lorimer & Company, Publishers
and
National Museum of Man,
National Museums of Canada
Toronto 1980

Copyright © 1980 by National Museums of Canada. Crown Copyright reserved. No part of this book may be reproduced or transmitted in any form or by any means, electronic or mechanical, including photocopying, or by any information storage or retrieval system, without permission in writing from the publisher.

ISBN 0-88862-388-7 cloth

Design: Don Fernley

6 5 4 3 2 1   80 81 82 83 84 85 86

Canadian Cataloguing in Publication Data

Roy, Patricia E., 1939-
Vancouver: an illustrated history
(The History of Canadian cities)

Includes index.
ISBN 0-88862-388-7 bd.

1. Vancouver, B.C. — History. I. Title: Vancouver: an illustrated history. II. Series.
FC3847.4.R69   971.1′33   C80-094674-X
F1089.5.V22R69

James Lorimer & Company, Publishers
Egerton Ryerson Memorial Building
35 Britain Street
Toronto M5A 1R7, Ontario

Printed and bound in Canada

Table of Contents

List of Maps

Appendix
List of Tables

Preface and Acknowledgements

This is not the definitive history of Vancouver; rather it is an attempt to sketch and explain certain aspects of the city's development. The topics examined have been selected to show some of Vancouver's unique characteristics and to provide material for comparison with other cities in the series. Such recurring themes as Vancouver's relationships with her British Columbia and prairie hinterland, her dependence on the provincial government, and the concern of local politicians with the preservation of law, order, and morality have received particular attention.

Researching and writing this volume has been a frustration and a joy. The sources for the city's history are rich and many episodes in it fascinating, but it was impossible to explore them in the depth many deserve. Students of Vancouver's history need not fear a lack of interesting and significant subjects.

The joy of historical research is partly the excitement of finding forgotten information; it is especially the pleasure of working with friendly and helpful archivists, librarians, readers, and editors. The staffs of the Vancouver City Archives, the Historical Photographs Division of the Vancouver Public Library, the Provincial Archives of British Columbia, the Legislative Library of British Columbia, the University of Victoria Library, the Public Archives of Canada, and the Directorate of History of the Department of National Defence are especially deserving of thanks. Robert A.J. McDonald, Robert Watt and other "anonymous" readers perused a draft of the manuscript, offered good suggestions, and caught several errors. Ann Cowan and her associates, notably Anne Carscallen who did photographic research, have cheerfully assisted in preparing the manuscript for publication while William Law efficiently saw it through the press. My colleague and general editor, Alan Artibise gave excellent advice at all stages of the research and writing, arranged for the production of maps, and patiently awaited the results. My parents provided warm hospitality and good companionship particularly while I was doing research in Vancouver. It is to them that I dedicate this volume.

Patricia E. Roy
July, 1980

Foreword
The History of Canadian Cities Series

The History of Canadian Cities Series is a project of the History Division, National Museum of Man (National Museums of Canada). The project was begun in 1977 in response to a continuing demand for more popular publications to complement the already well-established scholarly publication programmes of the Museum. The purpose of this series is to offer the general public a stimulating insight into Canada's urban past. Over the next several years, the Museum, in cooperation with James Lorimer and Company, plans to publish a number of individual volumes dealing with such varied communities as Halifax and Victoria, Kitchener and Quebec City, Ottawa and Montreal.

It is the hope of the National Museum of Man that the publication of these books will provide the public with information on Canadian cities in an attractive, stimulating and highly readable form. At the same time, the plan of the series is to have authors follow a standard format and the result, it is anticipated, will be a systematic, interpretative, and comprehensive account of the urban experience in many Canadian communities. Eventually, as new volumes are completed, *The History of Canadian Cities Series* will be a major step along the path to a general and comparative study of Canada's urban development.

The form chosen for this series — the individual urban biography — is based on the assumption that a community's history has meaning not discernible by a study of fragmentary portions only; that the totality of the urban experience is usually not present in thematic studies. The volumes in this series attempt to see the community as a whole and to relate the parts to a large context. The series is also based on the belief that, while each city has a distinct personality that deserves to be discovered, the volumes must also provide data that will lift the narrative of a given city's experience to the level where it will elucidate questions that are of concern to Canadians generally. These include such matters as ethnic relationships, regionalism, provincial-municipal interaction, social mobility, labour-management relationships, urban planning, and general economic development.

In this volume, Patricia E. Roy examines the city with the country's most spectacular setting. This account of Vancouver's development makes abundantly clear, however, that the city's history is also engaging and, at times, dramatic. Although a young city even by Canadian standards, Vancouver has in its brief history become Canada's third largest metropolis and a port of note in the international sphere. Dr. Roy is an Associate Professor in the Department of History at the University of Victoria.

Like other volumes in this series, this volume includes over a hundred historical photographs. This illustrative material not only enhances the text but also plays an essential part in recreating the past. While the photographs cannot by themselves replace the written word, they can be used as a primary source in a way equivalent to more traditional sources. The fine collection of photographs contained in this volume captures images of a wide variety of situations in Vancouver, allowing a later generation to better understand the forms, structures, fashions, and group interactions of an earlier period.

Alan F. J. Artibise
General Editor

Already available in this series:
Alan Artibise, *Winnipeg* (1977)
Max Foran, *Calgary* (1978)

Leonard Frank in the Rockies, c. 1924.

The Photographers

Turn-of-the-century Vancouver was a photographer's paradise. Not only were there new techniques with which to experiment, but for many, a new environment to record for relatives far away. The city's mild climate, varied geography, and lush vegetation created spectacular scenery that captured the photographer's imagination.

Particular natural settings have been favourite photographers' subjects throughout Vancouver's history. The more prominent of these are English Bay Beach, the Burrard Inlet harbour area, and Stanley Park, where generations of Vancouverites and visitors alike have been photographed in front of the "Hollow Tree". Vancouver's more scenic locations served more than eager photographers; many became favourite recreational areas and some were also centres of commerce.

The photographs of Vancouverites at work and play collected to accompany this social history were found in public institutions with formally designated photo archives, in informal collections in the community, and in the photographic collections of businesses which have been operating in Vancouver for generations. The bulk of the photographs, however, come from the collections at the Vancouver Public Library and the Vancouver City Archives. The former collection was initiated by Ron D'Altroy, the latter by the late Major J.S. Matthews.

The historical photographs in this book are the work of a number of early Vancouver photographers including Stuart Thomson, Richard Broadbridge, H.T. Devine, Philip Timms, and Leonard Frank. Timms and Frank, whose work is most prominently represented in this volume, deserve special mention. Philip Timms arrived in Vancouver from Ontario with his family in 1898, drawn to the West Coast by the prosperity resulting from the Klondike gold rush. Soon the Timms family established a printing business. Learning the fledgling art of photography from an older brother, Timms worked for a time for Edward Brothers Commercial Photographers, represented the Eastman Kodak Company, and established his own print and photography shop. The era of 1900-1910 was the period most carefully documented by Timms. This was due in part to the picture postcard craze during which everything possible was photographed. When the craze died out, he focussed his camera on reflections of people participating in urban life. Timms' work, located largely in the Vancouver Public Library, is a valuable documentation of the everyday activities of early Vancouverites.

Leonard Frank, a German immigrant, won his first camera in a raffle at a mining camp near Alberni on Vancouver Island. He soon decided that photography was his calling and travelled to Vancouver to establish Leonard Frank Photos. Known as an "all-round" photographer, Leonard Frank was a commercial, industrial, and portrait photographer. His logging photographs are world famous, and one of his photographs of Burrard Inlet appeared on a 1938 Canadian stamp. His attention to detail in his images of people at work creates a matchless record of the workplace. It is not surprising that the Frank collection has been described as one of the most significant in Canada. Recognizing the historical importance of the Frank collection, Mr. Otto Landauer, Leonard Frank's successor, contributed many Frank photos to the Vancouver Public Library where they form the cornerstone of the historical photographs collection.

A final note. Many of the photographs in this book were originally made from glass plate negatives. Sometimes cracks from these very fragile plates appear in the photographs. Such flaws, together with occasional unclear images and obvious poses are reminders of the recent evolution of photographic technology and the constraints under which early photographers worked.

Anne Carscallen

Oxen hauling logs in the 1880s.

An early view of Vancouver, c. 1893.

In this late 1880s scene of Burrard Inlet, an outbound trans-Pacific steamer passes a renowned coastal vessel, the Hudson's Bay Company's sidewheeler, the S.S. Beaver. In the background are the majestic Lions peaks.

Introduction

"By Sea and Land We Prosper"

Man did not make Vancouver's outstanding feature — its spectacular setting. On a clear day, the North Shore mountains, especially the Lions whose twin peaks symbolically guard city and harbour, dominate and seem within touching distance. When rain clouds hide the mountains, the sea is still present. When the sea is obscured, whining foghorns remind Vancouver of its maritime location. So too does the moderate climate. Scorching summer weather is as rare as an extended period of snowy cold, but a seemingly constant rain may come at any season.[1] Yet, the rain also nurtures the rich forests of coastal British Columbia from which the city has always drawn much of its wealth.

The rain also represents a link between mountains and sea. Clouds, after drifting westward across the Pacific picking up moisture, are forced to discharge their cargo when they meet the mountain barrier. Unlike the mountains, which long isolated British Columbia from the rest of Canada and still have psychological and economic effects, the waters surrounding Vancouver on three sides draw the city into contact with the world and are its *raison d'être*. The city's southern boundary, the Fraser River, home of a sometimes prosperous fishery, carries rich alluvial soil to the agricultural land of its delta and gives easy access to the sea for the lumber mills and other industries along its banks. The northern boundary, the narrow and deep waters of Burrard Inlet, separates the city from the mountains and provides miles of sheltered harbour. To the west, beyond the beaches of English Bay and Kitsilano, beyond the Gulf Islands and Vancouver Island, lies the open Pacific and the markets of the world. Not without reason did the city fathers choose as Vancouver's motto "By Sea and Land We Prosper."

The sea, its salmon and mollusks, gave a livelihood to coastal Indians whose culture flourished at Locarno Beach and Marpole as early as 500 B.C. By the time Europeans arrived, the Indian population was concentrated on the north shore, at Musqueam at the mouth of the Fraser River, and at Kitsilano at the entrance to False Creek. The Indian Reserves Allotment Commission of the late 1870s confirmed the confinement of the Indians to these tiny areas. Henceforth, the Indians were largely limited to the margins of society, although they participated economically in the larger community as commercial fishermen and cannery workers, as sawmill employees and longshoremen.[2]

The new industries developed long after the first European contact with the area, for explorers had not been noticeably impressed and made no significant impact. Captain George Vancouver who came in 1792 only observed that Burrard Inlet's moderately high and rocky shore was "well covered with trees of large growth, principally of the pine tribe."[3] The next Englishmen to record a visit, Captain G.H. Richards and the crew of H.M.S. *Plumper* in 1859, examined Burrard Inlet as a possible outer defence for New Westminster, the new capital of the gold colony, British Columbia. The gold rush, however, was a phenomenon of the Fraser Valley and of the commercial centre of the north Pacific coast, Victoria, and the gold seekers passed Burrard Inlet by.

Nevertheless, Captain Richards' discovery of coal led to at least two abortive mining ventures and, indirectly, to the arrival of the first permanent European settlers. In 1862, an English potter, John Morton, seeing samples of Burrard Inlet coal at New Westminster, associated the presence of coal with potting clay and walked the thirteen miles to the Inlet where he found that gravel, not clay, surrounded the coal. Despite his disappointment, Morton returned to the Inlet with two partners, Samuel Brighouse and William Hailstone. Together, they pre-empted land near present day Stanley Park and built a brickyard. The lack of local markets doomed the enterprise. The population of British Columbia and Vancouver Island was small and lumber was a cheap and readily available building material throughout the settled areas of southern Vancouver Island, the Fraser Valley, and the Cariboo. Undaunted, Brighouse later established a farm on his pre-emption, added to his land holdings, and died a wealthy man.[4]

The trees Captain Vancouver noted gave rise to Vancouver's most important industry. During the 1860s and 1870s, several sawmills shipped lumber as far as Australia, South America, and South Africa and formed an industrial base for three small villages: Moodyville on the north side of the Inlet; Granville, the service centre for the inlet communities; and Hastings, site of the Hastings Saw Mill, on the south side. Granville, colloquially known as Gastown after its garrulous hotel-keeper, Captain John "Gassy Jack" Deighton, eventually became Vancouver.[5] The mills could only export their output by sea. Only by narrow, muddy trails to New Westminster did Burrard Inlet have any other contact with the rest of British Columbia. From New Westminster, it was possible to travel by Fraser River steamer to the head of navigation at Yale and hence by wagon road to the gold mining regions of the Cariboo, which by Confederation in 1871 were rapidly declining in importance.

Confederation, however, brought the promise of the end of isolation in the form of a transcontinental railway linking the Pacific seaboard with the railway system of Canada. Prolonged delays in construction and a complex, bitter debate over railway routes and terminal sites bedevilled Ottawa's relations with British Columbia in the 1870s. Within the province, the railway dispute produced a new chapter in the story of conflict between the Island and the Mainland. The John A. Macdonald government finally decided in 1879 that the railway would terminate at Burrard Inlet rather than cross to Esquimalt on Vancouver Island.

Granville's transformation from a community of a few hundred people living in homes slashed out of the forest to the metropolis of Vancouver, however, did not begin until 1884 when William Van Horne, Vice-president of the Canadian Pacific Railway, announced that the railway would be extended twelve miles westward from its statutory terminus at Port Moody at the head of the Inlet. Even before visiting the Inlet in August, Van Horne had decided that the limited amount of flat land for industry and railyards, the tidal mud flats, and the need for ships to go through the treacherous Second Narrows to reach it made Port Moody an unsuitable terminus.

A first class harbour was essential to the CPR, whose local traffic would be light for some years. In association with Pacific steamers, the CPR could obtain through traffic from Asia to the east coast of North America and, in conjunction with Atlantic steamers, provide an "All-Red Route" linking Britain and her Asian and Australian colonies. Indeed, even before the driving of the last spike, the CPR arranged for chartered sailing ships to carry Japanese tea and other Asian products to Burrard Inlet. The success of these pioneer voyages led to a three-year contract between George B. Dodwell of Adamson, Bell and Company, a British shipping and exporting firm, and the railway. Dodwell named the line the Canadian Pacific Steamship Company and secured three former Cunard vessels to operate between the Orient and Burrard Inlet. By the time the *Abyssinia*, the first of these liners, reached Canada, Vancouver had replaced Port Moody as the terminus, and it was from the CPR wharf in Vancouver that the railway carried the *Abyssinia*'s cargo of tea, mail, silk, and general merchandise to Montreal, Chicago, and New York.[6]

While the CPR's need for a good harbour is obvious, the provincial government's motive in encouraging extension of the railway is less clear. A few weeks after the federal government relinquished its claim to railway lands west of Port Moody, the province announced that the lands were not open for sale. While visiting Montreal, Premier William Smithe had promised to hold them for the railway company until Van Horne could inspect the area. Van Horne agreed that if he could have the lands and "make reasonable arrangements with private holders of lands in that vicinity," the CPR would make Coal Harbour and English Bay its Pacific terminus.[7] After examining the site, Van Horne asked the province for approximately 11,000 acres including the Granville townsite and the north half of the Hastings reserve. He argued that the CPR could not afford to extend the line and build docks and other facilities without acquiring "sufficient property so situated as to be made immediately saleable for a sufficient amount to recoup the outlay

Indians making canoes at St. Paul's Mission, North Vancouver.

FIRST C.P.R. TRAIN ARRIVING IN VANCOUVER MAY 1887.

Vancouver celebrated Queen Victoria's Golden Jubilee and the arrival of the first CPR train on May 23, 1887.

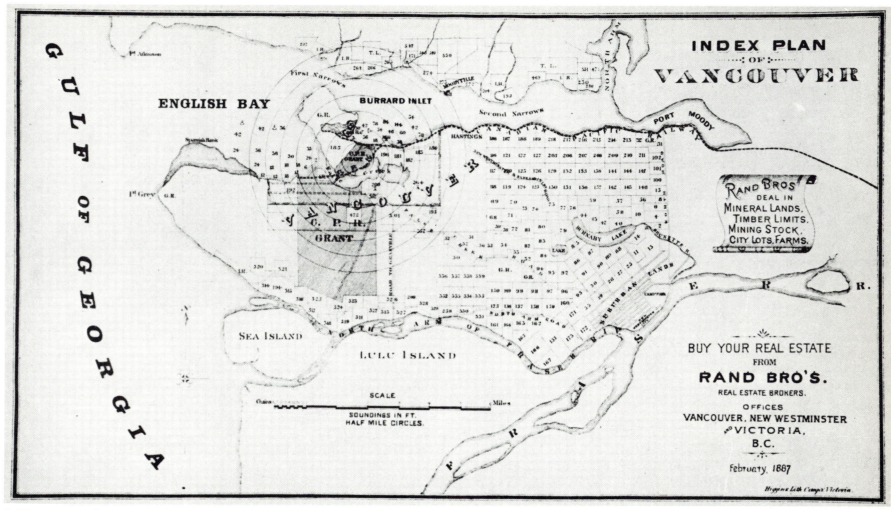

1 Vancouver in 1886

mentioned." Moreover, Van Horne claimed that the lands west of Port Moody would have been part of the overall land grant had the terminus been fixed at English Bay. Anticipating that the government was unlikely to be quite so generous, Van Horne privately informed Smithe that the CPR would accept less than 11,000 acres. The government donated all of its 39 lots at Granville plus 5,795 acres in District Lot 526 and 480 acres in District Lot 541. In total, the government gave the CPR more than 6,275 acres of crown land less two and a half acres in each of the two main parcels for public buildings and up to one-twentieth of the total for roads and other public works.[8]

Why was the province so anxious to give away crown land when the CPR was almost certain to come to Coal Harbour and English Bay? The most likely answer is that the crown hoped to make a quick profit from auction sales of its remaining lands in the area. Individual members of the government also saw an opportunity for private profit. John Robson, the Provincial Secretary, Minister of Finance and Agriculture, and Member of the Legislature for the New Westminster district, the constituency that included the future Vancouver, personally hoped "to realize on my 'Vancouver' lands."[9] Like most other private owners, Robson was pleased to donate a third of his holdings to the CPR as an inducement to extend the line. These private grants comprised about 200 acres.[10]

Not all private donors were eager to cooperate with the CPR, however. Squatters on the Granville townsite forced the company to accede to their demands for compensation or take them to court. And Port Moody land holders, who did not want the terminus moved, tried to prevent construction of the extension through their holdings by claiming that their town was the legal terminus. The CPR finally won its court cases, though, at one time, Van Horne threatened to carry the line out over the Inlet on trestles to by-pass stubborn land holders.[11]

John Robson may be called the father of Vancouver. In January 1886, while in the area looking for a school site, he told a public meeting of 250 Granville residents that they should incorporate as a city. Those present — about a quarter of the population — immediately chose a ten-man committee headed by R.H. Alexander, manager of the Hastings Saw Mill and a resident since 1870, to draw up a bill of incorporation. The committee consulted other city charters including that of the "boom" city of Winnipeg, a charter itself copied from Ontario models. They borrowed what they considered the best features of these charters and presented a draft bill to the Legislature. In addition, 124 "Vancouver" residents, including such oldtimers as L.A. Hamilton, the CPR's chief surveyor, and Dr. W.J. McGuigan, its medical superintendent, and newcomers including such real estate dealers as E.E. Rand, M.A. MacLean, W.E. Graveley, and F.C. Innes, petitioned the Legislature for incorporation. They cited the necessity of providing for the building of roads, streets, and bridges, and "the better preservation of law and order."[12]

The incorporation bill provoked a "spicy" debate since many of the charter's aspects were potentially controversial. Vancouver would be unique among British Columbia cities in having its own charter rather than being governed by the Municipal Act. Within the drafting committee disagreement arose about the means of electing the mayor; some citizens wanted election by Council rather than by the electorate at-large. There appears to have been no dispute over the principle of electing the aldermen from separate wards although in the first civic election they were chosen at large. The franchise, however, caused some discussion. Although based on property, it gave the vote to adult male and single female freeholders and to householders, pre-emptors, and leaseholders of six months' residence. Conforming to British Columbia custom, the only exceptions were Chinese and Indians. The corporation also had power to control gas and water companies and the erection of telephone and telegraph poles. At the same session the Legislature incorporated two water works companies and a street railway to serve Vancouver. Yet, the major focus of the Legislature's long debate was not these aspects of the charter but the city's name.[13]

In 1884, Van Horne suggested naming the city "Vancouver" since "Granville" gave no indication of its location. He thought Britons would remember Vancouver Island and Captain Vancouver from their school books and hence have an approximate idea of the city's locale. Many legislators argued that the proposed name would cause endless confusion with the Island and with Fort Vancouver in Washington Territory. Underlying this concern was the realization by Victoria MLAs and their friends that the capital city would soon be usurped as the province's commercial centre. This jealousy, however, did not

The Hastings Saw Mill, shown here about 1883, was one of the first industries of Burrard Inlet and, for some years after Vancouver's founding, a major employer.

prevent some of them from hedging their investments by buying Vancouver land at provincial government auctions. Their protest about the name was futile. John Robson had been converted to the name, and the government honoured the request of the "inhabitants of the Town of Granville" who wanted to be incorporated as the city of Vancouver.[14]

Following incorporation on April 6, 1886, the city held its first election on May 3. Almost all eligible voters turned out, and Constable J.M. Stewart was kept busy "restraining the combative instincts of the rougher portion of the community." The rivals for the mayor's office represented the city's old and new elements. R.H. Alexander was the candidate of the "old" element and the so-called "Victoria ring" of investors in Vancouver real estate and holders of charters for proposed utility companies. The Victoria investors did not hide their interest in the new municipal government. Premier Smithe, who owned at least one lot in Vancouver, personally campaigned on Alexander's behalf. About a hundred Victoria residents took advantage of a special Canadian Pacific Navigation Company excursion to vote and to look over lands the CPR was preparing to auction.

The "new element" was represented by M.A. MacLean. Like Alexander, MacLean was Scots-born and Ontario-raised, but he had arrived in Vancouver only in January 1886 after a brief sojourn in San Francisco. Before that he had farmed in the Qu'Appelle Valley and was in the wholesale business in Winnipeg before the real estate boom there collapsed. In Vancouver, MacLean was the partner of his brother-in-law, A.W. Ross, a Manitoba M.P., in a real estate firm. MacLean directed his election appeal to the working man. One of his election day dodgers alleged that Alexander did not consider Canadians to be much superior to Chinamen, that they required only a bowl of blackstrap and a piece of fat pork. Alexander's denial was lost in the wind as MacLean's supporters shouted, "No more blackstrap," "Winnipegers do your duty," and "Canadians for ever."[15]

The result was close; the count, slow. Five hours after the polls had closed, Postmaster Jonathan Miller, the returning officer, announced that MacLean had 242 votes; Alexander, 227. Pandemonium developed as the delighted crowd rushed to the Sunnyside Hotel where "artificial enthusiasm was pumped into them at the rate of fifteen cents a glass." Alexander's more sober supporters suggested that the election was illegal since neither MacLean's nominator nor at least a hundred of his supporters were eligible voters. A public meeting, chaired by J.M. Clute, opposed their petition as a disturbance to harmony and good feeling in the city and asked Alexander to have it withdrawn. No more was heard of the petition and MacLean remained mayor. Although Vancouver would remain the provincial government's legislative creature, it had shown its independence of the city of Victoria and its residents.[16]

In the aldermanic elections, L.A. Hamilton, who led the polls, represented the CPR but Vancouver was not a company town. The other aldermen were a mixed lot. Joseph Humphries, a carpenter by trade, had been at Burrard Inlet intermittently since 1862; Robert Balfour was a hotel proprietor; and Thomas Dunn, a hardware merchant. Illustrating the community's transient nature, two of the aldermen elected left before their terms expired at year's end.

The new council had much to do. It chose civic officials: a city clerk, a magistrate, an engineer, and a police chief. The most pressing need was a fire department, for the city was covered with stumps and other inflammable materials. Council agreed to have a volunteer fire department and authorized a public subscription to purchase uniforms. To induce residents to support the brigade, the fire company proposed to give the most generous donor the right to name it. Before the subscriptions were complete and before the company was named, clearing fires blew out of control on June 13, 1886 almost completely destroying the city and claiming at least eleven lives.[17]

The fire had some benefits. It hastened land clearing, destroyed ramshackle buildings on the old Granville Townsite, and gave invaluable publicity to the new city and the enthusiasm and optimism of its residents. The *Vancouver Advertiser's* first editorial after the fire proclaimed: "The location is here. Our harbour hasn't been destroyed, and Vancouver remains the terminus on the Pacific Coast of the Canadian Pacific Railway."[18] That editorial realized Vancouver's chief assets: nature's blessing of a fine harbour and Canada's gift of a transcontinental railway, which arrived on the eve of Queen Victoria's Golden Jubilee, May 23, 1887.

Chapter One

Laying the Foundations
1886-1897

Few of us came here for our health. We came to make money, to better our conditions. . . .[1]

Vancouver's residents were proud of having started to rebuild before the fire's embers were cold. Yet, for some years, the city was "not a very gorgeous place." Gradually, through the efforts of individuals, firms, and the civic government, an attractive and well-functioning modern city emerged. "We cannot afford to stand still," explained the *News*, "progress is our watchword, if we desire others to make their homes with us, we must give them streets and sidewalks, water and light, sewerage and protection from fire, schools and hospitals and all these essentials to our health, our prosperity and our comfort should be provided as rapidly as our means permit."[2] Although depression checked the city's development in the mid-1890s, the prevailing motif of Vancouver's first decade was remarkable growth and change during which the city's foundations were laid.

ECONOMIC GROWTH AND METROPOLITAN RELATIONSHIPS

If Vancouver was to grow, it required more than paved streets, pure water, electrical utilities and other modern amenities. It needed industry and it had to develop trade with a hinterland. Both the CPR and real estate agents recognized this and they dominated the efforts to promote civic growth. Both had land to sell, both were represented in the city government, and both agreed that what was economically good for them was good for the city as a whole. Their outlooks, however, were not identical. The CPR, seeking to "span the world," established a trans-Pacific trade as a means of generating traffic for its transconti-

nental railway. Local businessmen had more limited resources and horizons. Through advertising and bonuses they sought to encourage exploitation of the trade and resources of the provincial hinterland and the development of industry within Vancouver. At the best of times, loosening Victoria's long-established grip on provincial trade and attracting capital for new industries were difficult tasks, but in the depression of the early 1890s, they were almost impossible. Thus, real estate remained the most visible economic activity in Vancouver's first decade.

The anonymous early visitor who observed more real estate agencies than retail stores was not grossly exaggerating. In 1887 there were sixteen real estate firms and twelve grocers;[3] in 1890, fifty real estate agents and forty-two grocers. The real estate men fell into two basic groups: those mainly selling off their own holdings and those acting chiefly as agents for others. Their major common objective was to develop the city and make their individual fortunes.

The CPR was the largest single land owner but individual speculators had extensive holdings. Some, such as Samuel Brighouse, had owned land in the area since the 1860s, and a few had acquired crown grants in the 1870s and early 1880s. Most began acquiring property in 1884. That summer, a number of Victoria businessmen, some in association with A. W. Ross, who had made and lost a fortune in the Winnipeg land boom, began buying land around Coal Harbour, English Bay, and False Creek.[4] Once the CPR selected its bonus lands, Victoria residents added to their holdings at government auctions and some, such as the Oppenheimer Brothers, established their own real estate firms in the city.

The railway's arrival created quick, handsome profits. Prices rose as much as 200 per cent within the year and stories of rapidly increasing land values continued. At the end of 1890, the *News-Advertiser* reported the story of lots bought in July at an average price of $53.70 selling in December for an average of $184.37. Rand Brothers advertised that average prices in the business district had steadily risen from $50 a front foot in 1886 to $500 in 1891. By 1896, lots the CPR had sold in 1886 for $1,200 were selling for $10,000 to $20,000 depending on location.[5]

The depression of the mid-1890s created much unemployment and reduced the demand for Vancouver property, but the city escaped the collapse of land values that beset Winnipeg in the 1880s and 1890s. Although investors from Britain, the United States, and Germany put money into Vancouver land, no comparable boom occurred. Indeed, Vancouver prices were low by the standards of western North America. The *News-Advertiser* reported in 1890 that "here an acre at a certain distance from the post office can be purchased at the same price demanded for a similarly situated lot in Tacoma." Moreover, the CPR could afford to control the sale of its lands, and to discourage speculators it usually demanded one-third down and full payment within the year. To encourage development, it offered rebates to those who built within a year.[6] Other vendors might offer slightly easier payment terms but most major dealers did not depart from the CPR's pattern. Thus, little, if any, land was held on small margins.

Real estate was big business but it could not be sustained without economic growth. In addition to the existing sawmills and the CPR Vancouver needed new industries to provide permanent employment once the streets were built, the sewers laid, and the post-fire building boom complete. In 1890, the construction industry employed 700 men; the lumber mills, 885. The substantial increase in the lumber industry since 1886 was itself a product of the building boom rather than any increase in outside markets.[7] Despite an optimistic forecast that "smoke stacks will soon be much more common than telegraph poles," it was clear that Vancouver required manufacturers. "If we defer doing anything until the place grows," warned the *News-Advertiser*, "we shall never be called to take action, because we shall see our town stagnant and more people leaving than new arrivals coming in."[8] For the real estate men and merchants who

dominated City Council, sustained growth was essential if their businesses were to thrive.

Advertising local assets and the Interior's mineral resources to outside investors and potential immigrants was one means of promoting development. The timing was excellent for just as Vancouver was emerging prospectors were beginning to find the rich lodes of silver and lead that would make the Kootenays famous. The emphasis on the hinterland as well as the city proper illustrates Vancouver's metropolitan aspirations. Professional publicists in eastern Canada and the United States were eager to sell their services, but since the object of the exercise was to encourage local trade, the city subsidized local publications.[9] It bought a thousand pamphlets compiled by M. Picken and published in April 1887. This *City of Vancouver, British Columbia Handbook* forecast that Vancouver would "become the metropolis of the west, the London of the Pacific," and boasted of a 1600 per cent increase in population within the city's first year. It then presented an inventory of the city's assets, industries, businesses, churches, societies, and people. To promote hinterland growth, the city paid the printing and mailing costs of Mayor David Oppenheimer's pamphlet, *The Mineral Resources of British Columbia: Practical Hints for Capitalists and Intending Settlers with Appendix Containing the Mineral Laws of the Province and the Dominion of Canada*, and in 1890 spent $5,000 for 6,000 copies of R.E. Gosnell's *British Columbia a Digest of Reliable Information*, a volume dealing almost exclusively with provincial agricultural and mining prospects.[10] To interest potential British immigrants, the city sent a year's subscription to local newspapers to 350 workingmen's clubs in the United Kingdom and arranged to have the publishers print occasional general statistical articles about the city. The Board of Trade was also keen to advertise the city but was reluctant to spend money. It carefully debated spending $200 to have a Welsh lecturer include Vancouver in his illustrated lectures on Canada before deciding against it. The Board's annual report, however, contained considerable information about economic activities and prospects in the city and province and was itself a useful advertising device.

Advertising could draw attention to Vancouver's potential but city fathers and ratepayers believed new industries had to be encouraged with direct bonuses, indirect subsidies such as

One of the first steam logging railways in British Columbia carried logs from the nearby forests to the log dump at Kitsilano, c. 1890.

municipal tax exemptions or cheap water, and sometimes, both. Like elected officials elsewhere in Canada, they saw no conflict in using public funds to promote private industry. Nevertheless, most ratepayers agreed with Mayor David Oppenheimer that the city "should proceed with caution but not with timidity" in aiding new industry, and not all industrial projects received aid. Plans to bonus a flour mill, paper mill, woolen mill, an iron and steel works, and a shipyard did not get very far either because their establishment seemed inevitable given Vancouver's location or because those advocating these schemes could not present firm ideas. But when an energetic entrepreneur promoted his project well, ratepayers responded enthusiastically. Between 1887 and 1891 they overwhelmingly approved the sale of $25,000 worth of city debentures to bonus a smelter; the grant of a $30,000 bonus, tax exemption, and free water to a sugar refinery; and the issue of $100,000 worth of debentures to subsidize a graving dock.[11]

Neither civic subsidies nor enthusiasm could guarantee success to new industries. The first subsidized project, a smelter, failed before the city had to pay its bonus even though silver, lead, and copper were then being discovered in the Kootenay. Mayor Oppenheimer, confident that a smelter would "centralize the mining industry of the Province at Vancouver," conceived the idea of a smelter bonus; a "largely attended" public meeting unanimously endorsed the principle; and the ratepayers confirmed it. Claude Vautin, a London mining man, agreed to erect works costing $75,000 in return for the city's $25,000 bonus, and on February 14, 1889 the smelter was blown in. Alas, its promoters had not recognized the sulphurous nature of the ore and their unsuitable equipment functioned poorly. The London directors of the British Columbia Smelting Company Limited were so upset that they refused to provide further funds. After ten days of intermittent operations, the smelter ceased operating, and in December 1889, the plant was sold at auction. Because it had not reduced any ore, it failed to qualify for a civic bonus. The city continued to seek a smelter but refused to consider a bonus.[12]

The graving dock project floundered even before it got underway. When over 500 Vancouver residents met to discuss the project only a few questioned any details. The provision of ship repair facilities was a logical concomitant to Vancouver's development as a port. The ratepayers approved a $100,000 bonus, but the Glasgow firm, Bell and Miller, would not build the dock without provincial or federal aid and such assistance was not forthcoming.[13]

By contrast, the sugar refinery was a marked success. In 1888, Mayor Oppenheimer had the city distribute sugar beet seed to local farmers and discussed the possibility of establishing a sugar beet refinery with Europeans. The beets grew well but nothing evolved from the plan. Then early in 1890, Benjamin T. Rogers, an American who had the financial backing of such CPR directors as W.C. Van Horne, R.B. Angus, and Donald A. Smith, asked the city for a $30,000 bonus to cover the cost of buying and preparing the site, a fifteen-year tax exemption, and free water. With the warm support of CPR officials[14] and the ratepayers' approval of the bonus, the sugar refinery quickly came into being and made its first melt, using Phillipines raw sugar, in January 1891.[15] Some of the product was sold locally — although not at first on Vancouver Island, where jealous Victoria merchants refused to patronize a Vancouver industry — and eventually much was shipped eastward to Manitoba and the Northwest Territories. To Vancouver businessmen, the sugar refinery proved a valuable asset. Its payroll included approximately seventy-five men; it provided a market for other manufacturers such as the B.C. Cooperage and Jute Company; unlike most local industries, it drew on overseas rather than provincial natural products; and, in compliance with the bonus arrangement and British Columbians' anti-Chinese sentiments, none of its employees was Chinese.[16]

By choosing Vancouver as its terminus, the CPR demonstrated its desire to develop traffic by promoting trans-Pacific shipping. Despite a shortage of return cargoes, trans-Pacific shipping prospered as the CPR's efficient through service from Asia to the eastern seaboard cut into the American transcontinental trade. When the CPR secured an imperial mail contract in 1889, it ordered its own steamships. When the first of these, the *Empress of India*, arrived in April 1891, city residents celebrated much as they had when they greeted the *Abyssinia* four years earlier. A band played, hundreds of people lined the streets and stood on nearby housetops to get a good view, the Board of Trade entertained the captain at a banquet, and a lacrosse tournament and hospital benefit show were said to be in honour of the ship's

The meeting of land and sea, the CPR wharf in 1887. In the background is the Hastings Saw Mill and the forest that surrounded the city.

arrival. These celebrations were less elaborate than publicity-conscious Mayor Oppenheimer wanted, but neither City Council nor the Board of Trade believed in expensive pomp and ceremony.

Shipping stimulated local business. In 1886, even the relatively small ships calling for lumber cargoes spent approximately $2,000 each on provisions and for stevedoring. Larger ships meant more business. When the *Empress* liners arrived, the Vancouver Steam Laundry, for example, obtained a contract for washing 20,000 pieces of dirty linen from each sailing.[17]

The *Empress* liners were the most prestigious ships calling at Vancouver but were not alone. Individual vessels were occasionally chartered to bring cargoes direct to Vancouver, a practice that annoyed understandably anxious Victoria merchants. Then, in 1893, an Australian line, the Canadian-Australian, with the assistance of mail subsidies from Australia, New Zealand, Fiji, and Canada began calling regularly.[18]

Locally, the Victoria-based Canadian Pacific Navigation Company sailed regularly between Vancouver and Victoria after the railway's arrival. Vancouver merchants, however, sought to dominate the provincial hinterland, and even though they lacked the legal power to offer a subsidy, persuaded the Union Steam Ship Company to inaugurate a daily service between Vancouver and the coal mining centre of Nanaimo on Vancouver Island. Vancouver soon captured much of Nanaimo's wholesale trade and general business from Victoria and the steamship company introduced twice daily service.[19]

Vancouver businessmen were also keen to draw the Fraser Valley trade away from New Westminster. About 750 of them petitioned Council to bridge False Creek at Granville Street to connect with the road the CPR planned to build through its property on the south side and with the road and Fraser River bridges to be built by the provincial government and the municipality of Richmond. Although Alderman Bell-Irving claimed the bridge was simply "a bonus to the CPR," an overwhelming majority of ratepayers approved the bridge by accepting a $150,000 by-law for various improvements.[20] To gain rail access to the upper Fraser Valley, Vancouver City Council promised a $300,000 bonus to the local promoters of the Burrard Inlet and Fraser Valley Railway who proposed to build from Burrard Inlet through the agricultural districts on the southern side of the Valley as far east as Chilliwack and south to a link with the Northern Pacific Railway at the United States border. Even if the Northern Pacific had not gone into receivership in 1893, the difficulty and expense of bridging the Fraser River might well have thwarted them.[21] Not until 1910 when the B.C. Electric Railway completed its line from Vancouver to Chilliwack, did Vancouver successfully challenge New Westminster for control of the Fraser Valley trade.

The ambitions of Vancouver businessmen were not confined to the Fraser Valley; they also sought a direct rail link to the Kootenay to replace the cumbersome lake and portage routes to the CPR mainline at Revelstoke or the roundabout rail route through Washington State to Puget Sound and by coastal steamer to Vancouver or Victoria. They also wanted to displace Spokane as the Kootenay's economic centre. Initially, they could only take stalling action such as opposing the chartering of railways to build south from the Kootenay — an action that led some Kootenaians to boycott Vancouver suppliers. By 1892, however, some Vancouver risk capital was invested in the Kootenay mining industry, and as activity in the Kootenay increased, local optimists expected that Vancouver's investment, interest, and trade in the area would also expand. But the effects of the recession of 1893 seriously restricted the availability of local capital. In 1897, the forty mining brokers in Vancouver were far outnumbered by their counterparts in Spokane and in the Kootenay itself. Vancouver was so conspicuous by the absence of its influence that the Nelson *Miner* complained:

> The merchants of the capital [Victoria] and of Vancouver do not advertise, i.e., do not seek business in our interior mining camps, preferring to let it go to Winnipeg or to the States. The mining brokers of Vancouver and Victoria sit on their haunches and bewail the bad times, instead of trying to get a share of the mine brokering which is now done in Spokane.[22]

By late 1896, the Vancouver Board of Trade, in cooperation with Boards in Victoria, New Westminster, and Nanaimo, urged the provincial government to aid any company that would build a railway between the coast and the Kootenay. A firm of Vancouver contractors, the McLean Brothers, who had made a small fortune building dykes in the Fraser Valley after the 1894

The North Arm Bridge, completed in 1889, provided access to the settlement of Eburne and the farms of Sea Island. The speed limit is posted and reads, "parties driving faster than a walk over this bridge will be prosecuted according to law."

flood, secured a federal charter to build the Vancouver, Victoria and Eastern Railway through the Fraser Valley to the Kootenay. Gaining a charter and promises of provincial aid, however, was much easier than building a railway; only in 1916 did Vancouver get a direct rail link to the Kootenay region.

The cooperation of the Vancouver and Victoria Boards of Trade in supporting the V.V. & E. marked the beginning of a decline in the rivalry between the two cities. Only a few years earlier their respective newspapers had blamed sectionalism "on the other side of the Gulf," for such events as the stillbirth of the University in 1891 and a smallpox epidemic.[23] Victoria's hostility to Vancouver was well grounded on its recognition that Vancouver would eventually usurp it as Canada's Pacific metropolis although completion of the CPR had not immediately expanded the provincial resource base and the economy continued to depend on the traditional exports of canned salmon, lumber and coal. Even though Victoria was well located to benefit from that trade and her merchants, financiers, and transportation companies had the advantages of experience and capital over any Vancouver rivals, eastern firms opening British Columbia branches looked to Vancouver first.[24]

Vancouver's antagonism to Victoria was based, no doubt, on her inability to usurp Victoria's economic hegemony immediately, as well as on newspaper rhetoric and a tendency to confuse Victoria the city with Victoria the provincial capital. The Vancouver News had blamed "Victoria" influences for the temporary suspension of Vancouver's police powers after the anti-Chinese Riot of 1887 (see below, p.28). That act and subsequent amendments to Vancouver's charter raising the property qualifications for mayor, aldermen, and voters were particularly galling to the new city that, prior to 1890, lacked its own representative in the Legislature. Despite Vancouver's claim that the New Westminster district, of which it formed a part, had 4,500 voters and only four MLA's whereas the Victoria district had a similar number of registered voters and eight MLA's, the 1890 redistribution gave Vancouver only two members. The city responded by returning two independents, Francis Carter-Cotton and J.W. Horne. Although the provincial government promised to undertake a general redistribution after the 1891 census, not until 1894 and the Constitutional League's talk of separation did redistribution give the Mainland

a clear majority of seats and Vancouver, three seats in the thirty-three member Assembly. The new seats still did not give the city adequate representation but this seldom proved a significant handicap.

Inferior political status was much easier to bear because, despite Victoria's continuing economic leadership, Vancouver could be confident of eventually overtaking the older city. She not only had a direct transcontinental link via the railway and trans-Pacific shipping, but also had had some modest success in drawing trade from Victoria's doorstep when city merchants began doing business with Nanaimo. Her greatest disappointment in becoming the province's economic centre was her failure to draw the Kootenay into her hinterland, but that region's commerce had eluded Victoria as well. Furthermore, Vancouver had been growing at a much faster rate than the capital city.

POPULATION GROWTH AND ETHNIC RELATIONSHIPS

During its first five years Vancouver grew rapidly. Its population rose from approximately 1,000 at the end of 1886 to 13,709 at the time of the 1891 census (Appendix, Table I). Then, the growth rate began to decline. By 1893 and 1894, a drop in real estate prices, an increase in tax arrears, and a relatively stagnant growth rate revealed that the city was also suffering from the general North American depression of the mid-1890s.

Vancouver's distinctive demographic feature, as with most new communities, was the predominance of males (Appendix, Table V). As the city became more settled, the percentage of women increased, but in 1901 men still formed almost sixty per cent of the population. Many were transients who came to search for jobs or spend the winter while seasonal industries such as lumbering and fishing were closed. Some, especially during the depression of the mid-1890s, were "professional tramps." Their numbers became so great that in 1897 the voluntary Friendly Help Society called on the city to provide funds for meals and beds to spread the burden of poor relief and prevent abuses of indiscriminate charity. The city, however, recognized its obligation to assist the unemployed, and during the 1894 Depression, for example, City Council authorized the Board of Works to spend $5,000 on public works and establish

Rev. Hugh P. Hobson, rector of Christ Church Cathedral and some of his Chinese students. Several churches provided evening English classes as part of their missionary work among Chinese immigrants.

differential rates of pay for those granted relief work. Married men were paid $1.75 per nine-hour day for a maximum of four days a week while single men received $1.25 for a maximum of three days per week. Men who could prove need and at least six months residence in the city were given preference on such jobs. Thus, at an early date, Vancouver established the principle of endeavouring to "take care of its own."[25]

In the 1890s Vancouver was Canadian city with British overtones. Unfortunately, the exact statistics about birthplaces and ethnic origins readily available for older Canadian cities are lacking, since the 1891 and the 1901 census reported such information by federal constituency, not municipal division. And Vancouver was such a new city it did not have its own constituency. In 1891, it was part of the New Westminster district; in 1901, it was part of Burrard, an unwieldy constituency that stretched north from Vancouver along the mainland coast to the Yukon border (Appendix, Tables VII and VIII).

Probably about half of Vancouver's residents in the 1890s were Canadian-born and a steady influx of migrants from eastern Canada reinforced the Canadian presence originally supplied by the CPR. As well, some British-born business and political leaders such as Alderman Thomas Dunn, a hardware merchant; Alderman Robert Clark, a clothier; Mayor M.A. MacLean; Alderman W.F. Salsbury, CPR treasurer; and Alderman Edwin Sanders, a builder, had spent some years east of the Rockies. Most Canadians, of course, were also of British background but the few French Canadians gave evidence of their presence by organizing a reading room and benevolent society, L'Institut Canadien-Français de Vancouver, under the leadership of Dr. H.E. Langis. The handful of continental Europeans found few ethnic barriers to easy assimilation. Indeed the Oppenheimers, one of the most prominent families in business and civic politics, had been born in Germany of Jewish parentage. In sum, Vancouver had, with one very significant exception, a basically homogeneous society with few "outsiders."[26]

The exception was the Chinese, the only Asian group in the city until the Japanese began arriving in the mid-1890s. The Chinese were accustomed to hostility almost everywhere they migrated. In the Canadian context, British Columbia was the centre of intolerance since most Chinese resided there. Many had come in the wake of the gold rush of the 1850s and 1860s, and thousands had come to work on the construction of the CPR in the early 1880s. By the time Vancouver was incorporated, the provincial government had already passed laws designed to restrict Chinese immigration but had been thwarted by Ottawa's powers of disallowance. The province had slightly more success in designing regulations to limit the economic and political activities of Chinese already in the province. The frugal life style of the Chinese and their remittances to families in China led to complaints of "unfair" competition with white labour and of non-contribution to the country's development. The almost total absence of Chinese women made stories of moral depravity in the Chinese community almost believable.[27]

Before incorporation, there was talk of trying to keep the new city a white community. Then, early in 1887, through intimidation and a riot, some residents tried to expel Chinese land clearing crews in order to spare Vancouver "the evil which has cursed all Pacific Coast towns." Despite such attacks, and the city's refusal to hire them itself or to permit their employment on any city-assisted project such as the sugar refinery, the Chinese continued to come to Vancouver. After all they had few choices. Completion of the CPR had thrown thousands of them out of work, and an American law passed in 1882 barred their entry to that country. Apart from those employed as live-in domestic servants, most Chinese lived in their own small section of the city centred on Dupont Street. Although few had wives or families with them, federal head taxes discouraged immigration, and provincial laws restricted their economic activities, the Chinese continued to come to Vancouver and other British Columbia communities. As their population increased, so did hostility to them. By 1911, for example, their numbers had risen from 1,065 to 3,364 and while they formed a smaller percentage of the total population, they were a highly visible minority (Appendix, Tables VIII and IX).[28]

THE URBAN LANDSCAPE

In the 1880s and 1890s, Vancouver's chief concern was not its ethnic composition but the establishment of basic services: the protection of public health, provision of an adequate water supply, and introduction of electrical utilities as well as such mundane essentials as drains, streets, sewers, and sidewalks. Because of its concentration on what would become routine activities, City Council had little time to think ahead. Apart from the CPR surveyors who laid out streets on the Company's property, no one seems to have paid conscious attention to the distribution of activities within the city. Nevertheless, a discernible pattern of economic and residential locations did emerge.

In its early years, Vancouver was an ugly, smelly city. Hastily built frame buildings were often unpainted and much of the ground was covered with burned logs and stumps, themselves such a fire hazard that for some months after the Fire, insurance companies would not sell fire policies in the city. The absence of sewers or drains created foul odours in low-lying places. Beach gravel placed over worn-out planks provided a rough road surface.

Vancouver had no formal town plan. As a later planner observed, "Its history is that of Topsy, it just growed."[29] Lumbering and other industries dependent on water transport naturally gravitated to the shores of Burrard Inlet or False Creek. Noisome industries such as abattoirs and the tannery were located on the outskirts and although nearby residents complained about pollution they could do little about it. The city's one effort to place a heavy industry on a site of *its* choice had a high price. To get the CPR to build its yard on the north side of False Creek, the city exempted the yards from local taxes for twenty years. The City Council's precise motives are unclear: they may have resulted from fear of a rival commercial area developing on the south side of the Creek, but probably represented a desire to develop False Creek as an industrial area. If the CPR built its yard on the south side, it was unlikely to build a drawbridge necessary for marine traffic since the bridge would be busy carrying rolling stock between the yards and the main line. The settlement of CPR employees around the shops (at the south end of Seymour, Howe, and Hornby Streets) became known as Yaletown since many of its residents had formerly lived at the Yale construction headquarters in the Fraser Canyon.

In the centre of the city, commercial and residential buildings were intermingled, but Council's establishment of a fire limit in 1887 outlined the broad limits of what eventually became a clearly defined business district. To reduce the danger of fire spreading, and to lower insurance rates, all new buildings, within the designated area other than sheds or privies, had to be constructed of brick or stone.

Within the fire limit were several competing business districts. The most important commercial area along Water and Cordova Streets between Granville and Carrall Streets, included retail shops and most of the city's growing number of wholesale houses as it had easy access to the waterfront and the CPR. A second, less fashionable retail district developed along Westminster Avenue (Main Street). Here, Charles Woodward opened his dry goods store in 1892.

A third retail area emerged to the west along Granville Street and was strongly influenced by the CPR, whose luxurious Vancouver Hotel opened in 1887 at the corner of Georgia and Granville, then on the fringes of the developed city. A short time later, the CPR erected a 1,200 seat opera house nearby. Farther north along Granville were two of the largest privately owned buildings in the city, the Donald A. Smith and W.C. Van Horne buildings, named after their owners, two senior CPR officials. Because of its eagerness to develop Granville Street, the CPR dictated the permanent location of the main office of the Bank of Montreal and complained when the congregation of Christ Church Cathedral was slow to complete its building.[30] Granville Street also became important for the retail trade. The Hudson's Bay Company had first opened a store on Cordova Street but established a Granville Street branch in 1889. Three years later, it consolidated the two stores and opened a full department store kitty-corner from the Vancouver Hotel. Indicative of the trend towards separating the maturing city's retail and wholesale functions, the Hudson's Bay Company maintained a separate warehouse on Water Street.

Competition among the several commercial districts for hegemony came to the fore in discussions over the location of new public institutions. Attractions such as a public market and the post office would draw people to an area thereby increasing its business and its real estate values. Moreover, people liked to be within convenient distance of such services. In 1888, the city purchased a site at Westminster Avenue and Hastings Street in the eastern business district for a public market. Ratepayers in Ward I (the West End) were solidly opposed; Ward II was evenly divided; the eastern Wards III, IV, and V were overwhelmingly in favour. The market was built at Westminster and Hastings and became more popular as a place for public meetings and entertainments than for the sale of local produce.[31] West End property owners, however, were more successful in their efforts to obtain the post office and managed to persuade the federal government to build it on the west side.[32]

The competing business districts separated the two major residential districts, the varied East End and the generally affluent West End. Some of the "lumber kings," including R.H. Alexander still lived in the East End or Ward IV in the early 1890s and some real estate developers tried to lay out parks, alleys, and lots that sold for as much as $5,000 in 1890. Other real estate firms such as the Vancouver Improvement Company, an Oppenheimer family enterprise, realized, however, that because of proximity to the Hastings Saw Mill and the wharves and business section, the East End would be especially attractive to workingmen and mechanics. Thus, they subdivided much of it into twenty-five foot lots selling for as little as $450 each, erected modest frame homes on them, and sold them on the instalment plan. In the 1880s and early 1890s, the East End grew more rapidly than any other part of the city.[33]

Vancouver prided itself on being a "city of homes," but many residents, particularly bachelors and married men whose families had not yet joined them, lived in the crowded hotels and lodging houses of the business district. Some single men, both Chinese and white, especially the unemployed, the aged and the infirm together with a few families lived in shacks along the Burrard Inlet and False Creek waterfronts. East of the Hastings Saw Mill, a contemporary observer wrote, the shacks harboured "numerous disreputable characters, and are known locally as the 'rancherie.' Indians, Kloochmen and 'bad whites' inhabit this locality. . . [where much of what goes on] . . . would be more salacious than judicious, in the interests of public morality for publication." City officials were concerned about morality but also saw the shacks as a means of evading city taxes and a hazard to public health since they depended on tidal action to remove wastes. Not until 1896, however, did the Medical Health Officer report the destruction of a number of these cottages, the filling in of the sites, and the installation of sewers.[34]

The West End was a sharp contrast. By the mid-1890s, over two-thirds of Vancouver's "elite," led by Harry Abbott, superintendent of the CPR, had established homes there, especially along Seaton Street [West Hastings] overlooking the Burrard Inlet waterfront and along Georgia Street. For CPR officials, the area was convenient to their places of work in the CPR offices; the CPR, however, had had nothing to do with subdividing the area into large lots. In 1882, the original owners, Brighouse, Hailstone, and Morton had subdivided what they called the "City of Liverpool" with "primitive mathematical simplicity" into lots of one chain (66 feet) wide by two chains (132 feet) deep. Although the West End was home to many merchants and professional men, it, too, lacked many amenities. In 1895, some residents complained that apart from a three-foot-wide sidewalk and road maintenance, the city had made no improvements and had not even provided a street light. The exclusivity of the West End was also questionable; it was as subject to real estate promotion as any area in the city. The owner of some one hundred lots, for example, offered a one-third discount, financing, and a two-year free streetcar pass for each family in order to sell his land.[35]

A few individuals built homes and established small industries in Mount Pleasant, but, before 1890, the south side of False Creek (Ward V) was often viewed only as a suitable location for such nuisances as a tannery and a garbage crematory. Development south of False Creek really began in 1890 when the CPR auctioned city lots in its first major residential subdivision. The description of Fairview as "a gentle slope rising from the waters of English Bay" represented a salesman's fancy; few slopes were gentle and the neighbourhood had a better view of the False Creek industrial area than of English Bay beaches. Nevertheless, a widely advertised auction sold 314 lots at an average price of $378.93 each.[36]

A major attraction of Fairview was the prospect of street railway service. The CPR promised the Vancouver Electric Railway and Lighting Company sixty-eight lots in return for regular service. The street railway completed the line in November 1891, but in doing so effectively bankrupted itself and was unable to guarantee the service required by the CPR's terms. For almost a year during 1893-94, the street railway suspended its Fairview service. Fairview and Mount Pleasant had only about five hundred households and a number of

By 1894, Fairview was Vancouver's "Coming 'Nob Hill.'" Church spires, a large school and hundreds of single family homes in the background illustrate the city's growth. The Westminster Avenue (Main Street) bridge crosses False Creek where the CNR terminal now stands.

vacant houses. Many purchasers at the CPR auction had been local real estate dealers who expected to resell lots in this "Coming 'Nob Hill,'" and unfortunately for them, as for the street railway, Vancouver's first period of rapid growth ended just as Fairview was being opened to settlement.[37]

The presence of the electric street railway splendidly demonstrated Vancouver's modernity but seemed incongruous in a city where bears and panthers still roamed in nearby woods and open ditches drained even the fashionable residential areas. Private entrepreneurs had developed the street railway to enhance the value of their real estate holdings; when they got into financial difficulties, City Council, on which they were effectively represented, proposed to buy the street railway as it had bought the water works. City ratepayers, however, were a pragmatic lot. They rejected the street railway purchase as too costly, but approved the water works purchase because they knew that a reliable supply of pure water was essential for the encouragement of industry, fire protection, and especially for the maintenance of public health.

Vancouver was unusually conscious of public health. Several medical doctors who served on early City Councils established a tradition of "experts" influencing residents to accept health as a community concern. As a port, Vancouver faced constant danger from possible epidemics of smallpox, cholera, and typhoid fever. Within its first year, the city took several important steps for providing medical care. Under the Health Bylaw of 1887, the city provided medical and nursing care for the poor either at home or in the city hospital. It had already taken over administration of the hospital from the CPR, and in 1888 opened a new structure near the city centre. The hospital provided medical and nursing care, but many individuals — particularly women, for whom the hospital's facilities were limited — were treated at home. Fortunately, Vancouver had a surplus of doctors, and physicians were often willing to make several calls each day to a patient's home. Individuals suffering from contagious diseases, however, were often sent to the city's isolation hospital on the outskirts.

To maintain public health, City Council in 1887 overrode the objections of those who thought it an unnecessary expense and accepted the advice of Alderman J.M. Lefevre, a CPR surgeon, to appoint a medical health officer. The officer's main tasks were enforcing the provincial Public Health Act and persuading people to accept vaccination. Assisting him was an inspector who examined health-related conditions along with his varied duties as building, street, license and fire inspector. These officials and their successors regularly observed inadequacies in the city, but the expense of change and the unwillingness of some individuals to cooperate limited their success. The Medical Health Officer urged the inspection of milk to limit adulteration, and the milk inspector subsequently found almost half the samples tested unsatisfactory although he was more concerned about butterfat than impurities.[38]

Sanitation was a major concern championed by those who wanted a proper sewerage system. Once Vancouver grew, the simple system of dumping waste into the harbour no longer sufficed. Yet, city officials ignored the harbour master's protests against the city scavenger throwing garbage, including night soil, off the city wharf. In addition, the CPR's waterfront embankment cut off some natural drainage and contributed to an accumulation of "putrid and offensive" foul matter. The conditions of the drains were not improved by residents who threw slop, refuse, and garbage into street drains. CPR officials complained of an "unbelievable stench" that caused illness among its office staff, and stagnant pools appeared in many low-lying parts of the city, even the West End.[39]

In time the city recognized the need for a sewerage system. After an extensive engineering debate, it decided to install separate sanitary sewers and storm drains rather than a single system. Beginning in 1888, the city began laying a temporary network of wooden sewer pipes. Although ratepayers were willing to authorize expenditures on sewers, progress was slow. By 1890, the city had seven miles of sewers but over sixty-five miles of streets. Many areas, especially Mount Pleasant, Fairview, and parts of the Old Granville Townsite and the West End lacked sewers. Few areas had surface drains.[40]

Nevertheless, public health improved. In a congratulatory review of the city's first decade, the *Daily World* reported that as soon as Vancouver got pure water, the number of cases of typhoid fever declined. A reliable supply of cheap water was necessary for public health, fire protection, and industry. As long as Vancouver was small, it had few problems, but once the city grew, wells and creeks could not provide a potable supply.

An 1887 photograph of the D.W. Sheehan family home on Seymour Street in Yaletown. When the CPR moved its shops from the construction headquarters at Yale, some of the workers' cottages were moved via flat cars to be near the new shops and round house on False Creek. This home was demolished in 1949 to make way for the approaches to the Granville Street bridge.

J.M. Browning, the CPR's land commissioner, was the first of a succession of CPR officials to reside in this stone and shingle Queen Anne Revival home at the northwest corner of Georgia and Burrard Streets. After undergoing extensive renovations and serving as a residential hotel, it was demolished in the 1930s.

This building, at the northwest corner of Carrall and Water Streets, replaced the original Sunnyside Hotel which was destroyed in the fire of June 13, 1886. Both street and sidewalks were planked.

Vancouver was fortunate, however, since the nearby mountains offered a virtually unlimited source of pure water. Getting that water to the city and distributing it was a problem for engineers, while deciding who would take charge of the waterworks was the responsibility of municipal politicians. The city fathers had to decide whether the city itself should own the water works or, if the franchise was given to a private company, which one should be chosen. There had been no question that sewers, like the fire department, the streets, and the sidewalks should be publicly owned. In the case of other utilities, such as water, gas, and electric light, and street railways, there were opportunities for either private entrepreneurs or municipal government. In larger Canadian cities, the water works were usually publicly owned while in smaller ones they were often private enterprises.[41] Which pattern would Vancouver follow?

City Council decided to consider private proposals before seeking the necessary legislative authority to establish its own system. Two competing companies presented plans calling for a municipal guarantee on their bonds. The Vancouver Water Works Company, the creation of G.E. Keefer, a civil engineer, and several Victoria capitalists, proposed to bring Capilano River water through pipes laid under Burrard Inlet and distribute it throughout the city. The Coquitlam Water Works Company and its New Westminster backers planned to distribute Coquitlam River water. Because the Vancouver company required a lower rate of interest on a smaller amount of money and for a shorter term, the Council's Fire, Water and Light Committee favoured it. The Coquitlam company then made its terms more attractive and successfully worked behind the scenes with Alderman David Oppenheimer to get Council to adopt its scheme. An independent engineer confirmed the plan's feasibility but before ratepayers could approve the necessary guarantee, the Vancouver company announced it would build without any municipal guarantee and advertised extensively against the Coquitlam project. Both companies marshalled their forces on election day, but ratepayers agreed that the city should not risk its credit when private investors would provide a necessary service without any public cost. Within days of the vote, the Vancouver Water Works Company had its surveyors in the field. The arrival of Capilano water in the city on March 25, 1889 represented a major engineering feat for never before had

"water mains been laid across such a sheet of water as Burrard Inlet."[42]

Under the leadership of Mayor David Oppenheimer, who believed in public ownership of the water supply, lighting and the street railway, City Council was kept aware of the Vancouver Water Works Company's offer of the right to purchase company assets at any time. When the city and the company disagreed on the price the city should pay for water and Council became concerned about the adequacy of the pressure and service to sparsely settled areas, the city contemplated purchasing the system. During the prolonged discussions, the company did little to extend its mains. Finally, an arbitrator decided on a fair value, and the ratepayers, after little public discussion, approved the purchase by an overwhelming majority. In February 1892, the city took over the water works. Although the city laid some new mains, many neighbourhoods in Fairview, Mount Pleasant and English Bay still either lacked water completely or were victims of insufficient water pressure. Nevertheless, the city now owned a priceless resource. The water system remained the city's only municipally owned utility although serious consideration was given to taking over the electric light and street railway companies.

As in the case of the water works, outside investors were keen to provide telephones and gas and electric lighting. As Vancouver was undergoing incorporation, the New Westminster promoters of the New Westminster and Burrard Inlet Telephone Company secured provincial permission to extend their operation to the new city. Even before incorporation several Victoria residents had already secured a provincial charter to supply gas "to consumers at the terminus of the Canadian Pacific Railway Company." On November 27, 1887, "all evening long and far into the night, large crowds gathered in front of Rand Bros.' office...and gazed with admiration at the brilliant light." The gas light was soon obsolete. In August, the Vancouver Electric Illuminating Company, the creation of a Tacoma entrepreneur who sold shares to local investors, had turned on its "bright and steady light" and secured a one-year contract to light city streets. Although the News-Advertiser boasted that "Vancouver is better lighted than any other city of her size in the world," the street lights were not wholly satisfactory. Only when the company agreed to install better equipment did Council — several of

The Hotel Europe under construction at the corner of Water and Cordova Streets. Street layout in Gastown made the flatiron or triangular style of building appropriate. The towered building in the background, an example of the Victorian Italianate style of architecture, was built as an office block by J.W. Horne. On April 11, 1891, about the time this building was constructed, the Vancouver World *described Horne as the "heaviest individual property owner in Vancouver." Horne served for two years as an alderman and was elected to the Legislature in 1890.*

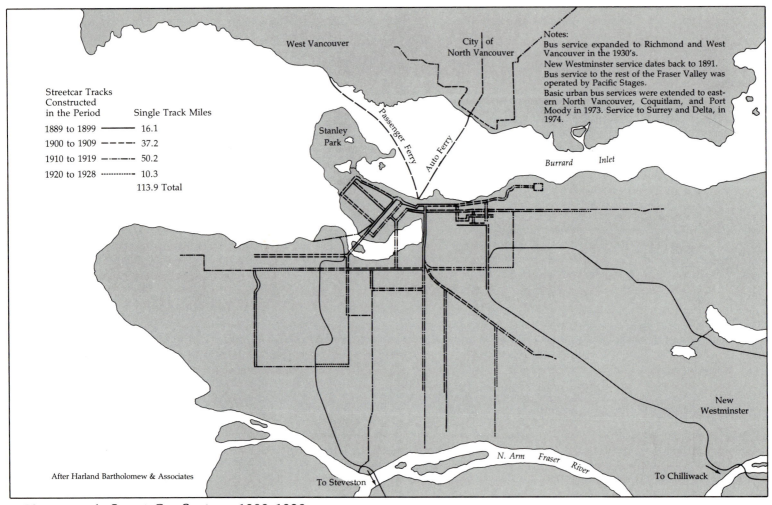

Streetcar Tracks
Constructed
in the Period   Single Track Miles

1889 to 1899 ———————— 16.1
1900 to 1909 – – – – – 37.2
1910 to 1919 –·–·–·– 50.2
1920 to 1928 ·········· 10.3
                        113.9 Total

West Vancouver

City of
North Vancouver

Notes:
Bus service expanded to Richmond and West
Vancouver in the 1930's.
New Westminster service dates back to 1891.
Bus service to the rest of the Fraser Valley was
operated by Pacific Stages.
Basic urban bus services were extended to east-
ern North Vancouver, Coquitlam, and Port
Moody in 1973. Service to Surrey and Delta, in
1974.

Stanley
Park

Passenger Ferry

Auto Ferry

Burrard   Inlet

New
Westminster

After Harland Bartholomew & Associates

N. Arm Fraser River

To Steveston

To Chilliwack

2 Vancouver's Street Car System, 1889-1928

whose members were company shareholders — give it a five year contract and abandon talk of municipal ownership. Private households were important consumers for "no one would think of putting up a house without a telephone and electric light."[43]

Although the electric light and the telephone had been invented only within the previous decade or so, they were well established elsewhere in North America when Vancouver came

into being. The electric street railway, however, was not successfully demonstrated anywhere until 1888. That same year, Harry Abbott, several other CPR officials and a number of real estate men, including David Oppenheimer, invested in the Vancouver Street Railway Company, and secured a provincial charter and a thirty-year civic franchise. In return for the use of certain streets, the street railway agreed to a six-mile-per-hour speed limit, a five cent fare, and an option allowing the city to purchase the system after thirty years. The franchise did not specify the motive power. The company, unsure whether electricity would replace horses, ordered cars and laid tracks suitable for either horse or electric power. But after making preliminary arrangements to buy horses, the company adopted electricity. On June 26, 1890, the Vancouver Electric Railway and Lighting Company, an amalgamation of the electric lighting and street railway companies, brought one of Canada's first electric street railways into operation. Its three and a half miles of track ran through the commercial districts and linked the peripheries of the East and West End residential districts. By February 1891, its four cars had carried 339,986 passengers and taken in an average of $76.14 per day. Since the daily average was highest in July and August, it is likely that once the novelty wore off, Vancouver residents again walked to work and to shopping.[44]

The electric company was soon in financial difficulty. It had grave problems raising funds because its own precarious financial state had been complicated by premature expansion into Fairview and because of depressed bond markets. One shareholder, Mayor David Oppenheimer, suggested the city purchase the company but ratepayers twice rejected the idea. The company remained in its creditors' hands until British capitalists took it over and formed the British Columbia Electric Railway Company in 1897.

"Municipal socialism" had not really been an issue in Vancouver. Most ratepayers decided the question of public or private ownership on pragmatic rather than ideological grounds despite the imprecations of mayors and aldermen whose interests may or may not have been influenced by their personal investments. In the case of the water works they preferred to have a private firm raise the necessary operating capital, but when city and company could not agree on water rates and the company failed to provide adequate service, the city took it over. In the case of the street railway, the circumstances were very different and it remained in private hands. Ratepayers had been able to raise the funds to buy the water works by selling four per cent debentures at an average price of $92.58. At the time they were considering the street railway purchase, they were borrowing funds to extend the water works; that issue sold at $88. The cost of the

street railway would have been high and its purchase would have strained the city's credit. The motives of the original promoters of the water works and the street railway were also very different. The water works company simply wanted to earn a profit from the sale of water whereas several original investors in the street railway wanted to increase the value of their real estate. The street railway promoters did not want to tie up money in capital intensive utilities unlikely to yield immediate returns, and the ratepayers naturally did not want to pay higher taxes to subsidize a street railway. Unlike their counterparts in Toronto who favoured public ownership because of poor service, Vancouver residents had adequate service. Moreover, unlike the water works, the street railway was a luxury in a city where most people still lived within walking distance of their work and shops.

By 1897, Vancouver looked like the modern city it was. Although the city had no formal plan, clearly defined industrial, commercial and residential areas had been established and within them there was some specialization of function: wholesaling and retailing had been separated; the well-to-do lived in the West End and the working classes in the East End. Private entrepreneurs provided gas, electricity, telephones and an electric street railway though in doing so they had sometimes allowed their enthusiasm for development to exceed reality and their financial resources. The city had bought the water works and was laying sewers and drains, building sidewalks, paving streets and maintaining its public health programme.

CIVIC POLITICS

Much of the responsibilty for developing the city belonged to the civic government whose role in shaping the physical environment was large. Most revenue from property taxes and debenture issues was spent on streets, sewers, and drains, but the city managed to plant a few trees and develop a magnificent park. City Council provided leadership. Ratepayers could actively participate in deciding the city's course by passing or rejecting money by-laws but usually they showed little interest in doing so. Possibly they were too busy with their own affairs to pay much attention to civic business; probably they recognized a consensus on most issues and saw no need to express an

The Vancouver Water Works built the Capilano Dam in 1888. Water from the North Shore mountains continues to give Vancouver one of its greatest assets, a virtually unlimited supply of pure water.

The Prior Street car barn in 1894. The Vancouver Electric Railway and Light Company was a locally-owned forerunner of the British Columbia Electric Railway Company.

additional opinion. From time to time when particularly controversial matters faced the city, mass meetings were held to discuss issues as diverse as a proposal to build a graving dock or the selection of the city engineer.

For real estate dealers and large property owners, their business and city business were closely related. Indeed, never again would there be such a close relationship between men who were privately working to develop the city and those who formally governed it. Of the six men who served as mayor between 1886 and 1897, three, including David Oppenheimer who served four terms, were actively involved in real estate. Nearly always one or two other real estate men served on Council, as well as a CPR executive, and several merchants.

All Council members were considerable property owners as demanded by the City Charter. In 1887, the Legislature amended the Act of Incorporation to raise the property qualification for mayor to $2,000 and for aldermen to $500. Some Vancouverites blamed Robert Dunsmuir, the Vancouver Island coal magnate and Nanaimo MLA who believed "property [was] the standard of intelligence."[45] A more likely reason was the government's fear of Vancouver becoming an unruly American-style frontier town after the anti-Chinese riot of 1887. In any case, in some wards only three or four men were eligible for election; in December 1887, all candidates were returned by acclamation. Because the franchise was also related to property ownership, some land owners had votes in all five city wards. Despite some public complaints, Council did not formally ask the Legislature for a change until 1889 when it requested that a $3,000 leasehold be deemed the equivalent of $1,000 ownership for aldermen. The change, however, had little effect on Council's overall composition.

Most Council members obviously shared the *News-Advertiser's* belief that "it is only proper and reasonable that those who made this city what it is and who contribute the greater portion of the municipal revenue should have the chief control of civic affairs." Certainly this was the CPR's view. During the December 1886 election campaign, L.A. Hamilton, the CPR's assistant land commissioner and an aldermanic candidate in Ward I, justified his candidacy by explaining that because the CPR paid more than a third of the taxes in the ward, it "had a perfect right to know how this money was to be expended and to see that a fair

portion was spent in Ward I." Although the CPR was influential in municipal government, "it was not all-powerful nor did it dominate civic politics" and its influence waned as the city developed. Others believed that men with a "stake in the country" were likely to manage the city efficiently and economically. "To lower the qualifications [for mayor and aldermen] to $500 would be to secure at the Council Board probably even a worse set of incompetents than we have here at present," declared the *World* in 1891.[46] The city's dependence on borrowed funds for improvements — by 1894 it had issued more than $2 million worth of debentures — made it essential to present a businesslike image to creditors.

Similar economic interests and ambitions to improve the city physically and encourage its growth did not guarantee political harmony and factions beset Council. Oppenheimer's chief critic was Francis Carter-Cotton, editor of the *News-Advertiser.* Their feud was as much personal as political, but since each man had press support (the *Daily World* spoke for Oppenheimer) and a number of friends on Council, their conflict seriously impeded city business even though Carter-Cotton was not a Council member. A bitter division over appointing a city engineer temporarily stopped all Council work and citizens began to look on Council meetings as "free entertainment, as interesting as a burlesque or comic opera." Only after a large public meeting complained that Council's shenanigans were affecting the city's credit and subjecting it to "ridicule and disgrace" and unanimously called for the resignation of the entire Council, did Councillors begin to work together to agree on an engineer.[47]

Because of their own property interest, Council members sought means of raising revenue to supplement the property tax, the main source of civic income. In 1889, as fixed annual charges were growing more rapidly than revenue, Council imposed a trade license fee on all ordinary traders and merchants, some of whom lacked the real property to qualify as candidates for municipal office. The Board of Trade condemned the general application of the license particularly the "injudicious" application of a $50 fee on real estate agents who "had done more to develop the city than any other class of businessmen." The agents refused to pay the fee and successfully challenged its legality in the courts. Council re-introduced the by-law the next year with lower fees, but, after more protests, abandoned trade licenses as a revenue source.[48]

While property owners did not get their way on the license issue, they readily rejected any proposals to tax land and not improvements to encourage building. The original City Charter permitted Council to exempt improvements from taxation, but, said Alderman J.M. Browning, "such Henry George suggestions were dangerous." In Vancouver's particular circumstances, he reasoned, absentee landlords were beneficial since they wanted to advance the city's progress to enhance their investments but did not require services. Other councillors argued that the single tax would make it difficult for working men to hold lots in anticipation of being able to build on them later. Only Alderman F.W. Sentell, a builder, and Alderman H. Mason, a dairyman who lived in suburban Fairview, voted for Alderman Carroll's resolution that real estate improvements not be assessed. For the time being, the single tax idea remained only a subject for debating societies, letters to the editors, and the Single Tax Club.[49] (See Chapter II for a full discussion of the Single Tax.) Vancouver City Council was too burdened with the daily routine of building a city out of the wilderness and trying to promote its economic development to worry about reform ideas. How could the city be "reformed" when it was not yet fully formed?

SOCIAL AND CULTURAL LIFE

The dominance of males in the population gave Vancouver certain social characteristics. The liquor trade flourished and prostitution was common but these activities were largely confined to a particular area. And, as later history would demonstrate, they were not unique to a town on the edge of the wilderness. Although Vancouver began as a largely masculine community, it rapidly became a settled one with homes, a variety of churches and schools, and a wide assortment of athletic and cultural activities.

Debate over liquor control was a staple of Canadian politics. Early in the 1890s the federal government appointed a Royal Commission to examine the Liquor Traffic. When the commission visited Vancouver in 1892, Mayor Frederick Cope reported that the city had fifty-five liquor places, eight saloons, and six or seven liquor wholesalers. He explained — though probably did not intend a pun — that most drinking was done by the "floating population." Proportionately, the number of liquor outlets had actually declined. Four years earlier, when the population was approximately seventy-five per cent less, Rev. Ebenezer Robson, on behalf of a number of city residents, complained that forty-nine hotel and saloon licenses and three retail and one whole-sale liquor dealer were "altogether an excessive number." City Council took no action to reduce the number of licenses since license fees provided one-seventh of its revenue. Nevertheless, the city did not greatly increase the number of licenses, and Mayor Cope boasted that the Sunday closing laws were so well observed, "it is as quiet here on Sunday as in Toronto."[50]

Vancouver may have succeeded in controlling the liquor trade, but it coped with prostitution only by trying to make it less visible. In 1887, after a delegation of churchmen complained that Indian prostitution was undoing the work of missionaries, Council's police committee instructed the police "to carry out most stringently the by-laws of the city relating to houses of ill-fame" and to charge both frequenters and inmates. Nevertheless, "the Social Evil" persisted and even children observed the "beautiful ladies in black, usually travelling in pairs on Cordova Street." Prostitution was, in fact, tolerated in the community at large. William Templeton's effort to make it a municipal election issue in 1889 failed, and five years later, the police committee merely suggested instructing the Chief of Police to regulate the seventeen or eighteen house of "ill fame" and make pursuit of trade less public. Prostitution, the committee said, should:

> be confined to bounds as limited as possible, that public driving in open vehicles be prohibited, sauntering around gates, front yards and sidewalks be stopped; sitting in the open windows whether up stairs or downstairs be ended, that smoking in view of public streets and all manifestations intended to solicit or attract attention either on the streets, in the yards, at the doors or windows be wholly restrained; and it is further recommended that those hotels and saloons under suspicion or known to be places of ill repute. . . be closely watched, and in the case of known violation be punished to the full extent of the law. . . .

For hotels and saloons, the supreme punishment was loss of their liquor license, a policy that was a convenient compromise.

British Columbia Sugar Refinery employees show off the trophy they won in a bicycle race with employees of the Hudson's Bay Company, Thomas Dunn and Company and McLennan, McFeely and Prior. The trophy is now displayed in the B.C. Sugar Refinery Company's museum.

A Chinese festival on Dupont (now Pender) Street, c. 1898.

The churches seemed more concerned about the liquor traffic than about prostitution and while those who desired to patronize ladies of the night would have little difficulty in finding them, the "Social Evil" was so well put out of sight that at least one tourist commented on the city's "refined and respectable" tone.[51]

Although the churches had only marginal influence in effecting moral reform, Vancouver claimed to rival Toronto for the title "City of Churches." As early as 1889, it had three Anglican, two Baptist, two Presbyterian, three Methodist (including a Chinese mission), Congregational, and Roman Catholic churches as well as a branch of the Salvation Army. Indicative of the British and Canadian composition of society, over half the population claimed membership in either the Anglican or Presbyterian churches when the census taker asked (Appendix, Table X).

The churches were one physical manifestation of the city's settlement; the schools another. The growth of the school system in particular paralleled the increase in population. In the fall of 1887, the School Board built a four-room school near Cordova and Jackson Streets in the East End. By the end of the school year it had 285 students and was turning others away. Recognizing the growth of the West End and Mount Pleasant as residential districts, the Board then built a four-room school on Burrard Street and a two-room school in Mount Pleasant. Henceforth, the School Board added new classrooms and built new schools almost every year, and by 1895 the city boasted 2375 students and 45 teachers. The students themselves appear to have had their parents' ambition. In his 1889 report, the principal of the East End school reported "pupils coming to this active city, to new homes, have more than ordinary zeal, so they make rapid progress in their studies."[52]

Vancouver had no high school until 1890, but some demand was expressed for university level courses. In 1890, a private entrepreneur, Charles Whetham, established Whetham College to prepare students for army, navy, civil service, and university matriculation examinations as well as for the first and second year examinations leading to the B.A. in any university. The pool of potential students was small — Vancouver High School opened with only 32 students — and Whetham College did not survive the 1893 Depression. "Hard times" also forced the

School Board to reduce its teachers' salaries with only a vague promise of restoration.

Adults also had educational opportunities. Beginning in 1889, the city made an annual grant to allow the Vancouver Reading Room to make its services freely available to all citizens. The grant did not cover all costs, however, and the library depended on donations of cash and reading materials. Because of the charitable nature of the librarian and his family, the reading room became a social centre for the lonely as well as a source of information and entertainment. The idea of a city museum was discussed as early as 1887, and in 1894 the Art, Historical and Scientific Association set up a museum featuring local ethnology, history, flora, fauna, and mineralogy as well as collections from outside the province. The museum's founders, such as Mrs. S.G. Mellon, the wife of a retired Royal Navy captain, and Rev. N.L. Tucker of Christ Church Cathedral, had planned that the city should own the museum, but Council did not grant financial aid until 1904. Thus, private initiative gave the city its first cultural institutions.[53]

Public parks, however, were a civic responsibility. Stanley Park was a show piece but was almost the city's only park. Neither the CPR nor private subdividers set aside any park land and neighbourhood parks had a low priority. Mayor Oppenheimer had encouraged planting trees and shrubbery to provide "breathing spaces" and "pleasant breaks from the present treeless expanse of the city" but did nothing to develop playgrounds. With vacant lots everywhere, children did not really need special play areas, and the School Board did not begin to concern itself with school yards until 1890.[54]

The proximity of the sea and its recreational possibilities diverted some attention from land-based parks. During the first summer after incorporation, the News had urged "our wealthy citizens" to take steps to build a first class hotel, bath, and boat houses and to furnish a supply of boats to encourage tourists to stay longer. That summer some of the more affluent residents did begin a tradition of July 1st sailing yacht races. Indian war canoe races were another holiday feature, but for most residents, of course, these races were merely a spectator sport. Swimming was a popular summer pastime especially after the Vancouver Trades and Labour Council persuaded the city to construct public bathing facilities at English Bay, the only readily accessible

*Dominion Day Parade on Cordova Street, 1887. The band of H.M.S. **Triumph** leads the parade, followed by the mayors of Vancouver, New Westminster, Victoria and Nanaimo.*

By 1898 when this photograph was taken, Stanley Park had been open for a decade. Its wilderness beauty and such man-made attractions as the aviary made it a popular destination for tourists and city residents.

waterfront with a good swimming beach.[55] Children, of course, found plentiful, though not particularly clean swimming places along the shores of False Creek.

The city's principal recreational interests were two large parks. Stanley Park, a former military reserve at the entrance to the harbour, was acquired from the federal government. Rate-payers approved the sale of debentures to build a road around it and agreed to allow the Brockton Point Athletic Association to build grounds for the Canadian game of lacrosse, the English sport of cricket, and the popular late nineteenth century activity, bicycle racing. In 1889, the city also obtained from the provincial government the site of Hastings Park, located just east of the city boundary. There it hoped to develop Exhibition Grounds and it gave the B.C. Jockey Club financial aid to build a race track. Both large parks served the interests of the business community since they were supposed to advance real estate values in their immediate vicinities and act as tourist attractions.[56] Stanley Park quickly became the tourists' symbol of the city, but development of the Exhibition Grounds came much later.

Although Kipling had found the Vancouver of 1889 to be "not very gorgeous," visitors in the 1890s almost always commented on Stanley Park's natural beauty and on the still new city's modernity. Many groups and individuals were responsible for changing the wilderness into a would-be metropolis. Without the CPR, Vancouver would not have come into being in 1886. As a means of communication with the outside world, a major employer and property owner, the railway company was the most important organization in the city. Yet, Vancouver was never a company town. Many individuals came to the city in the wake of the railway. A few made fortunes, and many left when depression in the mid-1890s slowed the city's growth. Business-men were especially prominent, and though largely disappointed in their ambition to control the provincial hinterland, many merchants established soundly based businesses catering to local trade. The real estate men were the most conspicuous members of the business community. Some were mere specu-lators; others, with large investments, played a prominent role in civic government for they recognized the symbiotic relation-ship between the city's well-being and their own prosperity. The city installed such basic services as streets, sewers, and public health programmes while private entrepreneurs initiated a water works, telephone system, and electrical utilities. Thus, a combination of public and private enterprise laid a firm physical foundation for the city.

A city is more than stores and streets, warehouses and wharves. The population increased dramatically from about 1,000 in 1886 to approximately 20,000 in 1897, but it was not a very cosmopolitan one. Apart from the Chinese minority, most residents were of British or Canadian origin. By building homes, raising families, and organizing various social and cultural activities, these residents had turned a wilderness settlement into a living city.

Dog-sledding was both a sport and a means of transportation to the Klondike gold fields. C.S. Douglas, the proprietor of the investment house shown in the background was a native of Wisconsin who came to Vancouver in 1889 after spending some years in Manitoba where he served in the provincial Legislature. His prosperous business reflected the return of good times to the city in the wake of the Klondike gold rush of 1897-8. In 1909, Douglas was elected mayor of Vancouver.

Chapter Two
The City Booms 1897-1912

I am the mayor of a cosmopolitan city — I should rather say of a city of cosmopolitans whose sense of cityhood . . . has . . . all the jealousy and . . . self-consciousness and the self-importance of youth.[1]

Business seemed to gravitate naturally to Vancouver, but her businessmen, aspiring to consolidate their metropolitan status pursued new markets within the province and beyond. By 1900 or so, the city was the undisputed metropolitan centre for Canada's Pacific Coast.[2] By every statistical measure the city grew rapidly. In 1897 it was home to 20,000 people, most of whom lived within about a mile of the business district; in 1912, 122,000 had settled in all parts of the city's 16.75 square miles. Thousands more resided in the bedroom municipalities of South Vancouver and Point Grey. Downtown, three-storey brick buildings had attracted comment in the 1890s; in 1910, the city limited new "sky-scrapers" to 120 feet or ten stories. The city's revenues rose more than ten-fold as did its expenditures. This rapid growth created many problems in providing basic services for new residents and absorbing a cosmopolitan population. As governing the city became more complex, Vancouver seriously contemplated new administrative structures including metropolitan and commission government.

ECONOMIC GROWTH AND METROPOLITAN RELATIONSHIPS

Though booster literature boasted of increases in Oriental trade, this formed a minute portion of Vancouver's trade.[3] The best opportunities were much closer to home — in the Yukon, the Okanagan, the Kootenays, and the Prairies. Speculation played very much a part in hinterland development and was also rife in Vancouver, but this growth based on "expectations" was sustained by real economic expansion.[4] British Columbia shared in the general prosperity and abundance of investment capital that created the wheat boom and stimulated the provincial mining industry benefitting directly from increasing prairie demand for lumber and such specialized agricultural products as fruit. The wheat boom was also the great era of railway building; two new transcontinentals were under construction as were innumerable feeder and branch lines. During the first decade or so of the new century, Vancouver businessmen individually and collectively sought to profit from hinterland growth. Their belief in the desirability of expansion was widely shared, and from 1903 through 1912 Vancouver elected the "Solid Five" Conservative MLAs in support of Premier Richard McBride who dreamed of developing the province's "vast natural resources through grandiose schemes which would make it almost an empire in itself."[5]

Good times returned to Vancouver dramatically with the Klondike gold rush of 1897-98. Seattle and Victoria initially benefitted as a lack of shipping, capital, and outfitting experience limited Vancouver's participation. Within months, however, Vancouver businessmen made such a successful effort to secure the trade that Edgar Crow Baker, a Victoria entrepreneur mused, "everything [is] going on in Vancouver and nothing in Victoria." Vancouver had replaced the capital as the province's economic metropolis. The city's quest for the Yukon trade began with an energetic advertising campaign. Some merchants published their own leaflets; the business community as a whole collected $8,164.70 to allow the Board of Trade to advertise in eastern Canadian, British, and American newspapers and to open a Bureau of Information in Seattle which, "on account of

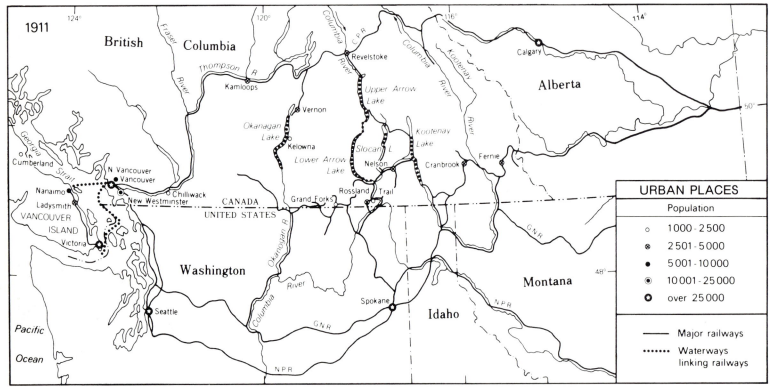

3 Vancouver and Region, 1911

the attack made on it by the press of Seattle did even more work than was expected of it." The frustration of gold seekers with the crush on Seattle's facilities and their concern about Canadian customs aided Vancouver's efforts to lure trade from the Puget Sound city. By the end of 1897, "every hotel in Vancouver and every boarding house" was filled with people from Europe, eastern Canada, and the northern United States preparing to head north. No houses were vacant and merchants were "overwhelmed with orders."[6]

By spring 1898, Vancouver was well prepared for the Yukon trade. Merchants brought in supplies from eastern Canada; the Union Steam Ship Company transferred two vessels to the northern service; the CPR purchased two ships for the Alaska run, and local firms such as Evans, Coleman and Evans,

wholesale building supply dealers, chartered vessels to carry goods northward. Soon there were more coastal steamers than passengers; rate wars lowered the fare from Vancouver to Skagway to as little as $10. To serve those already in the north, Vancouver merchants sent agents there or went themselves to take orders.

The start of the construction of the White Pass and Yukon Railway in the summer of 1898 brought new business; its completion in 1900 gave Vancouver merchants an almost complete monopoly of the Yukon trade. The opening of provincial and federal assay offices in 1899 and 1901 drew some Yukon gold directly to Vancouver and some of it entered the buoyant real estate market. Although the boom ended at the turn of the century, the Yukon trade remained fairly steady. By

An East Indian fisherman unloads his catch at Steveston, a village located at the mouth of the Fraser River.

Japanese shoreworkers at a local fish cannery. The industry employed men and women of diverse ethnic backgrounds.

The Billingsgate Fish Company wharves were located within the city limits.

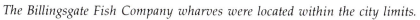

getting the Yukon trade away from Seattle and Victoria, Vancouver merchants restored their self-confidence, confirmed that their city had replaced Victoria as the economic metropolis of the province, drew attention to the city, and gained some new capital.[7]

The Klondike boom was a fillip. The prosperity underlying Vancouver's growth was part of a world-wide phenomenon. In Canada, this was the era of the wheat boom. The rapid settlement of the prairie grain growing areas by eastern Canadians and European and American immigrants created a demand for many products, especially lumber. The prospect of two new transcontinental railways promised new growth for Vancouver, already thriving as the province's established primary industries of fishing, lumbering, and mining flourished. Vancouver's pre-eminence within British Columbia guaranteed that when national businesses such as insurance companies established Pacific Coast branches or invested in the province's resource-based industries, Vancouver was the logical site for their offices. Similarly, when wholesalers such as Gault Brothers, textile merchants, or machinery manufacturers such as Canadian Fairbanks Morse established western regional branches, they chose Vancouver.[8]

In some respects, Vancouver could now sit back and wait for business. Apart from the work of the Vancouver Tourist Association which received some financial aid from the city, there was little civic advertising. The Tourist Association, founded in 1902, was predominantly, but not exclusively, a businessmen's group; among its founders was the President of the Trades and Labour Council. In time, real estate agents, whose numbers increased from 46 in 1901 to 650 in 1910, dominated the Association as it pressed for beautification of the city and circulated advertising pamphlets in eastern Canada, the United States, and Europe. The Board of Trade, in contrast, was mainly composed of lumbermen, major retail merchants, and wholesalers who were the city's economic leaders. Although its numbers were few, and many members apathetic, the Board proved an effective lobbyist. It did not ignore purely local issues, but its main concerns were the broad development of trade, securing better freight rates to the prairies, encouragement of "suitable" immigrants, and improvement of the harbour.[9]

By the turn of the century, Vancouver dominated the two primary provincial industries, fishing and lumbering. Most of the turn of the century consolidated salmon canning companies such as the Anglo-British Columbia Packing Company and British Columbia Packers established head offices in Vancouver. Although the enormous Fraser River salmon run of 1901 was not repeated, Vancouver continued to benefit from the industry despite fluctuations caused by the cyclical nature of the runs. So certain was the CPR that salmon canned at Steveston would be shipped eastwards or overseas from Vancouver, that it constructed a branch, the Vancouver and Lulu Island Railway, to serve the canneries and, incidentally, to make much of the CPR land grant available for residential development. Easy access meant the industry purchased most of its supplies, including machinery, from Vancouver rather than Victoria. Proximity also allowed the industry to draw on Vancouver for seasonal labour, a factor that contributed to serious labour unrest on the Fraser River in 1900.[10]

In contrast to vacillations in the fisheries, the lumber industry enjoyed steady growth to become the "king" of the city's industries with the Prairies as its the chief market. Of the 1,257 million feet cut on the coast in 1912, 812 million feet were sold there. To provide this lumber, old mills were expanded and new mills built in the established industrial areas along Burrard Inlet and False Creek as well as south and east of the city on the Fraser River. Even when major parts of their operations were outside city limits, the owners and managers of the mills often lived in Vancouver where they were among its "most influential" businessmen, its "most active entrepreneurs," and leaders in society. In 1903, John Hendry, head of the British Columbia Mills Timber & Trading Company, "the largest enterprise of its kind in the northwest" moved from New Westminster where he maintained an extensive mill to Vancouver, the site of his Hastings Saw Mill. A few years later, when William Mackenzie and Donald Mann of the Canadian Northern Railway organized the Canadian Western Lumber Company at Fraser Mills, east of New Westminster, their partner and general manager, A.D. McRae, built "Hycroft," the most palatial private home in Vancouver.[11]

The lumber industry was Vancouver's largest single employer, but it also supported such related industries as foundries, machine shops, and sash and door factories. By 1910, Vancouver

Even in 1906, sailing ships carried lumber cargoes away from the Hastings Saw Mill and other Burrard Inlet saw mills.

was the province's manufacturing centre with three-quarters of the provincial industrial output. This industrial growth occurred despite widely felt concern about a shortage of factory sites under public control. The CPR controlled most of the foreshore on Burrard Inlet and False Creek. As early as 1899, the Trades and Labour Council suggested creating a commission to control the foreshore and other public lands and create factory sites on land reclaimed from the eastern part of False Creek. This plan drew little support but interest in developing False Creek remained. From the turn of the century to 1912, "the city planned for, and from time to time the citizens voted on, schemes to dredge the mud flats, make the area navigable, and build docks and terminals in the proposed basin." Civic enthusiasm, however, was never quite sufficient to get two-thirds of the voters to endorse a particular scheme. Such plans may have reflected a desire to have shipping facilities independent of the CPR and certainly illustrated hopes of expanded coastal and overseas trade. The ultimate disposition of the east end of False Creek demonstrated a desire to cooperate with the CPR's competitors and as great a concern for inland as for seaboard trade. In 1910, the city gave the Great Northern Railway a strip of the foreshore in return for its dropping claims to riparian rights and building a station on its newly acquired False Creek lands. Three years later, the city gave 113 acres of False Creek land to the Canadian Northern Railway which promised to fill in False Creek east of Main Street as a site for its station and yards, establish deep-sea shipping facilities, base a trans-Pacific shipping line at Vancouver, and build two hotels. Over three-quarters of the ratepayers approved the controversial by-law and Mackenzie and Mann set out to raise the necessary funds.[12]

The CPR had provided Vancouver's *raison d'être* and remained essential to its continued growth and metropolitan status. Still, Vancouver faced a two-fold problem: high freight rates and inadequate communication with some parts of the province. Nevertheless, the city had a major advantage over eastern competitors: cheap ocean freight rates permitted the importation of foreign products such as tea, coffee, and spices and their processing, packaging, and distribution throughout western Canada. Vancouver's wholesale trade grew and by 1910, nearly one thousand commercial travellers were based in the city. Some

locally owned firms such as W.H. Malkin and Company and Kelly, Douglas and Company, both grocers, and McLennan, McFeely, and Prior, hardware dealers, had greatly expanded their activities during the gold rush and they built upon that growth to continue as important names in the business community. Some local firms, however, sold out to eastern entrepreneurs. Thus, local names such as George Trorey, Jeweller, Thomas Dunn, Wholesale Hardware, and Royal Crown Soap disappeared to be replaced respectively by Henry Birks and Son of Montreal, Woods, Vallance and Company of Hamilton, and the multinational Lever Brothers.[13]

Whether locally owned or not, the wholesalers and small manufacturers contributed to Vancouver's economy and through such agencies as the Board of Trade vigorously pursued the trade of the Interior. As the fruit industry expanded in the Okanagan Valley, they sought to make Vancouver a marketing centre. To publicize Okanagan apples, the city cooperated with the Vancouver Information and Tourist Association, the Trades and Labour Council, and a number of businessmen to sponsor the first Canadian National Apple Show in the fall of 1911. The city and the Board of Trade organized expeditions to the Okanagan seeking its trade. While apples could be shipped from the Okanagan to supply overseas and Vancouver markets, the lack of a direct rail link led Vancouver wholesalers to buy more perishable soft fruits for local sale from Seattle rather than from the still somewhat inaccessible Okanagan.

Control of the Kootenay mining industry and that district's trade still largely eluded Vancouver's grasp. Neither talk nor promises of provincial aid built a railway linking the coast to the Kootenay. In fact, completion of the CPR's Crow's Nest Pass line in 1899 and its special freight rates allowed Calgary and Winnipeg to share in the Kootenay trade. Despite the CPR's unwillingness to make more than minor concessions in freight rates from Vancouver, the President of the Board of Trade boasted of Vancouver becoming a distributing centre for the Kootenay and as far east as Calgary and Lethbridge.[14]

In dealing with the Prairies, Vancouver had effective rail links but suffered from British Columbia's high freight rates. The Board of Trade, with the provincial government's moral support, regularly complained to the federal Board of Railway Commissioners, but that agency upheld the CPR's claim that

*The close economic relationship between Alberta and Vancouver is illustrated by the presence in Vancouver of **a meat-packing plant** owned by Patrick Burns & Company of Calgary.*

Leonard Frank Photos

Many Chinese worked as domestic servants. Some lived in their employers' homes; others commuted from Chinatown.

By 1906, Chinatown was a well-established part of the city. The recessed balconies, evident in several of the buildings shown, were one of its unique architectural features. The Chinese Empire Reform Association of Canada building stands out in this photograph. A number of Chinese associations erected similar buildings in Chinatown. The ground floor was rented for commercial purposes; upper floors provided meeting rooms and some residential accommodation.

operating a railway in British Columbia's mountains was more costly than elsewhere. Nevertheless, Vancouver merchants copied Winnipeg enterprise and, in 1911, about a hundred of them made an excursion to the principal western centres to collect, record, and disseminate information in order to expand "our trade with our Sister Provinces." Such expeditions succeeded. One clothing manufacturer sold a half-million dollars' worth of goods in the three western provinces during 1912 and claimed the territory west of Winnipeg depended on Vancouver for ready-made clothing. Presumably, as fellow westerners, Prairie residents preferred the American styles popular in Vancouver rather than the British fashions produced by Toronto garment makers. Vancouver building styles also appeared on the Prairies in the form of the unique homes and commercial structures prefabricated by the British Columbia Mills Timber and Trading Company.[15]

The most exciting aspect of Vancouver's relationship with the Prairies was the prospect of becoming a grain exporting centre. The Panama Canal (opened in 1914) reduced the time during which ships carrying grain from Vancouver to Europe would be in the tropics where heat might damage cargoes. With the construction of the Canadian Northern underway by the summer of 1910 and the CPR double-tracking and reducing grades on its line through British Columbia, getting grain to the coast would be no problem especially since the CPR, early in 1909, announced special rates on export grain from Alberta.

Alberta interests pressed for Vancouver's development as a grain port. As early as 1902 they called for freight rate concessions and construction of grain handling facilities, including elevators, in Vancouver. The Calgary Board of Trade in 1912 organized a Panama Canal convention with the slogan "To the west with the wheat." The Vancouver Board of Trade joined the fight for better freight rates and discussed grain handling needs but took no firm action. There was disagreement over the formation of a Harbour Commission. City Council asked Ottawa to improve the harbour and create a Commission; the Board of Trade thought a Commission "an immature and inadvisable" idea, likely to make Vancouver an expensive port. H.H. Stevens, who became Conservative M.P. for Vancouver in the 1911 election, strongly advocated harbour expansion. Responding to his entreaties, the Borden government established a Vancouver Harbour Commission in 1913 and embarked on an active programme of harbour development including the construction of a grain elevator.[16]

Whereas in 1897 Vancouver's immediate economic goal was to complete the displacement of Victoria as the province's leading commercial centre, by 1913 the city was on the threshold of becoming the metropolitan centre for all of western Canada. In 1897, Vancouver businessmen had had to struggle to secure trade, while by 1913 business was often coming to them. And where in 1897 the coastal and overseas trade were potential sources of growth, by 1913 Vancouver's expansion was solidly based on the rapid development of the Interior of British Columbia and of the Prairie Provinces. By land and by sea, Vancouver seemed likely to continue to prosper.

POPULATION GROWTH AND ETHNIC RELATIONSHIPS

As Vancouver prospered, its population grew. "People are coming from everywhere," asserted the *Province* in 1907 as it reported the city was growing by fifty people per day. The booster group, the Hundred Thousand Club, formed in 1906, realized its immediate goal of increasing Vancouver's population in 1911 and changed its name to the Half Million League. Immigrants came from beyond the Rockies, from the United States, from Europe (especially Britain), and from Asia. In principle, most immigrants were welcome — if they were white — because of the "dearth of suitable labour for many industries and for domestic help throughout the province." Yet, even white immigrants found that Vancouver, though not overly hostile and sometimes even indifferent to ethnic backgrounds, could be unfriendly. And although they consciously mentioned it only in the context of Asian immigrants, Canadian-born residents in Vancouver were anxious to preserve their identity. In 1911, they represented just under forty-four per cent of the population (Appendix, Table VII).[17]

New British immigrants were generally treated as the equals of Canadians in such matters as the franchise, and in municipal employment shared the preference given to British subjects over foreigners. To a considerable extent their immigration was encouraged. In 1911, for example, the Board of Trade, copying a Winnipeg plan, established a branch of the Imperial Home

Reunion Association to provide loans "to deserving English-speaking men resident in Vancouver who desired to bring their wives and (or) families to this city from the British Isles." Yet, the English, the largest group of the British immigrants, were not always welcome and were "confronted everywhere by the sign: 'No Englishman need apply.'" At least one Englishman got a job by passing himself off as a Scot. The London *Times* correspondent wrote from Vancouver in 1908:

> There is an idea in eastern Canada that Vancouver is. . . English, and that Englishmen find a more congenial atmosphere here than in the cities of the central and eastern provinces. If this be the case, then the situation in the east must be indeed deplorable, for, "deplorable", is hardly too strong a word to employ in describing the situation in Vancouver. . . . A young Englishman arriving in Vancouver has less chance of obtaining employment than a European of almost any other nationality. In the best club of Vancouver, when an Englishman is put up for permanent membership, a whip has to be sent to the English members in order to overcome the black-balls which will almost certainly be used against the candidate, only because he is an Englishman.

This hostility, arising from the patronizing attitude of some Englishmen and the contempt for indolent "remittance men," who lived on payments from "home," may partially explain why "rather than being more British than the city as a whole as was the case in 1891, the top portion of Vancouver's business community had by 1911 become more Canadian."[18]

As the *Times* correspondent suggested, continental immigrants often faced little difficulty in being accepted. Nevertheless, by 1912, the mayor reported "continuous protests" against Italians "who were particularly suited to work" being given preference over British in civic work crews. The Italian population had, by 1905 or so, grown sufficiently large to have its own church, benevolent societies, and groceries. The Italians were largely concentrated in the east end of Strathcona, immediately east of Chinatown and Little Tokyo. Strathcona, in fact, was the only part of the city that had any claim to being an "ethnic" neighbourhood. The oldest residential district in the city, it had established its character as a working-class neighbourhood by the early 1890s. Attractive to newcomers because its houses,

mainly on twenty-five foot lots, were relatively cheap, the neighbourhood was also within walking distance of many places of employment including the docks and wharves, some saw mills, and the sugar refinery. It was also well served by the street railway. The city as a whole, however, paid little attention to Strathcona. From time to time the health inspector might complain of crowded or unsanitary conditions in the "foreign quarter," but Strathcona certainly did not play the same role in Vancouver that the North End immigrant district did in Winnipeg. Yet from at least the turn of the century, Strathcona School provided an education for children of differing ethnic origins. The children were aware of ethnic differences. Angelo Branca, the son of an Italian food importer, a one-time middleweight champion of Canada, and later a Justice of the Supreme Court of British Columbia, recalled:

> [At school] there was always a lot of fighting. We had a large Chinese population there, Japanese, Jewish — and there was always a lot of ethnic wars and the Wops were good fighters. I was one of the best. You know those who weren't of an ethnic group would call the Chinese people Chinks and they'd call the Wops Dagos — and the Jewish people Sheenies and Bohunks and things like that and this is what they used to do, the Canadian-born, English, Scots and so on. They always felt superior. There was a very distinct type of racism in those days. As a single group they were the majority, but not if you took all the other ethnic groups. Kids can be terribly cruel and this was the cruelty that made itself felt.[19]

Not all immigrants resided in Strathcona, and any non-Asian who had the means and inclination could live wherever he pleased and move about easily in society. The Swedes and Germans, for example, organized their own churches and clubs, but no definable Swedish or German neighbourhood became established, and the city was probably generally unaware of their presence — with one notable exception, Alvo von Alvensleben. An ostentatiously wealthy promoter, he arrived in Vancouver in 1904, secured money from Germany to invest in real estate and industry, and built up a varied industrial empire ranging from coal mines to tourist resorts. He belonged to the best businessmen's clubs, helped found the Hundred Thousand

Club, and welcomed the cream of Vancouver society to parties at his suburban Kerrisdale estate. "He is a type of which the province of British Columbia has every reason to be proud," commented a contemporary biographer. With the outbreak of the European War, however, von Alvensleben became *persona non grata* and spent the rest of his life in Seattle.[20] Such was the fickle nature of Vancouver society.

Americans also experienced the city's changeable affections. They had easily blended into the dominant Anglo-Canadian society, and "a most kindly feeling" existed between the resident Americans and the people of Vancouver. Many Americans, for example, participated in the 1900 Dominion Day parade while three days later the Stars and Stripes flew from many buildings and stores to honour Independence Day. Vancouver residents so favoured American styles in clothing and domestic architecture that a British tourist feared, "the Yankees, of whom there are naturally a large number here, are trying to make Vancouver into an American city." Adapting such an argument, the *Province* in 1910 suggested L.D. Taylor should not be elected mayor because of his American origin, a specious argument since C.S. Douglas, the candidate the *Province* favoured, was also American by birth! Individual Americans found a hostile climate if they were perceived as taking jobs that "could be just as capably filled by our own people." The B.C. Electric learned through bitter experience — the discontent of its employees and the threatened intervention of the provincial government — that "a British subject is better able to control the labour situation in this country, than an American citizen."[21]

The public often blamed American agitators for labour unrest. One such incident occurred in spring 1903 when clerks and other non-operating CPR personnel, members of the recently organized United Brotherhood of Railway Employees, walked out to support their demand for union recognition. Longshoremen, teamsters, and some coastal seamen refused to handle CPR freight; members of the Bakers Union and Building Trades Council would not work with "scab" goods brought in by the CPR, and some Vancouver Island coal miners joined the strike in sympathy. Although only slightly more than 2,000 men, scattered throughout the province, struck, the strike's four-month duration, the fatal shooting of labour leader Frank Rogers by CPR police in Vancouver, and the conclusion of the Royal Commission on Industrial Disputes that the strikes were part of an American-inspired socialist "conspiracy," contributed to lingering bitterness and suspicion on both sides. When unemployed men demonstrated early in 1912 to secure city relief, officials had little sympathy. They believed the protesters did not really want work but had been organized by American agitators. Their suspicions seemed confirmed when the American-based Industrial Workers of the World tried to turn the city's suppression of protests into a campaign for the right of free speech.[22]

Americans were useful scapegoats but opposition to them did not cause legal or physical conflict. They could become British subjects and enjoy all political rights; in contrast, Asians, even though they might become naturalized, could not vote and faced physical violence.

Until the mid-1890s, the Chinese were the only Asians in the province, but during that decade, the Japanese began to arrive. Most of the early Japanese immigrants settled at the fishing village of Steveston at the mouth of the Fraser River, but a small Japanese community also developed in Vancouver, adjacent to Chinatown. Here, they found boarding houses and employment agencies where newly-arrived immigrants, mostly male, could secure employment in sawmills, logging camps, the fisheries, and railroad construction, as well as in stores and services catering to their own community. Early in the century Japanese immigration declined sharply as the Japanese government, preparing for war with Russia, refused to allow potential soldiers to leave. In 1905, after Japan had won that war, emigration increased. As more Japanese came, they established "Little Tokyo" whose buildings, unlike those in Chinatown, had little distinctive architecture. Unlike the Chinese, many Japanese were able to send for their wives and families. Their community gained a reputation for being relatively clean and law-abiding. Nevertheless, their district:

> was a physically segregated area — as it was mentally. And from the physical, the immigrants gained a deep consciousness of their separateness. The area was apart as if a ghetto wall defined it. It was possible to shop at Japanese-owned stores, to live in Japanese-operated boarding houses or hotels, to congregate at street corners, to sit in soft drink and

A view north from the Fairview district, looking across False Creek to the industrial sector of downtown Vancouver, c. 1911.

ice cream parlours, to eat traditional Japanese foods in cafes, to go to the Japanese language school and hall close by, to watch the local athletic teams play on the sandlot, to worship in the Buddhist temple or Christian church.[23]

The Chinese and Japanese lived in distinct areas as a consequence of custom and informal suasion rather than of any laws. Dupont Street [now Pender] was the heart of Chinatown and most Chinese lived on or nearby it. Part of Chinatown's unsavoury reputation came from the adjacent white slums where both single men and families — many of them recent immigrants — lived in squalor. Some European immigrants eventually moved to more attractive parts of the city, but the Asians remained in what was essentially a ghetto.

Most Vancouver residents shared the anti-Asian prejudices of North America's west coast, and they endorsed senior governments' efforts to limit Chinese and Japanese immigration. By passing and enforcing by-laws regulating lodging houses and the keeping of livestock, the city eliminated many sanitation problems in the Chinese and Japanese neighbourhoods, but the image of filth there remained in white minds and was occasionally reinforced by illustrated newspaper articles suggesting that Chinatown, "smeared with filth and with no perceptible inclination to assist the authorities in their duties as regards sanitization of the city" stood for "all that is irregular and out of all conforming with city ordinances."[24]

The economic, social, and political bases of hostility to Asians are too complex to be examined here, but that hostility had been unusually virulent in 1907. The number of Chinese immigrants had been severely restricted by the recent imposition of a $500 head tax, but the number of Japanese immigrants had risen from nothing during the Russo-Japanese War to approximately 2,000 in 1906. More Asians, including East Indians whose numbers in the city to date were few, were expected. Asians formed probably no more than 10,000 of the city's population of 60,000, but the mayor claimed that a quarter of the population was of Asian origin. R.G. Macpherson, Liberal M.P. (Vancouver City) wired Prime Minister Laurier in August that 4,000 Japanese had arrived since January and that 2,000 more were coming. That figure was grossly exaggerated (many Japanese only stopped at Vancouver en route to the United States), but the larger figure was the one popularly believed (Appendix, Tables VIII and IX).[25]

On August 12, 1907, the founding meeting of the Asiatic Exclusion League in Vancouver declared that unless checked, the Japanese would "ultimately control this part of Canada." Four weeks later, on a hot, humid September evening, the Asiatic Exclusion League held a parade and mass meeting at City Hall to protest Japanese immigration. The crowd, estimated at anywhere from 8,000 to 30,000 heard speeches from such people as Rev. G.H. Wilson, an Anglican clergyman whose son became the chief anti-Japanese agitator in Vancouver during World War II; C.M. Woodworth, president of the Conservative Association, and A.E. Fowler, secretary of the Asiatic Exclusion League of Seattle. The meeting denounced Lieutenant-Governor James Dunsmuir for refusing to sign a provincial bill designed to curb Asian immigration and called on the federal government to permit British Columbia's immigration laws to stand. After the meeting, an effigy of Dunsmuir was burned while some speakers continued to make inflammatory statements. As the crowd wandered about the area, someone threw a stone breaking the windows of a tailor's shop in nearby Chinatown. The mob began smashing windows of Chinese shops and homes, then moved a few blocks to the Japanese quarter on Powell Street. The Japanese, armed with sticks, bottles, and knives repelled the invaders. There were some injuries but no fatalities. Nearly every Chinese-owned building had been damaged and fifty-nine Japanese properties were wrecked. The police had failed to halt the riot, but did prevent a recurrence the next night.[26]

The News-Advertiser and the World blamed young hoodlums for the riot; some blamed American labour agitators such as W.A. Young, a Seattle-based organizer for the American Federation of Labor who had spoken at the rally. In any case, the Vancouver City Council, determined to avoid a repeat performance of an incident that had drawn unfavorable international attention to the city, unanimously ordered the Asiatic Exclusion League to cancel its next meeting. While youths and outside agitators may have been directly responsible for the riot, among the 2,000 paid-up members of the Asiatic Exclusion League were representatives of Vancouver's political and social elite including Mayor Alexander Bethune as well as trade union leaders. During the 1908 civic election, the League, advertising

This comfortable house on 8th Avenue in the Fairview district of Vancouver with its large, cultivated garden was the residence of Lauchlan McLean, a railway and general contractor.

Not far from Fairview a scattering of natives maintained a traditional life style on the Kitsilano Indian Reserve.

"For Your Children's Sake Vote the Asiatic Exclusion League Ticket," endorsed eight candidates for aldermen of whom six were elected. Political leaders wanted to preserve order but did not wish to admit any more Asians. G.H. Cowan, a Conservative candidate in the 1908 federal election told campaign audiences that ninety per cent of the people of British Columbia wanted to stop "this torrent of alien yellow blood" that is "gradually encroaching, gradually monopolizing all the smaller industries in Vancouver." Cowan's stunning electoral success suggests strong support for his stand.[27]

Since the Asians were effectively hived off into their own neighbourhoods, Vancouver had the overall appearance of a relatively homogeneous city in which Chinatown and Little Tokyo were perceived as aberrations. To tourists they were an interesting curiosity; to residents, they represented a failure to check immigration, a source of cheap labour but a danger to the preservation of white society, specifically, an Anglo-Canadian society. To a police chief eager to increase the size of his force "the mixture of races in the population. . . makes it incumbent upon the City to be prepared for circumstances calling for the highest efficiency in the Police Force."[28] The Anglo-Canadian majority in Vancouver could absorb other whites, but could not cope with people of different colour, culture, and economic status. Immigrants were desirable, but only if they readily ceased to be identifiable as such.

THE URBAN LANDSCAPE

Prosperity and population growth created a housing shortage. Slums and dilapidated "cabins" continued to be a problem. Real estate dealers and contractors, however, sought to provide homes for all who could pay and to maintain Vancouver's pride in being a city of homes where even men of modest means could expect to own their own single family dwelling on its own lot. The real estate men spurred speculation, and the contractors created jobs.

Real estate dealers had always been prominent in the city. Although they became less important to its permanent development, their numbers were much greater in the boom years. The opportunities for a quick fortune seemed certain and little capital was required to enter the business. Especially between 1909 and 1912 many residents succumbed to the fever that was the symptom of speculation, a Western Canadian, if not national, disease. Nevertheless, Vancouver led among major Canadian cities "in the proportion of people employed in the building trades and in loan, trust, and real estate companies as brokers and clerks." Even clergymen were speculators, and one of the most popular opened a real estate office "so that he might serve his congregation in this world as well as in the next." So numerous were the real estate agents that one visitor, observing them swarming "hungrily in the place," suggested dumping them in the sea.[29]

Home building was a major industry employing carpenters, plumbers, and electricians and providing an excellent market for local saw and shingle mills and sash door factories. Individual contractors or speculators built many homes, and there were also some experiments in cooperative schemes. Organizations such as Vancouver Free Homes, modelled on a Los Angeles plan, offered savings to potential homeowners by buying land in large blocks and materials by the carload. Yet, these houses showed "an evident rivalry to produce in each home a front newer in design, more quaint and more attractive than its neighbour." Most of these "Free Homes" were in South Vancouver.[30]

Settlement patterns tended to be closely related to street railway development (see Chapter 1, Map 2). Although the B.C. Electric Railway seldom built in advance of traffic, its interurban lines, including the old Westminster and Vancouver Tramway, passed through South Vancouver and Point Grey. Thus, growth in the suburbs took place before the city itself was completely settled. As these areas grew, the BCER secured franchises and extended its city lines. Real estate firms inevitably referred to the proximity of the street railway or the prospect of service when advertising their lots and subdivisions. Occasionally, they were so enthusiastic in their promotional material that the BCER had to deny claims about proposed extensions, reduced fares, or improved service. Because of its importance for development, the BCER was also a divisive issue in municipal politics, especially in the suburbs. Nevertheless, public transportation helped Vancouver maintain its pride in being a city of homes.[31]

Much growth took place within the original corporate limits. Older areas became more fully settled while retaining many

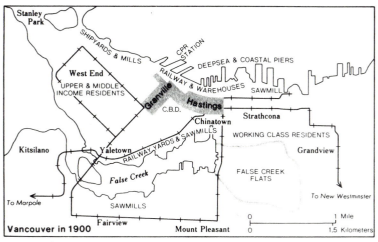

4 Vancouver in 1900

original characteristics (see Chapter 4, Map 4). The West End remained a prestige area but the opening of Shaughnessy Heights and the construction of apartment blocks presaged impending change. Though less fashionable than the West End, Fairview remained one of the "better class suburbs." Clerks and artisans found its land prices, property taxes, and terms of payment within their means. Fairview really began to grow in 1900-01 when more "handsome houses" were erected than in the previous ten years. Although the streets were muddy, the water supply spotty, the sidewalks bad, and the street lights far apart, it was then the city's fastest growing section. By 1907, its streets were well-graded, new water mains provided adequate pressure even in the higher areas, the lawns were neatly kept, the street railway gave a seven-and-a-half minute service, and it was the home of the city's new Vancouver General Hospital, an institution that rapidly became a first-class referral hospital for the entire province.

Mount Pleasant, an older district, grew slowly. In 1904, some property sold for less than it did during the 1890s boom, and in 1908, the eastern section was so thinly settled that the BCER could not justify constructing a short street railway line. A few residents listed farming as their occupation. Mount Pleasant remained uniquely free of speculation except along Westminster

Avenue, its main business street, where the temptation to profit led the Presbyterians and Baptists to put their property on the market and build new churches elsewhere. The East End, an even older area, grew more slowly still. It had relatively little vacant land and the influx of commerce and industry made it less attractive as a residential area. The city tried to prevent overcrowding, largely an East End phenomenon, through a building by-law allowing only one dwelling for every 2,000 square feet on any one lot. In fact the city did little more than complain about the continued presence of cabins and shacks along the Inlet.[32]

Two new suburbs, Grandview and Kitsilano, also grew up within city limits. Grandview, though named in the early 1890s when the Westminster and Vancouver Tramway opened the district, did not begin to develop rapidly until 1905 when it became a popular area for skilled workmen to build homes. By 1907, Professor Edward Odlum, a real estate dealer, told reporters that the anticipated fifteen minute street car service, the opening of streets, the introduction of electric light and the sewer would soon "add much to the comfort of the people" as he complained the whole East End lacked a sewerage system. Parts of the district were also without city water. The lack of city services was not confined to such working-class areas; the skilled workmen, salesmen and clerks who settled in the CPR's new "better class" and more expensive neighbourhood, Kitsilano, suffered similar problems.[33]

The most exciting growth, varied development, and spectacular speculation took place outside city limits. In the unorganized areas of Hastings Townsite and District Lot 301, the prospect of city improvements and street railway service raised real estate values but the areas remained working class. Low prices, easy terms (as little as $15 cash and $10 a month for a lot in "Scenic Heights, 'The Point Grey of Eastern Vancouver'") and easy communication made these areas attractive to men who desired "to have their families free from the contamination of such thickly populated and unsanitary conditions as men of our means are frequently obliged to live under in the centre of the city."[34] Hastings Townsite and D.L. 301 were small; most suburban growth was in South Vancouver and Point Grey (Chapter 2, Map 4).

South Vancouver was incorporated as a municipality in 1892.

After the completion of the Westminster and Vancouver Tramway, Cedar Cottage and Collingwood, two stations, slowly emerged as mixed rural-suburban neighbourhoods where real estate men usually quoted prices by the acre rather than the lot. The opening of the CPR's Vancouver and Lulu Island Railway in 1902 spurred development at Eburne (Marpole), a sawmilling centre on the Fraser River, and stimulated some settlement adjacent to the route.[35]

South Vancouver's original settlers were thrifty individuals who wanted to avoid taxation as much as possible. From 1893 to 1905, the municipality refused to issue debentures to finance improvements; in 1897, it adopted the single tax. The slogan of almost every candidate at every election was "Keep the debt down" and many ratepayers chose to work on the roads rather than pay taxes. Many did not, in fact, have roads to their homes. By 1905, property owners in the western sections were so frustrated by their inability to develop their land, they elected their own candidate as reeve and got the province to create a new municipality west of Cambie Street. Thus Point Grey came into being on January 1, 1908.[36]

Had the dissident western landowners not separated, they would have experienced expansion with a vengeance. As real estate dealers moved in, South Vancouver was about to undergo rapid change from a cautious, semi-rural society to a speculator's paradise governed by a boom psychology. Although the south slope overlooking the Fraser River attracted some affluent Vancouver residents, most of South Vancouver was a working class bedroom suburb. One real estate firm advertised its subdivision as "The Workingmen's Paradise"; another deliberately began selling lots at 2 p.m. on a Saturday afternoon to give workers a chance to buy on their weekly half holiday. Most important, South Vancouver lots were relatively cheap and the terms, easy. In 1907, a lot could be had for as little as $160 with a down payment of $25 and payments advertised as averaging less than fifty cents a day. South Vancouver was, as a contemporary wrote, "above all things, a place for 'home,' with all that envisions — that word so full of meaning to the British people." The British reference was appropriate since a large portion of the new settlers were recently arrived from England.[37]

By 1911, its 16,126 people made South Vancouver the third largest "city" in the province and its population was continuing to grow by an average of 200 families per month. Land was its chief asset and few sites were set aside for parks or extensive school grounds. Real estate developers successfully pressed for new public works and services, and ratepayers gave the BCER an extremely generous forty-year franchise and tax concessions in return for the company's agreement to lay more street railway lines. The street railway did promote growth. Between 1901 and 1911, assessments increased twenty-fold and, on streets where rails were laid, lot prices rose from $200 to $500 to $500 to $2,000. Unfortunately, extensive street railway trackage scattered the population and increased costs for such services as streets, sewers, and water pipes. The municipal debt increased from $209,000 in 1909 to $4,716,879 in 1912. Anyone who dared ask about taxes was a "knocker"; only a "booster" could survive in the atmosphere of these buoyant times (Appendix, Table III).[38]

Whereas South Vancouver was a working class suburb growing according to the whims of subdividers rather than according to any plan, much of Point Grey was an affluent, well-planned area. When the provincial government started to auction its West Point Grey lands in 1906, the land was mainly covered with timber; there were no roads, drainage or public utilities. Thus, Point Grey was virgin territory where City Beautiful ideas of curved streets and ample parkland could be applied without interfering with any existing land use. Unlike their neighbours in South Vancouver these well-to-do residents, who spent an average of $800 per acre for future homesites, could afford to spend more on municipal amenities that, in turn, increased the value of their properties. Before the municipality was incorporated, the Point Grey Improvement Association sought support for a public park, a marine driveway of the best possible construction, and the employment of a first-class landscape surveyor to plan the unsurveyed portions of Point Grey. In his inaugural address, Reeve S.L. Howe declared that the Municipal Council hoped to make Point Grey into a "thickly settled and most beautiful residential district." In its first year, the Council passed a by-law containing "the germs of the modern science of town planning." The Council built good quality roads, set aside $100,000 to conserve park sites, and adjusted municipal taxation to discourage speculative land purchases. Point Grey's real jewel, however, was the CPR's exclusive subdivision, Shaughnessy Heights. Sir Thomas

"Hycroft," built by A.D. McRae of the Canadian Western Lumber Company, was one of the first homes erected in Shaughnessy Heights. During World War II, General McRae gave the home to the federal government for use as a veterans' hospital. Since 1962 the University Women's Club has occupied and restored it.

At the turn of the century when this photograph was taken, the West End was the city's most fashionable residential district. The table is set for a lavish tea, part of the social routine known as the "At Home."

Samuel MacLure, a leading residential architect of British Columbia, designed "Gabriola" for B.T. Rogers of the B.C. Sugar Refinery in 1900. The mansion was probably named after Gabriola Island, the source of its stone exterior. In Vancouver, where lumber was plentiful, stone was rarely used for more than minor decorative features in residential buildings. "Gabriola" later became part of an apartment block and survives as a restaurant.

The Dominion Trust Building under construction on West Hastings.

The Post Office, built between 1905 and 1910, was in the centre of the financial district that developed on Hastings Street.

The completed Dominion Trust, one culmination of Vancouver's efforts to become a financial metropolis.

Looking northward towards the CPR station from the corner of Georgia and Granville in 1910.

Charles Woodward's second Vancouver store built in 1903 on Hastings Street.

The Birks Building going up in 1912–13 at the prime retail corner of Georgia and Granville.

The Toronto-based Canadian Bank of Commerce employed Toronto architects to design this "temple bank", constructed between 1906 and 1908.

Shaughnessy himself took great interest in developing this area which was first put on the market in 1909. In Shaughnessy, the CPR laid graciously curved paved streets and installed water, sewer, and other utilities before selling lots. Because land was sold in large parcels and carried building restrictions, Shaughnessy Heights escaped most speculation fever. Indeed, in 1911, Shaughnessy homesites were selling "for less than the average assessed price of the unimproved and unregulated area available for working people."[39]

Not all of Point Grey consisted of new subdivisions for the affluent. The area also included the old settlement of Eburne where employees of nearby saw mills, an abattoir, and flour mills resided. The conflict between the new and the old residents, between the well-to-do and the working class came to a head over the BCER franchise. The owners of undeveloped land including businessmen who had bought Kerrisdale land for country estates were prepared to accept almost any terms, including the forty-year franchise the BCER demanded in return for electric light and street railway service. The political leaders of Eburne, who dominated the first Point Grey Council, however, sympathized with municipal ownership of utilities. In any case, they had acquired electric lights while still part of South Vancouver and had street railway service (though they considered the fares excessive) via the Vancouver and Lulu Island Railway, so that their needs were not so pressing. Two municipal elections were fought on the franchise question; some Point Grey residents considered dividing the municipality or annexation to Vancouver as a solution. Finally, the BCER suspended its Point Grey service except on interurban lines, cancelled settlers' fares, and stopped all construction work. This forced the issue. After some months of walking and of waiting for building materials, Point Grey residents approved a forty-year agreement with the BCER.[40]

While the residential areas of the city and suburbs were growing, downtown was also changing. Despite the absence of zoning regulations, distinct retailing, wholesaling, and financial districts appeared. Competition for hegemony among downtown business districts ended as retailers gradually merged them into a "U"-shaped pattern along Westminster Avenue, Hastings and Granville Streets. Hastings Street, the base of the "U", became "one of the best business sections" with real estate values as high as anywhere in the city. The opening of Woodward's new department store there in 1904, the completion in 1908 of a nine-storey department store by David Spencer and Company, an old Victoria firm, and the presence of small specialty shops confirmed the importance of Hastings as a shopping street.

The wholesale district's general location was roughly determined before 1897. By 1911, wholesale houses filled the entire area from the CPR Station to the Hastings Saw Mill. Dammed between Hastings Street and the CPR tracks, wholesalers built skyward but crowding continued. When congestion forced the CPR to build new yards in suburban Coquitlam, some land near its roundhouse became available for general development. After 1910 a second wholesale district sprang up near the north end of the Cambie Street Bridge.

The appearance of a financial district and local financial institutions were the best indications of economic maturity. Several chartered banks had been present almost from the city's beginning; between 1895 and 1900, four eastern banks established Vancouver branches. By 1914, fourteen different chartered banks had branches in the city. Most followed the example of the first banks and established branches on Granville or Hastings Streets.

One of the most distinctive architectural additions to the city, the Dominion Trust Building on Hastings, a few blocks east of Granville, symbolized Vancouver's aspirations to be a financial centre. This thirteen storey building was "the most modern office building in Canada, the highest steel structure on the West Coast, and the tallest building in the British Empire" when completed in 1910. A locally owned enterprise, the Dominion Trust specialized in investments in British Columbia real estate. A second local financial institution, the Bank of Vancouver, incorporated in 1908, secured subscriptions for over half a million dollars' worth of stock. Soon after opening its Vancouver office in March 1910, it established branches in the suburbs as well as in New Westminster, Chilliwack, and the railway boom centres of Coquitlam, Fort George, and Hazelton. Another endeavour to secure financial leadership of the hinterland was the formation of the Vancouver Stock Exchange in summer 1907. It traded in local issues, Coeur d'Alene mining shares, and, by 1913-14, in Alberta oil stocks. Most of these local ventures were highly speculative, and, apart from the Stock Exchange, did not survive the depression that began in 1912.[41]

By 1913, Vancouver was a very different city than it had been in 1897. When the boom started the commercial area was small and exhibited only a primitive level of specialization of function. By 1913, definite retail, wholesale, and financial areas were evident. In 1897, the city had had only two heavily settled residential districts, the West End, where the affluent usually lived, and the more varied East End. By 1913, the West End was being challenged as the elite residential district by Shaughnessy Heights and Point Grey; the East End had become partly a "foreign" quarter and largely the home of labourers and their families while skilled workmen had moved to several new districts south and east of False Creek and into suburban municipalities. City "planning," aside from the affluent areas of Point Grey and Shaughnessy, was virtually non-existent and settlement was largely inspired by the extensions and franchise negotiations of the BCER. One sentiment dominated all areas of the city, however, and that was that Vancouver should be a "city of homes."

CIVIC POLITICS AND GOVERNMENT

Population growth and the dispersal of settlement placed heavy demands on Vancouver and its neighbouring municipalities to provide basic civic amenities. Prior to 1912, the city proper had no problem raising funds to expand its services. Every measure of civic finance — the value of assessable property, the amount of taxes levied, and gross revenue — rose almost without interruption. Taxpayers rarely defeated money by-laws. An English investment adviser reported that by 1912 Vancouver had borrowed $28,360,830 but had assets of $34,993,710. He had no doubt of the city's ability to pay off its debt. The borrowed money had been put to good use. Paved and gravelled streets replaced muddy roadways, and sewers and drains eliminated much of the stench that once pervaded parts of the city. R.S. Lea, a Montreal consulting engineer who examined the region's sewerage system, noted that despite justified complaints about False Creek, conditions there were "not as bad" as on the waterfronts of Toronto or Montreal. Moreover, people expected to have modern plumbing, piped-in water closets, and bathtubs as normal facilities in their homes

and apartments. By the end of 1912, Vancouver had 153 miles of sewers, 259 miles of water mains, 50 miles of asphalted or permanently treated streets, and 141 miles of rocked streets. Belying the fact that the city was still oriented to the pedestrian rather than the automobile, which was already damaging street surfaces, there were 191 miles of concrete sidewalks. And Vancouver still had its greatest asset, a pure water supply.[42]

Nevertheless, not all was well. Apart from the water supply, Dr. F.T. Underhill, the city's Medical Health Officer, found little to praise about health conditions. Deaths from tuberculosis and infant mortality were high. The city was eager to enforce regulations to improve the milk supply but lacked jurisdiction. The Vancouver Medical Association undertook a voluntary milk certification programme but only some dairies cooperated. Dr. Underhill told a provincial Royal Commission that "the milk is poor in quality, dirty, sometimes skimmed, and water is frequently added." The milk supply was only one public health problem. The Health Department's annual reports read like a litany of complaints about overcrowded old buildings and shacks in certain parts of the city, inadequate sewerage and drainage, and unsatisfactory scavenging.[43]

The state of the streets and sewers created greater public interest than any proposals for structural reform of the civic government. Though Vancouver was not immune to ideas of municipal reform then current in North America, her primary interests were practical and immediate. Mayor L.D. Taylor, publisher of the *World* and best remembered for his reluctance to wear formal dress, his red necktie, his Socialist leanings, and introduction of the single tax, spent more time during his first four election campaigns discussing plans to remedy inefficiencies in the city's Engineering Department than on theoretical reforms. Many Vancouverites sympathized with his rhetorical question, "Why it so often happens that after a street is macadamized the waterworks men begin to lay pipes at one end while the roller is hardly out of sight on the other?" The question was not really divisive; every candidate for mayor and most aldermanic candidates agreed on the need to reorganize the Engineering Department. Change came, but it was too late to aid Taylor politically. In analyzing his 1912 defeat, the *Province* suggested a major factor was muddle in the city, its streets, sewerage system, and all its public works.[44]

To outsiders, Vancouver's most notable civic experiment was adoption of the single tax in 1910, that is, a levy on land values only and not on improvements. Within Vancouver, the single tax was no novelty and its adoption aroused little interest. The City Charter had always provided for the separate assessment of land and improvements and empowered the city to exempt the latter from taxation in whole or part. In 1895, Vancouver reduced the tax on improvements to fifty per cent; in 1906, to twenty-five per cent. In 1903, South Vancouver withdrew taxation from improvements, and other British Columbia cities, including Victoria and Vernon, seriously contemplated the single tax. When Vancouver City Council held a special meeting on taxation in March 1910, the vote to eliminate the tax on improvements was close, but most debate was on an old and emotional question, exempting churches from taxation. To avoid tempting owners of valuable land from crowding their property Council secured the ratepayers' approval of a by-law putting a 120 foot height limit on new buildings.

Once Vancouver adopted the single tax, inquiries poured into city hall from all over North America. Single tax advocates including Henry George, Jr. and Joseph Fels visited Vancouver so to see for themselves. *The Single Tax Review* featured Vancouver in one issue, and a Henry George anniversary dinner in New York City congratulated Vancouver for "being the first city, approaching metropolitan proportions enterprising enough to adopt the single tax method of taxation." Vancouver had somewhat less than a pure Henry George product, for it had merely removed the tax from improvements. The city still collected business license fees, the much-hated poll tax, and special assessments and frontage taxes for local public works. Single tax advocates ascribed Vancouver's "phenomenal growth" to the single tax but overlooked the fact that growth was general throughout Western Canada, even in cities that did not adopt the single tax.[45]

Writing in *The Single Tax Review* in 1911, Mayor Taylor claimed Vancouver was "the only city of metropolitan size on the continent to elect a municipal government on a Single Tax platform." Taylor had either forgotten the previous election campaign or the *World* was incompetent in reporting it. Apart from a general statement advocating exemption of improvements from taxation as one of the many planks in his platform,

Taylor did not refer to the single tax at all. The only record of his advocacy of the single tax principle *before* its adoption was a *World* editorial published a month *after* the election. At that time he paraphrased a classic single tax argument that "Land has little or no value apart from population, trade and industry, and it is recognized as eminently just and fair that land should bear the burden of taxation incurred by communities in creating its value," and he argued the single tax would remove guesswork in valuing improvements. By then suggesting that the publicity accompanying the single tax would attract manufacturers, Taylor clearly indicated he had more in common with civic boosters than with socialists. His boosterism, in turn, was as much related to his desire to make the city grow as to the megalomania of which his critics accused him.[46]

The City Charter had permitted adoption of the single tax, but the provincial government was cautious in approving other civic reforms or any change in municipal government. The Legislature had to approve any change in the charter, a procedure that was not automatic, but it could also amend the charter, a provincial statute, without the city's approval as it did in 1904 when it transferred most powers of Council's Police Committee to a provincially appointed Police Commission. Similarly, Vancouver had to secure provincial approval when it sought to annex two adjacent unorganized districts and several neighbouring municipalities that were under the Municipal Act.

Vancouver had relatively little influence in the provincial government. In 1902, redistribution gave Vancouver only five of the Legislature's forty-two seats. Throughout the Conservative regime of Richard McBride (1903-15) Vancouver elected a "Solid Five" Conservative slate and had at least one member, either Minister of Finance or Attorney-General, in cabinet. The strength of Vancouver's support of the Conservatives is less significant than it seems. In 1909 and 1912, the Conservatives virtually wiped out the opposition; everybody in the province seemed to like McBride, the Conservatives, and their policies. Moreover, Vancouver MLAs tended to be loyal first to the province and then to the city. This was not inappropriate for the province was also growing rapidly in population and wealth, and Vancouver did not have the pre-eminent position that Montreal, Toronto, or Winnipeg had within their respective provinces.

Despite political debates over the efficiency of the city's engineering department, streets and cement sidewalks did get laid as this scene on Georgia Street near Seymour Street illustrates.

As a relatively new city, Vancouver was comparatively free of many of the problems of the continent's older cities such as acres of slums and entrenched corrupt politicians, but its administrative problems generated interest in two fashionable forms of municipal government, commission government and the board of control. Many municipal leaders, themselves engaged in small or medium business, particularly real estate, were eager to streamline the conduct of Council's day-to-day business. Aldermanic salaries were too low to permit anyone without private means to make municipal politics a full-time career and Vancouver had a few "gentlemen." "Prominent" residents were usually too fully occupied with their own business affairs to take on time-consuming aldermanic chores. The twelve aldermen who acted on a part-time basis often failed to conduct civic business with efficiency, speed, or thoughtful consideration. Because of the ward system, aldermen often had a special interest in a particular district.[47]

City Council and the Board of Trade began discussing a board of control in 1907. On two occasions, electors expressed no clear preference for a board of control over the existing system. Early in 1911, voters were able to choose among the existing system, the board of control, or a commission form of a government after Mayor Taylor, Alderman H.H. Stevens, the *Daily Province*, and an active Commission Government Association pressed for another vote. Yet as the election campaign progressed, the press and public gave more attention to individual candidates than to the plebiscite on the form of government. Of the 7,481 who voted for mayoralty candidates, only 5,005 bothered to express an opinion on the form of government. Nevertheless, all wards showed a strong preference for commission government, which had been explained to them as "a board of municipal directors" consisting of the mayor and four commissioners elected at large.[48] In addition to his legislative functions, each commissioner would be responsible for the administration of certain civic departments.

Council, agreeing with Alderman Stevens on the need to "make haste slowly," set up a special committee to examine commission government. By the end of 1911, Vancouver was ready to ask the Legislature to amend its Charter to allow the city to have its affairs administered by a mayor and four aldermen, all of whom would be subject to the progressive measures of

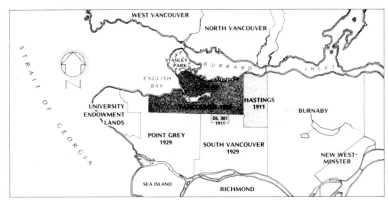

5 Vancouver's Boundary Extensions, 1886-1980

initiative, referendum, and recall. To allow the mayor and aldermen to maintain full-time office hours at City Hall and to attend daily business meetings, the city sought authority to pay the mayor $10,000 per annum and the aldermen, $7,500, each. The Legislature refused to amend the City Charter but appointed a Royal Commission to investigate municipal government generally and commission government particularly. Many councillors may have breathed a sigh of relief. Six of the seven aldermen who appeared before the Royal Commission opposed commission government and most agreed with Alderman Frank Trimble who declared, "I don't think we can better the present means of legislation for the City Council." Vancouver had flirted with reform but decided it was not necessary.[49]

While dabbling with new forms of civic government, Vancouver gave consideration to annexing its neighbours. In 1911, the city increased its area by almost fifty per cent through the annexation of two parcels of land administered by the provincial government: Hastings Townsite (2,950 acres) east of Grandview and the prosaically named 350 acre "squared bit of No Man's Land" south of Mount Pleasant, D.L. 301 (see Introduction, p.13). By 1907, real estate agents were busy selling lots in these areas to workingmen; in 1910, the city planned to extend its limits to include them and it promised water sewers, macadamized roads, and sidewalks. In both areas, only one voter opposed amalgamation. The perpetual street railway, light and power franchise the BCER had obtained for these districts in 1908

The Ladies Auxiliary of the Vancouver General Hospital started an ambulance service in 1902; the city took over the responsibility in 1910.

Photographer Philip Timms captured Fire Wagon No. 2 in action, c. 1900.

complicated matters, but on January 1, 1911 they became part of the city.[50]

The annexation of Hastings Townsite and D.L. 301 was accomplished with relative ease, but they formed only a small part of the Greater Vancouver movement. A Greater Vancouver and Contiguous Municipal League composed of delegates from Vancouver, the city and district of North Vancouver, South Vancouver, Point Grey, and Burnaby began meeting early in 1911 to discuss such subjects of common interest as a water system, trunk roads, local improvements, the investment of sinking funds, an isolation hospital, and tramway fares. The short run success of Greater Vancouver was confined to appointing R.S. Lea to examine the sewerage system and the creation of the Vancouver and District Joint Sewerage and Drainage Board in 1913. In the long term, the movement failed because of complications caused by the varying terms of the BCER franchises in the different districts and the lack of sustained enthusiasm outside Vancouver and South Vancouver.

In 1901, Vancouver had consolidated the separate, mainly short term franchises the BCER held for each street railway line into a common one expiring in 1919 when the city would have the option to buy out the street railway. In return for this eighteen-year franchise, the BCER accepted several conditions including annual payment of a percentage of its street railway earnings in return for the use of the city streets, a specified minimum service schedule, and a maximum five cent fare. To reduce the likelihood of the city exercising its option to take over the street railway, the BCER took special pains to negotiate long term franchises in the suburbs. The existence of two separate street railway systems with their own fare structures would be inconvenient for riders. If the suburbs were incorporated into the city, the situation after 1919 might be impossible. Beginning in 1909, South Vancouver, Point Grey, and Vancouver held intermittent, tedious, and complex discussions with the BCER on franchise consolidation. When a scheme for a common franchise expiring in 1937 was devised, Vancouver rejected it "with a thump which could be heard all over town." The aldermen were eager to take over the apparently profitable street railway in 1919, and they feared that franchise consolidation would reduce suburban interest in annexation.[51]

South Vancouver, however, persistently favoured annexation and enjoyed a warm courtship with Vancouver. Both parties knew a united Vancouver, with increased assets and population, would attract bond buyers. The city saw an opportunity for fresh water anchorage on the Fraser River while South Vancouver expected new public works (especially sewers), free mail delivery, and better fire insurance rates. Early in 1911, South Vancouver ratepayers voted 1,914 to 200 in favour of annexation. Vancouver ratepayers endorsed the idea by an even greater margin, 1,539 to 108, but turnout was low. Despite several mass meetings of Vancouver and South Vancouver residents, the provincial government refused to enact necessary legislation. It claimed the people were not unanimous, that British bondholders had been insufficiently consulted, that a sewerage system could be dealt with under the Municipal Clauses Act, that Vancouver had enough problems providing services within its existing limits, and that any scheme for Greater Vancouver must include Point Grey. In short, the province believed it must "hasten slowly" and ensure that the measure was in the public interest. Early in 1913, the two municipalities again sought annexation legislation but Premier Richard McBride again rejected their request until Burnaby was included and the BCER franchise question resolved. By 1913, however, British Columbia was deep in depression. South Vancouver, on account of its heavy borrowings and the speculative nature of much of its development, suffered more than most areas.[52]

Troubled times were not the occasion to take on new schemes or obligations. This was especially true in Vancouver where most municipal political leaders, like their constituents, did no more than flirt with reform or change. Mayor Taylor, with his enthusiasm for the single tax and commission government, was a political aberration whose eccentricities were tolerated only until the electorate realized his administration was in a muddle. As in the province as a whole, such mundane matters as streets and roads were more important to the average voter than any grand scheme of reform.

SOCIAL AND CULTURAL LIFE

The social and cultural activities of Vancouver residents were varied. Class differences were evident in many activities but many recreational pursuits, particularly outdoor ones, could be

The children shown in this 1910 Leonard Frank photograph enjoy dancing as part of their physical training class. That year the School Board's supervisor of drill boasted that the "Daily Movements of the pupils [were] now uniform, so far as it is possible."

Leonard Frank Photos

enjoyed by anyone. Although Vancouver was noticeably deficient in small neighbourhood parks, except where real estate subdividers used them as sales attractions, few children lacked a place to play. Many parts of the city still had vacant lots but in 1911-12, when it became apparent that few such natural play sites remained in some areas, the Local Council of Women initiated action that led City Council to establish supervised playgrounds in school yards.[53]

The many organized outdoor sports reflected the cosmopolitan origins of city residents. By 1912 there were ninety baseball teams, five amateur leagues, and a professional team that played against Victoria and several American teams. Cricket had its adherents among British immigrants, but the most popular spectator sport was the Canadian game, lacrosse. Vancouver professional teams sometimes competed successfully for national championships but were often beaten by their greatest rivals, the New Westminster Salmonbellies. So keen was intercity competition, that the BCER had to put on special trains for playoff games. Vancouver's mild climate delayed the introduction of ice hockey, but on January 5, 1912, the Vancouver Millionaires made their debut in the 10,500 seat Denman Arena, built by the Patrick family who established a professional hockey league composed of teams from Vancouver, New Westminster, and Victoria. The availability of artificial ice made skating a popular sport among the elite who organized the fashionable Connaught Skating Club.[54]

Indoor entertainment was abundant in variety. At least ten downtown theatres offered a varied diet ranging from touring American vaudeville companies, including the Pantages circuit, to Shakespeare, from touring opera stars such as Madame Melba to Hollywood movies. Vancouver, in fact, had Canada's first movie theatre and by 1913 had eight of them.[55]

The theatres also served politicians in search of an audience. After the 1903 CPR strike, the Socialist Party of Canada, whose base was Vancouver, doubled in size. Over the next few years it regularly drew 1,500 to 1,700 people to its Sunday evening meetings at the Empress Theatre but it had little measurable influence. Many of the audience were dressed in evening clothes and were there to be entertained, not proselytized. The *Western Clarion*, the Socialist newspaper, frequently complained that only nine or ten attended regular Socialist Party meetings.

Vancouver before the Great War was "not a hot-bed of socialism." The Socialist Party and its potential ally, the Vancouver Trades and Labour Council, were long divided over political strategy. The Socialist Party thought it should be the labour party whereas the Council wanted to form an Independent Labour Party as in Winnipeg. Moreover, the Socialist Party's class analysis was "difficult to justify when people were able to move up the economic ladder as more immigrants came in to replace them at the bottom." Individuals of modest backgrounds did rise to become part of the economic elite but wealth did not provide automatic entrée to the more exclusive social elite. Bankers, railway executives, and lawyers were more likely to belong to such socially prestigious groups as the Vancouver Club than self-made entrepreneurs or promoters who were prominent in the "second rank" Terminal City Club.[56]

Class differences did exist in Vancouver and can be seen clearly in the lives of its women. The fashionable women of the West End had their "At Homes" so well organized that a modern geographer has mapped them. These women did not work outside their homes and often employed others to help with domestic duties. As one of them recalled:

> Women in business were unheard of and the career girl was still to come. The daughters of the house, after finishing school, either abroad or in Vancouver, and "coming out" stayed at home and helped their mothers in light household duties or with the entertaining.

The idea that women's place was in the home was not confined to the elite. By custom, and sometimes by regulation, only women without husbands or fathers to support them sought employment. The largest number were in domestic service, but women also worked in stores and offices as well as in traditional female occupations such as teaching and nursing.[57]

Women did have some political influence. Single women property owners had always had the municipal vote. In 1912 married women in similar circumstances were enfranchised, and indeed, in that year, a woman led the poll in the School Board election. Through such organizations as the Local Council of Women, the auxiliaries to the Vancouver General and St. Paul's Hospital, and other philanthropic groups, women were often influential in pressing for improved public services for

From the 1890s until his death in 1922, Joe Fortes, a native of Barbados, was a volunteer lifeguard at English Bay where he taught countless children to swim. A drinking fountain with the motto Little Children Loved Him stands to his memory in a nearby park.

The construction of a new concrete bathhouse at English Bay in 1909 made swimming an even more enjoyable sport.

women, children, and the poor. The Municipal Creche or day care centre and its related employment centre for daily household workers was an excellent example of such a service.[58]

One group of women were the subject of much political controversy — the ladies of Dupont Street. Late in November 1903, the city announced a plan to close the disorderly houses. Shortly thereafter, eighteen of the twenty-five candidates of the Electors Union, a moral reform group, won seats on Council and other elected bodies. They wanted "fearless enforcement against all places of vice" and succeeded in placing their supporters on the police committee. Mayor McGuigan, however, believed "the street" should be retained as a restricted district and every effort was made to keep the "loose women" there. The provincial government apparently endorsed McGuigan's idea for it amended the City Charter to transfer most of the police committee's authority to a new three member provincially appointed Police Commission. Most aldermen were incensed by provincial interference with the City Charter and sought disallowance; the Trades and Labour Council protested the supervision of the police by an appointed rather than elected body, but the Police Commission remained.[59]

In the meantime, a three month warning period for disorderly houses expired. Although personally favouring a segregated district, Police Chief North had carried out the committee's instructions and began laying charges against owners of Dupont Street houses. With the police court magistrate's cooperation, a practical compromise was devised. The police continued to arrest inmates of houses of ill-fame but fines on Dupont Street were only $20; elsewhere, they were $50. By 1907 there were forty-four bawdy houses on Dupont Street. Some had Chinese agents; many were rented through such "respectable" real estate firms as Rand Brothers and Ceperley and Company. Nevertheless, by 1909, the police claimed to have driven all the women of ill fame from the Chinese quarter and out of the city. In fact prostitution was simply relocated, from Dupont Street to Alexander Street. After persistent pressure from the Social and Moral Reform League, the Good Government League, the Ministerial Association, and the Japanese community (which had no political influence because it lacked the franchise), the Police Commission ordered the Police Chief "to rid the city of undersirables, no particular district being designated nor the method employed." The moral reformers were delighted but incredulous. The police closed the premises on Alexander Street, but no police force could cope with the houses scattered throughout the city. Vancouver had disposed of its "restricted district" but had not eliminated the basic problem.[60]

Alexander Street was an outlier of the Skid Road district where liquor flowed copiously from legal outlets and "blind pigs." As the metropolitan centre for the province's resource industries, Vancouver always had a population of transient men in between jobs. Many came to town with a season's wages in their pockets; many left as near indigents. The temptations of Skid Road for lonely men were great. The foreman of a grand jury complained, "almost every criminal case before us is justly chargeable to liquor procured from unscrupulous dealers. In the section of the city lying between Water, Hastings, Carrall, and Cambie Streets the hotels take up at least 45 per cent of the land actually occupied by buildings. . . . A worthless and dangerous class of persons is to be found in the neighbourhood of some of these hotels, and in a number of the licensed premises such people are given encouragement." The license commissioners attempted to stop all-night drinking in grills and restaurants and considered restricting licenses to a definite area but failed to "clean up" the district.[61]

Despite its immoral underside, Vancouver was a city of churches and churchmen. When Rev. R.G. MacBeth visited Vancouver in the summer of 1911, he was impressed by the "numerous, handsome and well attended [churches], men being in the majority in the congregations." The churches expanded to meet the needs of a growing population but by 1912 were confronting problems of suburbanization. Many downtown churches found it difficult to maintain their structures as commercial buildings displaced residents. Nevertheless, most Protestant churches opposed any plans to exempt church property from municipal taxation. Some churches, such as the Scandinavian Methodist Mission on Cordova Street, surmounted the problem nicely by building a business block including church quarters, offices, and apartments.[62]

Cooperation rather than competition often governed relationships between denominations. The Anglicans and Presbyterians each accounted for about a quarter of the city's population; the Methodists for about fourteen per cent; the Roman Catholics

Picnics organized by churches, companies, unions and various societies were a popular group entertainment until well after World War II. P. Timms photographed this splendid feast at the butchers' picnic in North Vancouver in 1904.

Probably the most photographed site in Vancouver is the "Hollow Tree" in Stanley Park. Pauline Johnson, the famous Indian poetess, stands at the right in this 1904 group photograph. After Miss Johnson died in 1913 her ashes were scattered off nearby Siwash Rock.

for about ten per cent and a variety of religions and non-believers formed the remaining quarter (Appendix, Table X). Thus, the city's religious composition reflected its overall Anglo-Canadian ethnic homogeneity. In an early example of ecumenicism, Roman Catholic Archbishop Neil McNeil and a prominent Anglican clergyman, Rev. Lashley Hall, led clergy of several denominations to endorse the Canadian Industrial Peace Association and its efforts to seek an alternative to strikes and lockouts as a means of settling labour disputes.[63]

Church groups were also active in traditional philanthropic roles. Responding to social surveys made between 1910 and 1913, both the First Presbyterian and the Central Methodist Church began to emphasize social work among the immigrants and other residents of the slum areas in which they were located. Many charities, however, operated independently of denominational affiliations, and, as in other western Canadian cities, some services were provided by a combination of private charity and municipal grants. Vancouver, like any community, had its poor, its orphans, its aged and infirm, but its newness denied it a class of wealthy private philanthropists and its metropolitan position gave it an unduly large share of certain classes of unfortunates. Large hospitals and a Children's Aid Society Home drew sick people and orphan and abused children to Vancouver. The City Hospital does not seem to have discriminated against out-of-town patients, but the city was reluctant to aid the Children's Home before the provincial government in 1910 required all municipalities to contribute to the support of those children committed to the care of the Children's Aid Society. A greater strain on the city's charity were the fishermen, loggers, seamen, miners, and construction workers who fled from the hinterland in times of unemployment. Generally, private charities, including the Salvation Army and such inter-denominational groups as the Strathcona Institute for Sailors and Loggers, the Canadian Camp Brotherhood, and the Central City Mission coped with the demand for beds and meals. At times of severe unemployment, the city itself had to step in. In December 1907 the city provided meal tickets and turned the old city hall building into a dormitory, so great was the number of unemployed drifting into Vancouver. At the same time, the city organized some temporary relief work under the Board of Works and set up a labour bureau where "full

information can be secured from [the] applicant and employment secured for him."[64]

During boom years, the need for such special civic services was exceptional, but in times of depression, caring for the unemployed was a major problem. In both cases, it was a price to be paid for metropolitan status. And, as in the conduct of civic government generally, the city responded according to pragmatic considerations rather than from any theoretical ideal. As self-conscious and self-important as the cosmopolitan citizens of Vancouver might been, they were prepared to share a part of their wealth. During the next quarter century that willingness would be severely tested.

"Stevens' Folly." Built as a result of the urgings of H.H. Stevens, M.P., the Canadian Government Grain Elevator was completed just as World War I was beginning. It was little used until the grain trade really began in the early 1920s.

Chapter Three

Depression and Consolidation 1913-1939

Vancouver is much like stage scenery. All tinsel and glitter one side (the side the audience sees) and black and white behind the scenes.[1]

In August 1914, volunteers arranging to distribute the proceeds of the Citizens' War Fund to aid soldiers' dependants had their meeting interrupted by the wife of a British reservist who became their first beneficiary. She had walked into the city from South Vancouver with her recently weaned baby. A neighbour had lent her some tea but she had no food for the child.[2] Her plight — as much as statistics of population decline, drastic cuts in building activities, vacant houses, and increases in unemployment and tax arrears — illustrates the extent of the depression that had hung over Vancouver since 1912. While the War provided some relief for the poverty stricken, it also accelerated the depression and completed the ruination of the paper fortunes of speculators. In fall 1914 both the Dominion Trust Company and the Bank of Vancouver closed their doors. The sharp drop in real estate values on which they had secured many of their loans pushed them into insolvency, wiped out the savings of many small investors, and ended Vancouver's hopes of becoming the financial centre of Western Canada. Even "gentlemen" suffered. The records of the Terminal City Club in the early war years are filled with resignations, suspensions, and the erasures of names for failing to honour club obligations.[3] Despite growth in the mid and late 1920s, depression dominated Vancouver's next quarter century and was finally relieved only by the outbreak of World War II.

ECONOMIC GROWTH AND METROPOLITAN RELATIONSHIPS

In 1914 there were few indications that the depression that had struck in 1913 was more than a temporary aberration. When the prominent booster group, the Progress Club, established in 1912 as the joint effort of local businessmen and the city to attract new industries, population, and tourists fell victim to the depression in 1913, the city took over much of the Club's work. Vancouver appointed an industrial commissioner and established the Vancouver Industrial Bureau. There was reason for optimism. In anticipation of the Panama Canal's opening, new trans-Pacific ships were calling; the completion of new railways was imminent; the Canadian Pacific and Great Northern Railways were improving their facilities; the federal government had announced plans for a new public wharf equipped with heavy lifting apparatus and a subsidy for a dry dock; and federal grain commissioners were building Vancouver's first grain elevator.

For several years, the elevator — known as "Stevens' Folly" after H.H. Stevens, the Conservative M.P. for Vancouver City who had agitated in Ottawa for its construction — stood empty. The war diverted shipping to the Atlantic, landslides impaired the Panama Canal's effectiveness, the Board of Railway Commissioners reduced export grain rates only slightly, and financial embarrassment prevented the Canadian Northern from constructing its own terminal facilities. Not until the Harbour Commission built a terminal railway in the mid-1920s was the Canadian Northern, by then part of the Canadian National Railway, completely independent of its chief rival, the CPR.

The provincial government also expressed an interest in

harbour development by purchasing the approximately eighty acres of the Kitsilano Indian Reserve at the mouth of False Creek in 1913. The sale was controversial. According to Liberal critics in Ottawa, the price of $300,000 was a great bargain for the province but did not protect Indian rights. Slightly more than two-thirds of the sale price was distributed among twenty members of the Kitsilano band, but later, other Indians claimed a share and the provincial opposition questioned the generosity of the commission paid to the agent in the deal. In addition, the federal government, especially H.H. Stevens, believed the Reserve's development should be under the Harbour Board's jurisdiction while the province claimed authority to make arrangements with the developer of its choice. In any event, the depression left the Kitsilano Indian Reserve a virtual wasteland.[4]

Eventually, the War stimulated overseas demand for such British Columbia products as copper, pulp, paper, and lumber, and private owners improved terminal and harbour facilities. The Canadian Northern filled in the eastern portion of False Creek for its terminal, the Great Northern extended its buildings and trackage on adjacent property, and the CPR began extending Pier D. Vancouver manufacturers also secured some shell contracts but the most important wartime industry was shipbuilding. Initial interest in shipbuilding was closely tied to the problem of shipping lumber overseas. During 1915, half the local mills had to close. The Board of Trade, seemingly hesitant to commit local resources to new developments, rejected as "unwieldy and unpracticable" a cooperative shipbuilding scheme but helped persuade the provincial government to provide the necessary credit to start a wooden shipbuilding industry. By early 1917, the Imperial Munitions Board was awarding contracts for steel steamers to Vancouver area yards. Coughlan's of False Creek, a machine shop and manufacturer of construction steel before the war, had been almost idle since the building boom collapsed. By May 1918 it was Vancouver's largest single employer with over 7,000 employees. The shipbuilding industry began to decline before the war ended. The Western Canada Shipyards on False Creek completed their contracts for wooden ships in August 1918. Vancouver had plenty of skilled shipbuilders but high wage scales and the city's distance from such essential raw materials as steel made peacetime competition difficult.[5]

Once the war and immediate post-war unrest ended, Vancouver tried to resume her previous course and to become a major grain exporting port. An experimental shipment of prairie grain from Vancouver to Europe via the Panama Canal was very successful and the Armistice made shipping available again, but high freight rates on westbound grain handicapped the development of Vancouver as a grain exporting port. Premier John Oliver hired G.G. McGeer, a Vancouver lawyer and former Liberal MLA, to represent the province before the Board of Railway Commissioners. With the support of the government of Alberta and the Vancouver Board of Trade, McGeer led the crusade against inequalities in freight rates. As the Railway Commissioners gradually ordered reductions, the volume of grain shipped through Vancouver increased (Appendix, Table XIII).

By 1922, shipping had become one of the city's largest industries. In that year, the Board of Trade estimated that each of the 720 ocean-going vessels that called spent an average of at least $5,000 in addition to stevedoring, storage, and cartage charges. During the decade, the number of deep sea ships calling at Vancouver increased 260 per cent. To cope with the expanded general trade, both the CPR and the Harbour Commission built new piers of which the largest was the Harbour Commission's Ballantyne Pier. The Panama Canal also made the markets of the United States eastern seaboard accessible to Vancouver lumbermen. Lumber exports increased almost ninety-three per cent between 1920 and 1928. The grain trade, however, dominated the skyline. In an eighteen month period during 1923 and 1924, the Harbour Commission and private companies built new elevators quadrupling grain storage capacity from 1.25 million bushels to 6.5 million bushels. And by the end of the 1920s, Vancouver had changed from "an inconspicuous lumbering and small exporting centre to one of the leading grain ports of the world." The inconspicuous horizontal wooden warehouses and anchorages that once characterized the waterfront were overshadowed by the tall grey grain elevators built along the eastern part of the harbour while new office buildings housed an increased number of shipping agents, customs brokers, and others providing specialized services for overseas trade.[6]

During the 1930s, the port remained busy. Although the

The Union Steamship Company whose docks are shown in this 1925 Leonard Frank photograph served coastal communities with passenger and freight service and provided summertime day excursions to nearby resorts.

In the foreground, the old CPR station, built in 1898, is being demolished. Behind it is the new CPR station, opened in 1914.

The primitive Lulu Island airport shown in this 1929 photograph was replaced in 1931 by a modern airport on Sea Island.

volume of grain exports fluctuated annually, some years were as good as any in the previous decade. Nevertheless, depression and drought on the Prairies reduced other aspects of Vancouver's business. During the 1920s, Vancouver merchants had actively campaigned to increase trade with the Prairies and especially to wrest wholesale business away from Winnipeg. As in the fight for the grain trade, freight rates were the key. Vancouver merchants wanted reductions in the "mountain differential" to enable them to compete with Winnipeg for control of the wholesale trade of the British Columbia Interior and the western Prairies. Knowing that "Vancouver's trade would be increased at the expense of Winnipeg [a city] that had established the right to a monopoly of all the trade east of the Rocky Mountains,"[7] the Manitoba city vigorously opposed any changes in freight tariffs. A partial reduction of the "mountain differential" in 1914 and in 1921 had allowed Vancouver merchants to increase their prairie business. In 1928, Woodward's, a major local department store, entered the prairie market directly by opening a branch in Edmonton.

To consolidate their position in the western prairie, some Vancouver businessmen in 1926 joined Mayor L.D. Taylor in the Western Canadan Unity and Development League, an organization composed of representatives of municipal councils, Boards of Trade, property owners' associations, and similar bodies in the three most westerly provinces. One of the League's objectives was the opening of the Peace River District. This scheme was dear to the hearts of many Vancouver businessmen who had realized since 1911 that northeastern British Columbia was falling into Edmonton's economic orbit with the building of the Grand Trunk Pacific from Edmonton to Prince Rupert. The Pacific Great Eastern Railway, promised by Premier McBride in 1912, had become a financial and political nightmare rather than the answer to Vancouver's dreams. Nevertheless, late in 1929, the Vancouver Board of Trade organized its own On-to-the-Peace-River Association to lobby support for the construction of a rail link to the Peace River.

Mayor Taylor also sought to re-establish the Industrial Bureau that Council had abolished in 1919. He believed it should be separate from the tourist bureau and should have "a definite policy. . . for securing new industries and assisting, with advice, such smaller industries as are now established here." His efforts led to the formation of an industrial survey committee including representatives of the adjacent municipalities, the appointment of an Industrial Survey Commission, and the production of a booklet outling the "existing state of industry in Vancouver and its future possibilities." Despite the election of businessman W.H. Malkin, a wholesale grocer, as Taylor's successor, there was no obvious follow-up such as the creation of a civic industrial department. Two years later, in 1929, the Board of Trade published its own survey. Although the city's booklet focussed on showing the city why it needed a Bureau of Industry and the Board of Trade's survey on potential manufacturers, both surveys emphasized how potential hinterland and overseas resources and markets would ensure Vancouver's metropolitan status, and both stressed the need for manufacturing industries to increase the city's population. Although Vancouver was the province's leading manufacturing centre, apart from the sawmills that employed 3,309 of the city's 13,334 workers in manufacturing in 1925, the major employers were industries such as bakeries, print shops, and laundries catering chiefly to a local market (Appendix, Table XI).[8]

Civic subsidies for promotional activities were used largely to encourage tourism. The Vancouver Publicity Bureau often developed campaigns in cooperation with similar organizations in the American Pacific Coast states and while it advertised in Ontario and Quebec, the Prairies were its prime interest. So successful were these efforts that in the 1920s Vancouver's golf courses, accommodation, and parking spaces overflowed with visitors. The construction of new luxury hotels, such as the Georgia, did not completely solve the problem. The Canadian National Railways began construction of its hotel in 1928, but the Depression delayed completion of the new Hotel Vancover until 1939. Poor business conditions on the Prairies led the Publicity Bureau in 1933 to shift its advertising emphasis to the United States, but Vancouver's Golden Jubilee celebrations in 1936 drew hundreds of prairie tourists on special railway excursions and automobile cavalcades.

During the 1930s the city did invest in one new industry, a civic airport. Vancouver's pride was insulted in 1928 when the world's hero, Charles Lindbergh, refused to visit because of inadequate landing facilities which consisted then of a forty-acre field on Lulu Island. Ratepayers enthusiastically approved by-laws to spend $300,000 to buy land on Sea Island, which aviation and engineering experts had suggested was the best location available for an airport, and they approved a second by-law to develop an airport on that site. Although the official opening in July 1931 was an exciting event for citizens, the aviation industry was stagnating in the Depression. Nevertheless, the city gradually improved the airport and scheduled daily service to Victoria and Seattle began. But not until 1939 did the federal government's Trans-Canada Airlines begin regular passenger and mail service from Vancouver to eastern Canada. By the end of the decade, Vancouver claimed to have "the leading commercial airport in the Dominion."[9]

Vancouver's enthusiasm for the airport reflected her citizens' long-standing realization of the paramount economic importance of transportation. The completion of the CPR had allowed Vancouver to displace Victoria as the provincial commercial centre; freight rate reductions, the establishment of grain handling facilities, and, especially, the Panama Canal had permitted Vancouver to make the western Prairies tributary to her and to replace Winnipeg as the metropolis of the Canadian West. A modern airport would equip Vancouver to preserve her position if any shift in trading patterns emerged in the air age. By taking an active role in promoting development rather than a sometimes passive one as they had during the pre-war boom when they often waited for business to come to them, Vancouver residents recognized that theirs was, indeed, a leading city.

STRIKES, LABOUR DISCONTENT, AND UNEMPLOYMENT

Despite ample evidence of past growth and future opportunities for economic development, a significant part of Vancouver's population was not always content. Workers who struck for higher wages and to express sympathy with such fellow workers as "Ginger" Goodwin, the Winnipeg General Strikers, and the Relief Camp Workers frightened some local officials and businessmen who expected a breakdown in law and order. Similarly, although the unemployed were a perennial problem since Vancouver was the traditional "end of the road," dealing with them was never easy and contributed to the near polarization that sometimes occurred between organized labour and the business community.

The war and immediate post-war years were marked by great tensions between organized labour and business. Socialist ideas, hitherto on the fringes of the labour movement, had gained considerable currency. The rapid growth of wartime industry and problems directly related to the War revived union activity. Membership had been flagging since the failure of an attempted general strike in 1911[10] and the increase in unemployment in the pre- and early war years. The War gradually ended unemployment, but caused prices to rise more rapidly than wages and led to the introduction of conscription in 1917. The Trades and Labour Council joined the Socialist Party in sponsoring mass protest meetings and in calling for a referendum on a general strike to oppose all forms of compulsory service. Delegates to a special B.C. Federation of Labour convention overwhelmingly endorsed the idea of a general strike; however, their militancy did not extend to a walk out when a Vancouver unionist was jailed for refusing the draft.[11]

Federal orders-in-council concerning censorship, sedition, loafing, and the ever-rising cost of living continued to anger organized labour. During the spring and early summer of 1918, civic outside workers, shipyard workers, BCER electrical workers, and letter carriers struck for higher wagers. None of the strikes lasted more than ten days, but to Mayor R.H. Gale and to the business community, they were distressing. Support for unions was widespread among employees; even city police had formed a union in affiliation with the Trades and Labour Council. Talk of sympathetic strikes continued and it was possible to perceive the strike of shipyard workers as a German plot.[12]

The shooting of Albert "Ginger" Goodwin set off what has been mistakenly called "Canada's first full general strike."[13] Goodwin, a union organizer, had been reclassified from medically unfit and called up for active service after he led a smeltermen's strike at Trail. To avoid military service, Goodwin disappeared into the woods around Comox. Eventually, a Dominion police officer found and shot him. To the labour movement, Goodwin became an instant martyr. By a vote of 117 to 1, the Vancouver Trades and Labour Council endorsed a twenty-four hour "holiday" beginning at noon on August 2, 1918, the day of Goodwin's funeral. The "holiday" confirmed many of the "establishment's" worst fears about "Red Socialists with pro-German ideas"[14]; it led to violence, and ended any prospect of the business community and labour movement working together to resolve outstanding conflicts. It was, however, far from a general strike. Workers in the steel shipyards went out, but those in the wooden yards remained on the job; the long-shoremen struck, but CPR dock handlers stayed at work; the BCER's city street railwaymen took their cars back to the barns, but the interurbans continued to operate. Although a few machine shop workers and some B.C. Telephone electrical workers also struck, telephone operators, printers, teamsters, postal workers, hotel and restaurant employees did not join the strike. The president of the Civic Workers' Union refused to order his members out.

Intervention by several hundred returned soldiers — many convalescents — turned what might have been a small scale protest and temporary public inconvenience into a dramatic confrontation. The veterans, who had no sympathy for those who had not volunteered to serve their country, attempted unsuccessfully to prevent the street railwaymen from turning in their cars. In mid-afternoon, 1,000 veterans, formed into a self-styled "Defence of the Realm League," marched on the Labour Temple, invaded it, "and literally forced some of the labor leaders into the city jail — for their own protection."[15] As the soldiers roamed the streets, several fights developed between them and the "holidayers." Despite their violent actions and Mayor Gale's urgings that they refrain from further action, the veterans clearly had the sympathy of a significant portion of the community. That evening, an overflow crowd filled the meeting the veterans organized at the Empress Theatre to hear various speakers, including some union members, denounce the Trades and Labour Council's executive as tools of the Kaiser.

The Goodwin protest completed the temporary polarization between organized labour, the Trades and Labour Council, and the business community, represented by "a central citizen's committee" composed of businessmen and returned soldiers. Mayor Gale threatened to declare martial law if there were any indications of renewed violence. Vancouver City Council sought legislation to make it illegal for policemen to organize and to affiliate with any Trades and Labour Council. Some members of the business community set about to revive the Employers' Association of British Columbia to consolidate and coordinate the "employers of capital and labour on a sound and equitable basis." The Armistice ended the conscription problem but further exacerbated tensions between labour and capital as the winding-down of the munitions industry and the return of the soldiers increased unemployment. Moreover, the "Red Scare" was sweeping the western world.[16]

The outbreak of a general strike in Winnipeg in May 1919 created some panic in Vancouver. Householders stocked up on groceries, businessmen bought $10 million worth of riot insurance and MLA G.G. McGeer advised Premier John Oliver:

> a serious feeling of unrest exists in this City among a great number of the best men in the Community, fearing an outbreak of a similar nature here. It is a well recognized fact that there is an element associated with the cause of labor in this City, who are decidedly inclined to Bolsheviki tendencies, openly endorsing Soldiers and Sailors Councils and open-ing [sic] endorsing the Spartacans, the Bolshevists and the Soviet rule. I do not mean to suggest that this element represents, either the majority or a large minority of the people, but yet, at the same time, I feel that under certain circumstances they are sufficiently powerful to do a great deal of harm and to cause a great deal of trouble.

McGeer feared that not all members of the city police would assist in maintaining law and order, but the general public was less worried. The active militia had difficulty getting recruits and the Citizens' League formed by Mayor Gale initially had problems getting volunteers to carry on any essential services that might be interrupted. Eventually, the League signed up 6,231 members, produced *The Vancouver Citizen* to give "authentic news about the strike" and to counteract the *Strike Bulletin* when typographers of two of the three dailies struck, and provided volunteers when some telephone operators walked out. The League considered its chief accomplishment to be "in what was prevented."[17]

During Vancouver's month-long strike, the street railwaymen, electrical workers, some telephone operators, most civic em-ployees other than police and firemen, sugar refiners, and metal trades workers were out at least part of the time and there were interruptions in coastal shipping. Enthusiasm for the strike was not universal. Many strikers were tired of strikes, were aware of serious unemployment, and had struck reluctantly. Of the approximately 16,000 union members in the city, only 5,804 had cast ballots on the strike, and of these, only 3,305 favoured it. The street railwaymen, for example, walked out only after the longshoremen and other strikers intimidated them. Public transportation was not seriously disrupted as the city temporarily lifted its ban on jitneys, the privately owned automobiles that had earlier competed with the street railway. The strike was remarkably free of violence. Military observers reported that the most exciting demonstrations were large football matches between strikers.[18] This lack of violence, the minimum public inconvenience, the insignificant "alien" element, the absence of a solid front among either labour or the rest of the community, and the fact that the Winnipeg General Strike, to which it was clearly a response, ended, spared Vancouver a legacy of bitterness, though not of fear. The Citizens' League dissolved itself after the strike. The Trades and Labour Council was beset by internal problems. Although R.H. Neelands was elected a Labour MLA for South Vancouver in the 1920 election, labour and socialist candidates generally fared poorly at the polls.

Throughout the 1920s, the labour movement in the province was "balkanized" and labour seemed so peaceful that the city's industrial survey boasted of "experienced, reliable, home-loving, home-owning and anti-radical workers in every branch of industry."[19]

The only major strike in the 1920s involved longshoremen in 1923. That strike led to the formation of a company union, the Vancouver and District Waterfront Workers' Association. In spring 1935, the Waterfront Workers who had been taken over by progressives briefly demonstrated in support of the Relief Camp strikers who were then in the city but stopped short of a sympathetic strike. When they refused to handle a cargo of "hot" newsprint from Powell River, the Shipping Federation cancelled its agreement with them and signed with a new company union, the Canadian Waterfront Workers Association. Deep sea shipping virtually ceased until the Shipping Federation secured replacements for striking longshoremen and police protection for them. When strike leaders were forbidden to address the strike breakers, about a thousand strikers led by a Victoria Cross winner marched towards Ballantyne Pier. They responded to the tear gas and batons of a combined force of city and provincial law enforcement officers and the R.C.M.P. by throwing bricks and stones. Small skirmishes followed. Two hours later, twenty-eight people had been injured and a number arrested on charges relating to participation in a riot.

The waterfront riot gave Mayor G.G. McGeer reason to assert that Communists controlled both the relief camp and waterfront workers. The polarization that had threatened to develop in 1919 reappeared as McGeer prepared to establish a Citizen's Army under Brigadier-General V.W. Odlum to maintain law and order. The Citizens' Army never materialized but a Citizens' League composed of a number of prominent residents warned of the danger of Communism. One of its full page newspaper advertisements featured a diagram showing the "connection" between Vancouver and Moscow.[20] Given the circumstances — the Relief Camp Workers were on their On-To-Ottawa-Trek — the revival of the Red Scare is understandable, especially since, for other reasons, residents did not have full confidence in the administration of the city police. Mayor McGeer may have exploited the Communist threat because of his ambitions in the forthcoming federal election, but he was also eager to maintain a strong anti-Communist image to attract investors to the "Baby Bonds" he was selling to finance construction of the new city hall.[21] The Waterfront Workers themselves remained off the job until December when the strike ended with their union at least partially broken.

The presence of the Relief Camp Workers in Vancouver was unhappy evidence of Vancouver's established role as Canada's "end of the road," as the "Mecca for the unemployed." Early in World War I, the local press blamed the unemployment problem not only on the completion of railway construction and shutdowns in mining and logging but also on the influx of men who "had been hounded away from the prairies by the mounted police." During a severe unemployment crisis in the early 1920s, Mayor W.R. Owen told an unemployment conference at Ottawa that Vancouver could not fairly be expected to support transients from the Prairies during the winter and he requested federal funds to allow the Greater Vancouver Sewerage Board to provide work for the unemployed. For several years, the city also sent a team to post handbills in cities and small towns along main railway lines warning harvesters that no winter work was to be found in Vancouver. Nevertheless, drifters continued to

Reverend Andrew Roddan of First United Church presides over the soup kitchen established by his church to help feed the thousands of unemployed men who drifted to Vancouver during the Depression of the 1930s.

During the Depression unemployed men camped in these "Jungles" near the railway tracks.

This snapshot and the one above were sent to Prime Minister R.B. Bennett to show him the wretched conditions endured by the unemployed who had found Vancouver to be the end of the road.

Striking Relief Camp Workers march along Hastings Street in the 1935 May Day Parade.

Nearly 1500 children played hooky to attend the May Day demonstration though not all marched in the parade.

come and their numbers greatly increased as the economic situation deteriorated in the 1930s. During that troubled decade the movement of the unemployed from the Prairies as well as from the British Columbia Interior was often blamed for Vancouver's problems. In December 1929, J.H. McVety of the British Columbia office of the Employment Service of Canada advised the Department of Labour that:

> Every district [in the province] has a surplus of men and, generally speaking, there is not reasonable ground to expect that employment will be available to them in the near future. Vancouver is, of course, the Mecca of the unemployed from the interior of our province and also from the Prairie provinces. They are attracted here by milder weather conditions and the prospects of obtaining some kind of work throughout the Winter.

The city was reluctant to give relief to transient single men especially since many resident families required help. Registration under the federal Unemployment Relief Act in the fall of 1930 "brought to light the hidden sores of unemployment. Men who were too proud to ask for charity promptly applied for the work they so grievously needed."[22]

Though the problems of families were great and were only partially eased by city relief and voluntary schemes to distribute shoes and clothing, the single men attracted the most attention. Not only did the city, province, and federal government dispute responsibility for them, but they were numerous and Communists organized their demonstrations well. Their presence made the unemployment burden seem greater than it was; in 1935, for example, Vancouver had a lower percentage of its population on relief than Montreal, Toronto, Winnipeg, Calgary, Regina, or Halifax.[23]

McVety wrote about Vancouver as a "Mecca of the unemployed" in the wake of the first of many Depression parades and mass meetings. From a spectator's point of view, this first "display was a dead loss. Not a voice stirred, not a banner fluttered." The calm was mute testimony to the discipline exerted by Communist leaders; the absence of flags was a subtle protest of Police Chief Bingham's order to display the Union Jack as well as the Red Flag. The Vancouver Unemployed Workers claimed to have 1,000 members among the approximately 12,000 to 14,000

During the 1935 Relief Camp Workers Strike many citizens agreed with Mayor McGeer that the strike was the prelude to "a revolution to bring about a soviet government in Canada." This advertisement appeared in the Vancouver Daily Province, *May 29, 1935.*

unemployed. It demanded immediate relief, in cash not kind, for all unemployed regardless of colour, nationality, or length of residence, and work at union rates, that is, $4.50 per day rather than the $1.00 and $2.00 offered to single and married men respectively for city work projects. Alderman W.C. Atherton, a realtor, suggested that protesters get jobs decorating store windows for Christmas to which Comrade McEwen facetiously replied that at Easter they could paint eggs red, white, and blue. When another alderman asked why they had not approached the senior governments, their spokesman replied, "Simply because the problem is centred in Vancouver." On that point the City Council agreed but the tone of future confrontations between Council and the representatives of the unemployed had already been set.[24]

The "floating population which congregates in the city in time of stress" threatened to become permanent. During the summer of 1931, a number of men established "jungles" in the Great Northern Railway yards, on Harbour Board property, and under the Georgia Viaduct. The original orderly conditions of the "jungles" deteriorated until by September they were "a hot-bed for every form of disease, physical, moral and social" and the city and Harbour Board destroyed them. Former "jungle" residents were among the 2,000 men who left Vancouver that fall for provincial government road camps. The road camp scheme failed as senior governments fought over its cost and scope, and many unemployed refused to go. On March 3, 1932, approximately 4,000 men formed a Hunger March to protest the policy of cutting single men off relief if they refused to go to the camps. City Council refused to meet the marchers; mounted and foot police armed with clubs tried to disperse them and the marchers used their flags and banners as lances. Several people, including two policemen, required hospital treatment. A May Day demonstration may have been kept in check by the presence of a destroyer cruising off Point Grey. When new demonstrations occurred in November and December, Mayor L.D. Taylor told citizens that the demonstrations had been organized in Toronto by the Communist Party of Canada whose motto was "To Communize All the World or Else Destroy It" and he upheld police efforts to maintain the peace. Meanwhile, the demonstrators, through the Block Councils of the Unemployed, complained of "the wanton and sadest [sic] methods" of the police in putting protests down.[25]

When the R.B. Bennett government established work camps under the management of the Department of National Defence, the camp workers became prime targets for organization by the Workers' Unity League, a Communist organization. In December 1934, over 1,200 men marched on Vancouver to protest work camp conditions and the "black listing" of dissidents. After private citizens provided the protesters with a few days' food and shelter and after an orderly parade through downtown department stores, City Council gave them relief for the duration of the Christmas holidays. When the provincial government agreed to urge the Department of National Defence to hold a public investigation of the camps, the men returned to them. But the appointment of the Macdonald Commission on April 1, 1935 was too late; the Relief Camp Workers' Union had already organized a strike. The first of approximately 4,000 Relief Camp strikers began to arrive in Vancouver on April 4, 1935 and they remained until they left on the On-To-Ottawa-Trek on June 3 and 4. Their object was to protest the existence of the relief or "slave camps." In Vancouver, the peaceful strikers found so much public sympathy they were able to collect $4,600 at a Tag Day.[26]

After three weeks, the orderliness of the strike disappeared. On April 23, some three hundred strikers paraded into the Hudson's Bay Company department store and damaged fixtures and merchandise as police evicted them. When a crowd gathered at Victory Square, Mayor McGeer, who thought the relief camp strike the prelude to "a revolution to bring about a soviet government in Canada," read the Riot Act. Many citizens agreed with McGeer that the Communist leadership had to be exposed and law and order preserved, but others listened attentively at strike rallies, donated money to the strikers' support, and joined the strikers' May Day parade to Stanley Park. Arguing that the strikers still had plenty of public sympathy, McGeer used the demonstrations to underscore to senior governments the need for new relief policies and new methods of financing public works and services. Meanwhile, the strikers staged unauthorized tag days to support themselves, tried forcefully to enter Woodward's and Spencer's Department stores, and briefly took possession of the museum on the Public Library's top floor until they were promised temporary relief.[27]

In his recollections, *Bloody Sunday,* Steve Brodie, one of the strikers, recalled how the hundred or more sit-downers who occupied the Art Gallery for thirty days took special care not to damage the art work there.

Police evict a sit-downer from the Post Office.

A sit-downer enjoys "Government Hospitality" at the Post Office.

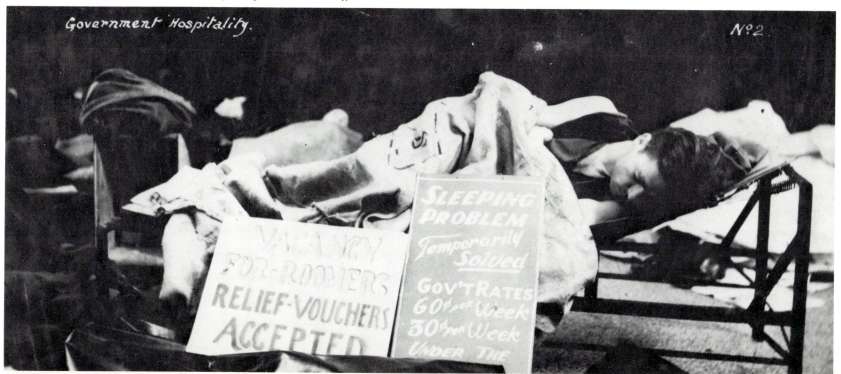

The strikers' departure on June 3 and 4 on their ill-fated On-To-Ottawa-Trek, which the federal government stopped at Regina, eased the situation as did the closure of the Defence Department work camps. The new Mackenzie King government replaced those camps in the fall of 1935 with railway maintenance work and temporary winter work camps. When the winter camps closed in spring 1938, the men drifted to Vancouver and once again confrontations occurred.

The provincial minister of labour announced that the only aid British Columbia would give interprovincial transients was transportation back to their prairie homes. Since work was not available in the Prairie provinces, many of the unemployed, led by Steve Brodie, a Communist, launched a surprise demonstration and occupied the Post Office and Art Gallery for almost a month until city police, assisted by the R.C.M.P., forced them out by using tear gas. When two city plain clothesmen clubbed Brodie, the former "sit-downers" smashed plate glass windows on Hastings and Cordova Streets. Prime Minister King had ordered that the eviction from the Post Office should take "place at an hour that would be least embarrassing to the public," and by 6:30 a.m. the confrontation was over. Over thirty people, including five policemen, were in hospital, an unknown number were given first aid treatment at a station set up at the Ukrainian Hall by the Young Communist League, and twenty-two strikers were under arrest.[28]

Once the city wakened and learned of "Bloody Sunday," sympathy developed for the strikers. "We want something done for these people," Dr. Lyle Telford, C.C.F. MLA for Vancouver East, told Premier Pattullo. Ten thousand people met at the Powell Street grounds on Sunday afternoon to protest "police terrorism" and demand the resignation of the Pattullo government. Under persistent protest from the public and ex-sit-downers alike, Pattullo persuaded the federal government to cooperate in an emergency relief scheme to disperse the unemployed.[29] The worst of the unemployment problem was now over. The outbreak of World War II, little more than a year later, ended it, and the introduction of unemployment insurance in 1940 meant that while Vancouver might again become a "Mecca" for the unemployed, it would not have to provide sustenance for large numbers of them.

POPULATION GROWTH AND ETHNIC RELATIONSHIPS

Throughout the interwar years, Vancouver's population increased at a relatively moderate pace. Indeed, between 1911, the peak year of the boom, and 1916, the population actually dropped by 15,000. From that wartime nadir, growth was slow but steady and in 1929 was artificially inflated by amalgamation with South Vancouver and Point Grey (Appendix, Table III). The population's composition also changed as natural increase and internal migration rather than immigration from overseas caused the greatest growth. The portion of Canadians gradually rose from 43.8 per cent in 1911 to 60.7 per cent in 1941 (Appendix, Table VII). Increasingly, the Canadians were western natives, but this had no immediately discernible effect on Vancouver's attitude towards the rest of Canada.[30]

The Prairies replaced Ontario as the main source of migrants from other provinces. Indeed, so numerous were prairie emigrés and winter visitors that they organized such groups as The Prairie Peoples Association, "A Social Club for Social People," to arrange gatherings where they might "inculcate that old Prairie spirit" and assist each other in finding homes and jobs. That association disappeared but picnics of former prairie residents became an annual event at Stanley Park.

Many of the unemployed transients also came from the Prairies but little attention was given to their ethnic origin. Apart from Asians, ethnic groups in Vancouver had a fairly low profile. The dismissal of many "enemy aliens," chiefly Germans and Austrians from their jobs during World War I, was simply a manifestation of wartime xenophobia. Of Europeans, only Italians, the largest European ethnic group, experienced any sustained discrimination. During the war, for example, Vancouver denied all relief to men of Italian descent not because of Italy's position in world affairs but because Italians were often found "drinking and carousing." Like other Europeans, Italians, on first arriving in Vancouver, often settled in the so-called "foreign quarter" in and around Strathcona where accommodation was cheap. Although the various ethnic groups built their own churches and meeting halls in this area, they usually moved on to other parts of the city when they established themselves economically. Thus, the churches and halls remained the most visible evidence of a "foreign" presence. Ethnic identity was also commemorated in an annual festival of folk dancing and crafts begun in 1933 to combat racial prejudice. The festival featured many ethnic groups and attracted attention from many parts of North America, but its location in a hotel ballroom rather than in a large hall or outdoors suggests a narrow base of local support.[31]

In contrast to Europeans, Asians were highly visible and very unpopular. The Asian population was almost exclusively Chinese and Japanese as pre-war immigration legislation requiring immigrants to come directly from their homelands effectively barred immigrants from India. When 376 Indians challenged that law by sailing directly from India on a chartered Japanese vessel, the *Komagata Maru,* they were held on board ship in Vancouver harbour for six weeks in spring 1914 before finally being denied entry. Since few early immigrants from India had brought wives with them, the Indian population remained small.

The Chinese and Japanese, who lived mainly in the most densely settled parts of the city, were highly visible and the latter were rapidly increasing in number as Japanese men sent for their wives and raised families. Except for the proprietors of small neighbourhood shops who lived on the premises, most Chinese resided in Chinatown. Most Japanese lived in Little Tokyo but some moved into other neighbourhoods where they often met hostility. The Japanese families who moved into Kitsilano, for example, had their children unjustly blamed for spreading contagious diseases. Such complaints were trivial compared to the reaction when Chinese and Japanese merchants began opening small grocery, confectionery, and cleaning shops throughout the city. The Retail Merchants Association, representing large and small white merchants, urged the public to patronize white merchants and lobbied for immigration restrictions. Despite the passage of what was essentially a Chinese exclusion act in 1923, competition continued. White merchants regularly complained of violations of the law, especially by-laws relating to closing hours, by Chinese and Japanese merchants. From time to time, municipal politicians called for severe restrictions on the number of trade licenses issued to Asians, but such measures were beyond the authority of both provincial and city governments. In 1937 and 1938, anti-Japanese sentiments were especially strong because of Japan's aggressive actions in Asia.

This increased tension gave Alderman Halford Wilson an additional excuse to take up the cause of the white merchants. Although the majority of Council rarely sympathized with Wilson's suggestions, his crusade was a major factor in creating such a strong hatred of the Japanese that federal authorities feared even a minor provocation might lead to riots.[32]

Thus, throughout the interwar years Vancouver maintained its tradition of welcoming only those immigrants who were likely to contribute to its economic growth and only those who were white. Moreover, the distress and migration patterns produced by the Depression rekindled memories of earlier riots and demonstrations and allowed municipal politicians to pander to the fears of their constituents. Although these fears were often much exaggerated, the possibility of confrontation was high.

THE URBAN LANDSCAPE

The most visible changes in Vancouver between the wars were along the waterfront where grain elevators and new piers were built to serve the city's expanded role as a port. In the commercial district new hotels and office buildings including the Royal Bank Building, the Stock Exchange Building, the Medical-Dental Building and especially the Marine Building were constructed. The last building, designed by its architects to bring to mind "some great crag rising from the sea, clinging with sea flora and fauna, tinted in sea-green, touched with gold," was long the tallest and finest office building in Vancouver. The three major department stores also undertook major expansion during the 1920s. When the Depression halted new construction, the skeleton of the new Hotel Vancouver dominated the skyline and seemed a ghostly symbol of the end of prosperity.[33]

In the residential areas, as Vancouver slowly regained the population lost between 1913 and 1916, there was some construction in older areas and considerable growth in the city's eastern part. Workingmen built homes in the old Hastings Townsite and adjacent areas. Extensive building activity in the 1920s also took place in the suburbs of South Vancouver and Point Grey but they remained the least densely populated districts. Vancouver was able to boast of an "unusually high level of home ownership" as fifty-one per cent of its homes were owner-occupied in 1931. A Board of Trade *Industrial Survey*

By 1939 when this photograph was taken from the Hotel Vancouver, apartment blocks and rooming houses dominated parts of the West End. In the far right of the photograph is the Marine Building, an office building completed in 1930.

As he stood on Georgia Street facing westward in 1933, Leonard Frank saw the Strand Theatre and the Birks Building with their sidewalk canopies. Beyond, are the old Hotel Vancouver and the new, but then uncompleted, Hotel Vancouver.

Looking eastward on Georgia Street in this 1934 Leonard Frank photograph is St. Andrew's Presbyterian Church on Richards Street. Beyond, lie several blocks of frame homes that were demolished in the 1950s to make way for the Post Office and Queen Elizabeth Theatre.

explained: "The individual of moderate means, through the assistance of financial houses, with a very small initial outlay of cash, secures his lot and proceeds with his home." The dominance of single family dwellings meant the population density was relatively low for a city of Vancouver's size and visitors often commented on the city's spaciousness. With only 5,609 residents per square mile in 1931, Vancouver had considerably lower density than any other Canadian city with a population over 100,000.[34]

Before 1914, Vancouver had grown without obvious direction or planning. Apart from establishing fire limits, the city did little to guide the location of development. Definite commercial and industrial districts emerged only because businessmen found it convenient to be near each other or adjacent to required trackage or waterfrontage. Residential development was widely scattered especially in the suburban municipalities which were well-served by north-south street railways. Even in the city proper there were many problems including streets located on sixteen per cent grades. Bogs and deep ravines were used as building lots. Speculators had touted any paved street with a street car line as a commercial street thus creating an inefficient mix of stores, houses, and vacant lots, discouraging homebuilders and denying storekeepers the local customers vital to their economic survival. Servicing the debt caused by illogical land development imposed a heavy burden on taxpayers. During the boom years, few Vancouverites worried about long term costs. Moreover, the city's natural attractions lulled residents into taking beauty for granted. When City Council in 1905 tried to have the BCER put proposed high tension power lines underground, it was less concerned about ugly power poles and lines than with the danger of accident from the still somewhat mysterious power of electricity.[35]

A few Vancouverites did recognize the need to keep their city beautiful, to replace its haphazard development with organization. Inspired by the Local Council of Women, a number of interested citizens, including prominent Board of Trade members, copied an idea already implemented in several prairie cities and formed the Vancouver Beautiful Association. Their objectives of beautifying "the city in every way possible" and "in a deeper sense" promoting "higher development" were ambitious; their immediate goals of planting trees and window boxes and keeping boys and girls off the streets were modest.[36] They secured City Council endorsement and assisted in lobbying the provincial government to donate the old court house site at Hastings and Cambie Streets for a civic park to provide open space in the heart of the commercial district. The Association also gave English landscape architect Thomas Mawson a forum to present his plans for beautifying Stanley Park. The collapse of the boom prevented Mawson's scheme and a related civic centre proposal from being implemented. The only immediate result of Mawson's work was the beginning of the construction of a seawall and a lighthouse at Stanley Park, projects subsidized by the federal government.

During the Depression and the War, the federal Commission of Conservation kept the idea of town planning alive. In 1920, the Vancouver Board of Trade, which had already called for a town planning act, invited Thomas Adams of the commission to speak to it. Soon after, the Board pressed the provincial government for town planning legislation. The Real Estate Exchange and other groups, including the Associated Property Owners, favoured it as did the half-dozen members of the Town Planning Institute of Canada living in Vancouver. There was already a good local example of the benefits of town planning in Point Grey. The CPR had applied town planning principles in laying out Shaughnessy Heights and early Councils had passed by-laws containing "the germs of the modern science of town planning." In 1922, Point Grey became the first Canadian municipality to pass a town planning by-law. In 1925, under persistent pressure from the Vancouver City Council, the province passed legislation permitting municipalities to establish town planning commissions to advise them on town planning and educate the public. Like Point Grey, Vancouver quickly took advantage of the new law and appointed a commission in March 1926. Council expected the commission would save it the task of playing "Solomon" between rival interests, halt the incursion into residential districts of inappropriate buildings such as stores, apartments, laundries, and factories, end the speculative holding of vacant land by those who hoped to turn their property into commercial or apartment sites, and solve traffic congestion.[37]

To further the work of town planning, Vancouver, in August 1926, joined Point Grey in hiring the American firm Harland

Large, well-tended gardens and half-timbered Tudor revival style homes were common in Shaughnessy Heights as this 1920s photograph of a garden at the corner of Angus Drive and Granville Street illustrates.

Bartholomew and Associates to prepare a comprehensive town plan for greater Vancouver. The Bartholomew Report, "the most comprehensive general plan" for any Canadian city in the interwar years, drew much favourable attention to Vancouver. The final report, published in 1929, was distributed throughout the world. Although Council agreed to spend $40,000 for three years of Bartholomew's work, neither Council nor private citizens would subscribe the funds necessary to publicize the virtues of town planning.[38]

The Bartholomew firm prepared a town plan designed for the next thirty or forty years or until the population reached one million. The scheme reflected both the City Beautiful ideal of making the city an attractive place to live and the City Efficient concept of giving priority to economics rather than aesthetics. Council never officially approved or adopted the plan, but as late as 1972 a local planner described the Bartholomew plan and its revisions as "the only really effective plan in the field of roads and streets" with its most important feature being "the fact that it exists." Despite its unofficial status, the city implemented many of the report's recommendations, especially if they were likely to relieve practical problems such as conflicts over zoning regulations or traffic congestion.[39]

Shortly before formally receiving the report, the Council passed a comprehensive zoning by-law. Under this by-law, the Town Planning Commission was able to control the many requests from distressed property owners who sought immediate gain by having their property re-zoned from residential to apartment or commercial. The Depression also helped enforce zoning regulations as frustrated speculators let vacant property go for taxes. Until amended in 1939, the zoning by-law could not restrict the creation of housekeeping suites in single family districts. Moreover, attempts to limit the construction of new buildings to those in harmony with their neighbours failed because the Architectural Board of Control established in 1936 was neither "sufficiently broad nor restrictive."[40]

Zoning was most important and controversial in the West End. Once the city's prestige residential district, it had been supplanted by Shaughnessy Heights. As well-to-do residents moved out, apartments and commercial building appeared. A few of the new apartments catered to the luxury trade but many covered almost the whole lot. Others were conversions — old mansions divided into housekeeping rooms or small apartments while their speculating owners waited for land values to rise. Such blighting made the West End the first area to get attention from the Town Planning Commission. When the commission proposed to confine apartment blocks to six stories and to the area near Stanley Park, land owners charged that without the possibility of apartments, the value of their land would fall. The owners, however, accepted requirements for front, side, and rear yards as this would make new apartments "a good neighbour while we live in our homes in the West End awaiting a buyer for our property." When the Depression halted apartment building, some property owners blamed site area restrictions for their problems and called for the abolition of all zoning restrictions. Other residents opposed any further relaxation of zoning rules since with 27 persons per acre the area was already crowded and the Depression was hastening the conversion of old houses into suites and rooms. City Council eased zoning regulations in what the *Province* called the "first retrograde step in [the] planning of Vancouver."[41]

The city did endeavour to provide some of the new physical facilities recommended by the Bartholomew plan, particularly those designed to relieve traffic congestion caused by the increasing popularity of the automobile in the 1920s. During 1929, the city prepared by-laws asking ratepayers to approve construction of the Burrard Street Bridge across False Creek. The first by-law just failed to get the necessary sixty per cent majority as voters tended to express sectional interests. A second by-law, presented in December as unemployment was increasing, was advertised with a reminder that building the bridge would create jobs. It passed. Despite the Depression, the city also undertook to eliminate a number of railway level crossings and street jogs, to widen Kingsway, to construct the First Avenue Viaduct over railway tracks, to lay new railway yards east of False Creek to serve the grain trade, to acquire additional park land including the Crystal Pool site on Beach Drive, and to develop, by using relief labour, the Fraserview golf course on a 1,250 acre tract of tax sale land in South Vancouver.[42] Such projects created jobs and improved both the city's appearance and efficiency.

The Bartholomew Report noted how shopping areas had developed along suburban street railway routes. By confirming

Gas stations sprang up rapidly in Vancouver. This photo, taken during World War I, shows four women from well-to-do families who pumped gas as a part of their contribution to the war effort.

By 1929, neighbourhood gas stations were common. Austin Taylor, a prominent businessman founded the Home Oil Company in 1928 to market gasoline and fuel oil. In 1937 the Company became a wholly owned subsidiary of Imperial Oil Limited but the Home Oil name did not disappear from service stations until 1976.

this in commercial zoning by-laws, town planners insured that ribbon-like commercial growth would continue away from downtown. As far as public transportation itself was concerned, the Bartholomew Report found that Vancouver was "more or less adequately served" by street cars and motor buses and proposed only modest change and additions for the future. By 1914, the BCER had laid out a fairly comprehensive street railway network. During the 1920s, it completed a few short extensions and bought additional cars to meet increasing demand. In outlying areas such as the Point Grey campus to which the University of British Columbia moved in 1925, the BCER introduced a feeder motor bus service. On the interurban run to New Westminster, the BCER retained its electric railway, started its own motor bus firm, the B.C. Rapid Transit Company, and answered private motor bus competition by secretly buying controlling interest in the Pacific Stage and Transportation Company.[43]

Town planning laid a basis for Vancouver's orderly development but the 1930s were essentially a decade of marking time. There was little commercial building, and, apart from a few new homes built in the former Point Grey municipality by owners who could take advantage of low construction costs, there was little residential construction. Although the city carried out parts of the Bartholomew scheme, it could not afford such luxuries as the proposed Burrard Street civic centre. Park development in the 1930s was primarily a means of hiring the unemployed and only incidentally a means of beautifying the city. Nevertheless, the city launched one major new project during the depths of the Depression, the new City Hall. A new city hall had long been needed. Since at least 1910, the limitations of the old Market Hall had been apparent, and by 1927 it was unsightly, unsanitary, in danger of collapsing from dry rot and twisted roof beams, and an inefficent and poor place to work. To accommodate the increased staff created by amalgamation with Point Grey and South Vancouver, the city abandoned the Market Hall and leased the Holden Building, an office building at 16 Hastings Street East, as temporary headquarters. Completion of the new City Hall ended Vancouver's embarrassment as the only major city in North America without a proper city hall.[44]

Vancouver residents had talked about a new city hall since 1910, and a city hall was part of a grandiose town planning scheme outlined in 1914 but fell victim to depression and war. The persistent problem was choosing a site. On several occasions between 1912 and 1935 ratepayers were asked their opinion on one or more proposed locations. The most commonly mentioned site was the Central School grounds at Cambie and Pender in the heart of downtown. An illustration of the complexity of the choice is the December 1933 by-law asking voters to authorize Council to make tentative plans for a new city hall and to name their preference from among five proposals. The voters definitely wanted a new city hall but showed little agreement about its location. When all the voters were tabulated, the first choice was Thornton Park on Main Street by the Canadian National Railway Station. The other choices followed closely with the last being Strathcona Park at Twelfth Avenue and Cambie Street.[45] The site selection vote was not a binding one, and the next year City Council asked ratepayers to approve the transfer of $630,000 from unexpended by-law balances to build a new city hall on the Central School site and replace the school. By a mere twenty-nine voters, the by-law failed to get the necessary two-thirds majority. Mayor McGeer then by-passed the voters. He got the provincial government to authorize the sale of "Baby Bonds" (see below, p.114) and though he personally favoured Thornton Park, he avoided the east-west split within the city by referring the site problem to an independent committee composed of the Chief Justice of British Columbia, the President of the University of British Columbia, and the Chairman of the Town Planning Commission. When the committee recommended Strathcona Park, Council unenthusiastically accepted their choice. During Vancouver's summertime Golden Jubilee festivities in 1936, former Prime Minister R.B. Bennett laid the cornerstone, and the official opening took place at the end of Jubilee Year.[46]

Behind the facade of such new structures of the 1930s — the City Hall, the CNR's Hotel Vancouver, the Marine Building, and the Burrard Street Bridge — Vancouver was more than a little shopworn. In spite of the Town Planning Commission's efforts to use zoning to prevent blight, some neighbourhoods, particularly east of Main Street, deteriorated as homeowners were often unable to afford repairs or taxes. The lack of repairs caused a deterioration of housing. The non-payment of taxes made the task of administering the city difficult.

This residence at 61 West 57th Avenue shown in a 1929 Leonard Frank photograph was typical of the single family homes characteristic of South Vancouver.

CIVIC POLITICS AND GOVERNMENT

Governing Vancouver was never easy and the prolonged Depression made it exceedingly difficult. The city's overriding problem, inadequate finances, was similar to that of many western Canadian cities. Property taxes, a relatively inelastic source, continued to be the major provider of revenue, yet, the city's expenses were increasing. It had to meet its ordinary operating expenses, find funds to cover public works debts incurred when money was easily raised, and cover the cost of furnishing relief and work for the unemployed. Paradoxically, G.G. McGeer, who as mayor in the mid-1930s faced the most serious financial crisis in the city's history, had, as an MLA in 1918, successfully opposed introducing a business tax that would have spread the tax burden more widely throughout the community. In 1918 the city was still faced with the need to provide work on sewer construction and road grading as a form of unemployment relief. By broadening the tax base, it could avoid the self-defeating measure of raising the mill rate. Many taxpayers were already delinquent and depressed real estate markets made tax sales an uncertain source of revenue. When it failed to get approval for the business tax, the city effectively abandoned the single tax system and imposed a tax on twenty-five per cent of improvements. To meet its day-to-day obligations, the city discontinued sinking fund payments and began using money authorized for specific purposes to meet general expenses. In his 1920 inaugural address, Mayor Gale declared that "all ranks should pay according to their several abilities." A broadly based committee recommended that instead of raising property taxes, the city should seek larger provincial grants and introduce a civic income tax. The Associated Property Owners of Vancouver persistently complained that they represented only a quarter of the population but paid almost eighty per cent of the taxes. Nevertheless, Vancouver continued to rely on the property tax as its main source of revenue. The addition of South Vancouver and Point Grey increased the number of property tax payers but created new problems as assessors tried to equalize assessments throughout the new, enlarged Vancouver.[47]

The Depression seriously underminded Vancouver's finances by increasing its relief costs to unprecedented levels and reducing its tax revenues. At the end of 1930, City Council wired Prime Minister Bennett of its need for thousands of dollars to provide food, clothing, and shelter for the unemployed. During six weeks of registration under the federal Unemployment Relief Act in fall 1930, 4,503 married men and 5,244 single men applied for aid. Unfortunately, from the city's point of view, the act depended on matching grants rather than on the number registered. Throughout the decade, Vancouver officials constantly complained of the enormous burden of relief costs; rarely did they admit that Vancouver was actually in a good financial position relative to other Canadian cities.[48]

Yet the city did have serious problems. Many residents could not afford to pay their taxes and few wanted to buy tax sale land. In November 1933, the city put 2,481 properties on sale but sold only 125, and only one property yielded a surplus over taxes owing. Since there was slight chance of sale, the city held no tax sale in 1934. Because of its reduced income, Council advised city departments to cut back and civic service suffered greatly. By temporarily closing special classes, all social service work, and the dental department, and by reducing medical services, vocational guidance, home economics, and manual training classes, the School Board reduced its costs by $654,200 despite increased enrolments. The Fire Department, over the protests of insurance underwriters, closed two halls and introduced a rotation system whereby each fireman worked one day a week without pay.[49]

During the December 1934 civic election campaign, G.G. McGeer repeatedly claimed that Vancouver had been bankrupt since 1929. McGeer's interest in financial affairs was not confined to the city. As he took office, he published a 359-page book, *The Conquest of Poverty,* to show how "the management of the monetary system can be easily changed from an institution which threatens the destruction of civilization into one of enduring service to human progress." Calling on the wisdom of Jesus Christ and Abraham Lincoln, he called for money management by government officials rather than private bankers and for the creation of money by government. He strongly attacked usurers for having established "a hell on earth." Although McGeer got Council to endorse the idea of a municipal savings bank, he recognized that reforming the monetary system was a matter of federal rather than municipal jurisdiction. He took his ideas to meetings of Western Canadian mayors and secured

The view from Little Mountain in 1938. The sparsely settled area in the foreground had been on the edge of the city limits until amalgamation with Point Grey and South Vancouver in 1929. The large building to the right of centre is the new City Hall; beyond is downtown. In the background are the North Shore Mountains.

support for his plan of a new system of national credit.[50]

Given that he equated usurers with the devil, McGeer's attack on municipal bondholders was predictable. While campaigning for mayor, he promised to reduce interest rates on existing city debts and to make an impact that would "be heard on St. James St., Montreal." Interest payments accounted for almost a third of the city's expenditures and McGeer saw no reason why the city should pay an average of 4.65 per cent interest when 3 per cent money was readily available. The angry bondholders were unwilling to make the sacrifice as long as the city could actually meet its obligations. At their urging, the city had Thomas Bradshaw, a well-known municipal financial consultant and Toronto insurance executive, examine Vancouver's finances. Bradshaw concluded that the city's problems were not "unsurmountable" and suggested more efficient tax collection. McGeer did not welcome this admonition to put the city's house in order. In the meantime, a City Council taxation committee, a "Brain Trust" including representative citizens, also considered tax problems. It accused Bradshaw of offering no useful solutions, declared that the city's problems were not temporary, and that the Depression had only made a bad situation "worse and more acute." The root of the problem was "absurd, uncertain, and impossible taxation," the legacy of the single tax and its heavy burden on land. To lift the load on real property they urged replacing the partial single tax with the British system of taxing improvements on the basis of their use and income value. They wanted the federal government to help with relief and airport administration costs and the province to take over policing costs and give the city a larger share of provincial tax revenues. In addition, the "Brain Trust" called for rigid economies, strict limits on capital borrowings, the re-organization of the Tax Department and the appointment of a city manager. McGeer considered the report an "outstanding accomplishment of his administration."[51]

To accomplish the re-organization of civic finances, G.G. McGeer, MLA asked the province to assist with costs relating to unemployment relief and police services, authorize the practice of suspending sinking fund payments, permit the issue of "Baby Bonds," and approve the plan to reduce bond interest. The Pattullo government sympathized with the bondholders and had already warned McGeer it would not approve any unilateral reduction in bond interest lest such action impair provincial credit. Part of the quarrel between the city and province also reflected their differing interpretations of the actual size of the city's deficit on current account.[52]

Although the province — itself facing serious financial problems — had little sympathy for Vancouver or for McGeer's plans to reduce the deficit, it did authorize the issue of "Baby Bonds." These bonds proved the most imaginative and successful of McGeer's financial schemes. McGeer had alienated outside investors with his threat to cut interest payments and upset ratepayers' associations by not seeking their approval of the bonds; he knew local capital was available. Both the BCER and the B.C. Telephone Company had sold securities locally. A local sales campaign would also stimulate local pride. McGeer sold almost $1.5 million worth of the three per cent debentures in denominations as low as $100 each, hence their name, "Baby Bonds." Much publicity was given to small individual purchases, including those by children, but over half the bonds were taken up by contractors who accepted them as part payment for work on city projects or by large local businesses such as the oil companies, the B.C. Telephone Company, the BCER, the B.C. Sugar Refinery, and several large merchants. Executives of some of these firms also served on a businessmen's committee organized to assist the sales campaign. Some corporate buyers may have hoped to influence city decisions on such matters as the location of the new city hall; others undoubtedly accepted McGeer's argument that the bonds would put idle local money into circulation to create jobs. Moreover, the interest rate was competitive; two Dominion bond issues of 1935 offered only 2.5 per cent interest. Proceeds from bond sales were used to repair winter storm damage to Stanley Park and the Forum (a sports arena on the Exhibition Grounds), to construct new roads, bridges, sewers, and water mains, and, especially, to construct a new city hall. All the projects were labour intensive, a point emphasized in the sales campaign. The "Baby Bonds" were a practical manifestation of McGeer's theory that given a sound monetary policy, an "abundance of money" could "be made available to promote the public enterprise of peaceful progress."[53]

Despite the success of the "Baby Bond" campaign and an increase in the percentage of taxes collected from seventy-one

Mayor G.G. (Gerry) McGeer at the ceremony marking the laying of the City Hall's cornerstone, July 2, 1936.

per cent in 1933 to eighty-one per cent in 1936, the city continued to plead financial problems and again tried to have the bondholders accept three per cent interest. The bondholders refused to budge and the city continued to pay bond interest at the regular rates. Near the end of his term, McGeer issued a statement noting how the financial situation had improved. Assets and the sinking fund had been increased, collections were up, tax rates had been reduced, and some services restored. A tax sale had been held though only 380 of some 11,755 available lots were sold.[54]

The city still cried poverty in its appeals to senior governments for better financial terms but the situation was improving. In 1937, ninety per cent of the taxes owing and some arrears were collected. By the end of the decade, the finance committee was able to draw up a budget that, save for the sinking fund and depreciation, was balanced.

In the course of his fight with the provincial government for financial concessions, McGeer, who also sat as a government backbencher, accused the Pattullo administration and its Finance Minister, John Hart, a Victoria investment dealer, of "deliberately forcing Vancouver into bankruptcy." Vancouver, of course, often considered herself to be the milch cow for the rest of the province while the rest of the province sometimes complained of Vancouver interests directing the government of British Columbia. In terms of political representation, Vancouver had reason to feel aggrieved. Although home to approximately a third of the province's people (Appendix, Table IIa), the city had as few as one-eighth of the provincial members. Moreover, the city was often seriously underrepresented in cabinet. Only two Vancouver MLAs, Joseph Martin (1900) and William J. Bowser (1915-16), ever served as premier, and both had exceptionally short and controversial terms. At times, Vancouver was sometimes completely shut out of the cabinet. After Attorney-General J.W. de B. Farris resigned from the Oliver administration early in 1922, Vancouver lacked a cabinet post until the election of S.F. Tolmie and the Conservatives in 1928. Despite the complaints of Vancouver's Liberals about their "humiliating position," the election of Liberals to five of Vancouver's six seats in 1924, and Oliver's declared sympathy for the situation, the premier refused to appoint a Vancouver member to his cabinet since neither the Vancouver MLAs nor the city's Liberal party

organization could agree on a candidate and because he seriously doubted the Liberals' chances of winning the by-election which would be made necessary by a cabinet appointment.[55]

The Tolmie administration (1928-33) was only nominally more generous in providing the city with representation. Tolmie appointed three Vancouver MLAs to his cabinet as ministers without portfolio after an intraparty squabble. Dissension involving Vancouver Conservatives was not new. In 1923, opponents of Bowser's leadership formed the short-lived Provincial Party under the guidance of Vancouver millionaire General A.D. McRae. Vancouver business interests, however, considerably influenced Tolmie. In 1931, after a number of prominent Vancouver businessmen insisted that an outside committee examine government finances, Tolmie appointed George Kidd, the recently retired President to the BCER and several prominent provincial businessmen to such a committee. The subsequent Kidd Report recommended drastic reductions in provincial expenditures and condemned the party system. Before Tolmie recovered from the shock of their proposals, his government had disintegrated. In the subsequent election, T.D. Pattullo and the Liberals trounced him while the brand-new CCF party formed the Opposition. The Pattullo administration, though not giving Vancouver all that it wanted financially, did include two Vancouver MLAs in the cabinet and one of them, Dr. George Weir, was instrumental in initiating social and economic reforms. In 1933, Vancouver elected nine MLAs spread among four constituencies. Except for the two CCF members elected in Vancouver East, all the Vancouver members elected in 1933 were Liberal.[56]

The increased number of MLAs given Vancouver in the early 1930s partly reflects the city's increased size as a result of the amalgamation with South Vancouver and Point Grey in 1929. The story of amalgamation also illustrates the provincial government's influence over municipal affairs. The history of South Vancouver and Point Grey offers an interesting contrast in municipal development.

With the help of provincial legislation in 1914 guaranteeing that Shaughnessy would remain a single famiy residential district until at least 1925, Point Grey overcame internal division. Because the CPR, which owned one-third of Point

Grey's land, was able to pay its taxes during the wartime depression, Point Grey, with careful management, remained solvent. South Vancouver, in contrast, provided "an illustration of how not to conduct the affairs of a municipality" as it suffered from political turmoil, administrative inefficiency, and financial chaos that gave it a comic opera image and undermined confidence in the municipality. With the collapse of the real estate boom in 1912-13, population growth stopped, tax collections fell by half, the money markets were dead, the banks refused further credit, and South Vancouver was forced to lay off most of those engaged in municipal works thus increasing the unemployment problem. By the end of 1917, South Vancouver was in such poor circumstances that it could not always meet its payroll, was borrowing from the sinking fund, and using by-law revenues for other than authorized purposes. In 1918, the province agreed to assume payments on a three-quarter million dollar loan that had come due on condition that it administer South Vancouver through a commissioner with all the powers of the reeve, council, police commission, and school board.[57]

Commissioner F.J. Gillespie set out to restore South Vancouver's finances. He had all buildings re-assessed, abolished the single tax by taxing improvements at one-third their assessed values, and raised money by collecting back taxes and other debts and selling municipal property. As well, he reduced the number of municipal employees and so cut back on municipal services that some plank sidewalks decayed beyond repair and the Fire Department complained of the impassibility of some roads. Some improvement in the overall economic situation and population growth helped Gillespie and his successor, A. Wells Gray, restore South Vancouver's treasury. In April 1923, the province restored self government to South Vancouver. Though they had recently regained their independence and were offered no tax relief, South Vancouver residents in January 1924, overwhelmingly indicated support for amalgamation with Vancouver.

The province's paternal attitude towards municipalities was very clear in the revival of the amalgamation plan. In March 1924, T.D. Pattullo, Minister of Lands, invited lower mainland municipalities to discuss their water supply and other matters in which cooperation could bring about economy of administration

and better service. That year the province created the Greater Vancouver Water District to take effect in January 1926. During the next few years most lower mainland municipalities joined the system and some municipalities considered other metropolitan ventures. Late in 1926, the three core municipalities worked out a joint arrangement to purchase land from the CPR and develop Little Mountain Park. Discussions about a metropolitan police force failed but a Metropolitan Board of Health including all lower mainland cities and municipalities came into being in 1936 with financial aid from the Provincial Board of Health and the Rockefeller Foundation.[58]

Once the scheme to amalgamate Point Grey, South Vancouver, and Vancouver was underway, its progress, though not always smooth, was relatively quick.[59] The BCER franchises that had helped wreck the pre-war scheme, were no longer an issue. The decline in the number of street railway passengers during the wartime depression and future uncertainties caused by increased automobile use meant the street railway was no longer an attractive investment for the city even if the financial resources were available to purchase it.

The first amalgamation scheme presented to Vancouver voters in the 1920s affected only Vancouver and South Vancouver. Because municipal services in the suburb were inferior, the plan provided for separate budgets until South Vancouver services reached city standards. Ratepayers in both municipalities enthusiastically endorsed the principle of amalgamation. When a revised proposal calling for an integrated budget was voted on in June 1925, South Vancouver ratepayers again endorsed amalgamation but Vancouver voters, fearing higher taxes, rejected it. Nevertheless, Mayor Taylor continued to press for amalgamation. As he explained early in 1926, "To the outside world, Vancouver with a population of over two hundred thousand would be an entirely different city than Vancouver with one hundred and twenty-eight thousand."[60]

To assuage sensitivities in Point Grey, whose officials attended joint meetings only for "courtesy's sake," Taylor was willing to consider the county council or metropolitan system of government in which Reeve J.A. Paton had expressed an interest. Under this plan, the components would turn over some responsibilities to a central authority but would retain separate identities; under amalgamation individual identities would be

The Point Grey Municipal Hall in Kerrisdale with its Tudor revival architecture and large garden blended well with the Point Grey surroundings.

submerged. In a plebiscite held at the December 1927 municipal elections, Vancouver ratepayers clearly preferred amalgamation to the county council system or retention of the *status quo*. A month later, Point Grey and South Vancouver voters expressed similar views. With this evidence of support, representatives of the three Councils worked out amalgamation principles. Before January 1, 1929 the whole area would be reassessed, the wards redistributed, the system of local improvements made uniform, provision made to include as many as possible of the employees of the three municipalities on the new city payroll, and representation of the School and Park Board increased. On June 25, 1927, Vancouver and South Vancouver approved the plan by a large majority. The Point Grey Council, which was divided on amalgamation, did not submit the plebiscite to its ratepayers until December. Though Council members vigorously discussed the question, ratepayers showed little interest. Then, in spite of snow-covered streets, a relatively large number of Point Grey residents voted and showed strong support for amalgamation. A month later, they defeated Reeve Paton and all but one of the anti-amalgamation councillors.[61]

With Point Grey's participation assured, planning for amalgamation began in earnest. The solicitors of the three municipalities and representatives of their Councils drafted an amalgamation bill that the Legislature readily passed. Committees also began to work out such necessary details as the incorporation of suburban police and fire departments into the Vancouver system. The resolution of such anomalies as duplication of street names was deferred until after amalgamation. In October 1928, the three municipalities chose a mayor for the new Vancouver, councillors for each of its twelve new wards, and School and Park Boards. Under the guidance of Mayor-elect W.H. Malkin, a deliberate attempt was made to centralize services and "to think Vancouver."[62] On January 1, 1929, the new Vancouver, now the third largest city in Canada, came into being.

One of the most controversial matters in working out amalgamation was the question of wards and ward boundaries. Within Vancouver there had been intermittent discussion of the ward system and the possibility of change. In 1920, the voters approved a proportional representation scheme, actually a preferential scheme, advocated by the Vancouver Proportional Representation League and endorsed by the Board of Trade, the

Trades and Labour Council, veterans' groups and many other societies. Proponents of "P.R." claimed it would provide efficient civic government and ensure minority representation. Although the original plebiscite was not clear on the matter, aldermen were elected from the city at-large and each voter, no matter how many pieces of property he owned, had only one ballot. On the ballot, the voter marked his choices for all civic offices, other than the mayoralty, in order of preference. This preferential system was confusing, especially for those who had to count the votes and it seemed to have no significant effect on the outcome of the election. Proportional representation, commented the *Sun*, "is extremely fair and highly moral, but deadly dull." In 1923, ratepayers dropped "P.R." and restored the wards.[63]

In the amalgamation discussions, Vancouver wanted to retain its existing wards and give South Vancouver and Point Grey each two aldermen; South Vancouver wanted to abolish wards and Point Grey submitted a plan for a complete redrawing of ward boundaries south and east of False Creek and south of English Bay. Instead of paying attention to existing neighbourhoods, the wards were divided by a series of parallel lines drawn on a north-south axis south to the Fraser River. Since Point Grey was the reluctant party to amalgamation, she got her way. The chief advantage of the new ward boundaries was supposed to be the obliteration of old loyalties. Since the new wards were largely artificial creations, they were expected to make people think of themselves not as residents of a neighbourhood but of the new city. Few of the new wards were composed of any one particular economic group. Moreover, the Asians, the only minority ethnic group sufficiently concentrated to be numerically significant, had never had the municipal franchise.

The blurring of the wards had a detrimental effect at City Hall. Instead of making aldermen work for the city as a whole, the new wards seemed to encourage "sectionalism, log-rolling, and the you-scratch-my-back-and-I'll-scratch-yours of making policy and plans" and led aldermen to try "to dabble in every civic department." Only the aldermen themselves seriously objected when the provincial legislature in 1935 insisted that the city hold a plebiscite on abolishing wards and reducing the number of aldermen. Few public bodies expressed an opinion. The Associated Property Owners of Vancouver, an organization dominated by large property owners, thought the time was not opportune for

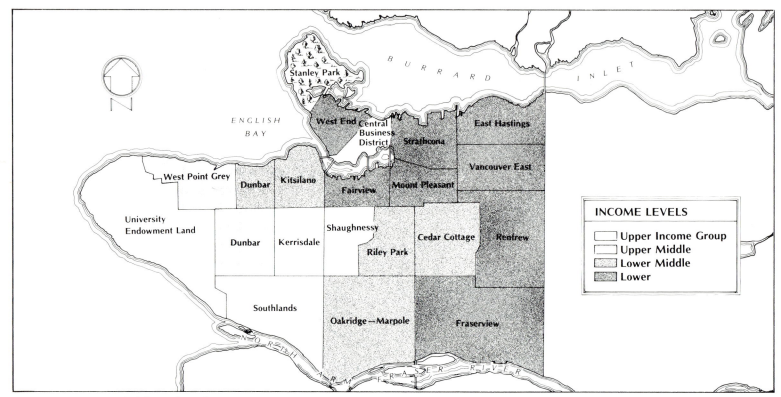

6 Vancouver Neighbourhoods, c. 1925

INCOME LEVELS
- Upper Income Group
- Upper Middle
- Lower Middle
- Lower

change, and the Trades and Labour Council endorsed the at-large system. The election campaign was marked by apathy and an unusually low twenty per cent of the electorate actually voted. Nevertheless, the result was clear. Two-thirds favoured abolishing the wards and eighty per cent favoured reducing the number of aldermen from twelve to eight.[64]

The at-large system, in contrast to the ward system, presented voters with dozens of names on a ballot. The newly formed CCF took advantage of this in 1936 and ran a full slate of aldermanic candidates of whom three were elected.[65] Only two declared CCF incumbents were returned. The existence of party politics at City Hall was confirmed the next year under the paradoxical name of the Non-Partisan Association. The NPA was non-partisan only in the sense that it included a carefully

balanced number of Liberal and Conservative candidates. Acting chiefly as a publicity agent advertising candidates, it did not oblige successful candidates to follow any party line or principles. Despite many challenges, the NPA remains a force in Vancouver civic politics. As some supporters of the ward system had forecast, the at-large system and the NPA's management of it, gave the business and professional classes and the residents of the west side of the city a disproportionate influence on Council, a complaint that recurs throughout the city's recent history.

SOCIAL AND CULTURAL DEVELOPMENT

One of the persistent paradoxes of Vancouver, as with many

other cities, is the contrast between the widespread interest in such socially acceptable entertainments as theatrical and sports events and the seaminess of the lives of a few of her residents. Given such conflicting outlooks on leisure time activities, it is not surprising that morality became a political issue.

Vancouver remained on the circuit of touring movies, vaudeville acts, and concert artists but there was also much local activity. The Vancouver Symphony Society, established in 1919, could afford to give few concerts until financed by Mrs. B.T. Rogers of the sugar refining family. In 1930, using local performers, it began a successful annual series of subscription concerts at the Orpheum Theatre. During the Depression, the BCER and Home Oil sponsored free summertime concerts in Stanley Park. Amateur actors were also busy. The Vancouver Little Theatre, founded in 1919, acquired its own theatre in 1923, and productions of the Players' Club drew Vancouver residents to the University campus.

Professional sports did less well. In 1915 the Vancouver Millionaires defeated the Ottawa Senators at the Denman Arena to win the Stanley Cup; they narrowly lost to the same team in 1921. By 1927, the Patrick family had sold their Pacific Coast Hockey League to the National Hockey League. Vancouver did not have another professional sports team until after World War II. Amateur sport flourished, however. Team sports occupied many people and some individual sports produced stars such as Percy Williams, who won gold medals in the 100 and 200 metre dashes at the 1928 Olympics in Amsterdam. Thousands welcomed him home.

Because of the enthusiasm Vancouver demonstrated on such occasions, Mayor McGeer aparently believed that parades and new sports facilities would help promote "civic spirit" and restore confidence during the Depression. In the summer of 1936, he became "Jubilee King" as Vancouver celebrated its fiftieth birthday with parades, pageants, a new stadium at Brockton Point and a Jubilee Fountain in Lost Lagoon. Poor attendance forced the city to drop the entrance fee to some events and caused a $50,000 deficit, but McGeer justified the expense by noting that the festivities had attracted approximately $20 million worth of tourist business. The effect on "civic spirit" and confidence is impossible to assess.

The establishment of the University of British Columbia in 1915 to replace McGill University College, essentially a junior college, provided Vancouver with some cultural leadership. Dr. F.F. Wesbrook, the University's first president, established the Vancouver Institute in 1916 to provide free weekly lectures on matters of general interest pertaining to literature, the arts, nature studies, and science. At least one member of the University's faculty was a founder of the Vancouver Poetry Society in 1916. Members read and criticized each other's work, and, in 1922, published what they believed to be the first Canadian chapbook.[66]

Members of the business elite and their wives worked for an art gallery. H.A. Stone, who desired a memorial for his only son who had been killed in the war, approached twelve family friends and persuaded them to offer $100,000 to the city for the purchase of paintings if the city would build a gallery. Though the public seemed keen on the idea, City Council and the ratepayers rejected it. Nevertheless, by 1931, the founders raised $135,000, sufficient to provide a fully equipped gallery on a city-owned site on West Georgia Street, Meanwhile, a second group of artistically inclined individuals, including some active journalists, organized the B.C. Art League in 1920 to encourage "education and cultivation in arts and crafts." The culmination of their efforts was the opening of the Art School in October 1925.[67]

In contrast to these cultural developments, Vancouver still had problems of crime and immorality of a proportion to cause police scandals and provide several mayors with election issues. In 1926, the "moral administration" of Vancouver, particularly as related to the policing of illegal liquor outlets, was a minor civic issue though G.G. McGeer blamed the maladministration of the liquor business and the odium it gave provincial Liberals for the failure of federal Liberal candidates in the 1926 federal election. Two years later, the state of crime was a major issue. The Police Commission, no friend of incumbent Mayor L.D. Taylor, had been aroused by rumours that some members of the morality squad had been accepting bribes not to interfere with keepers of disorderly houses, gamblers, and bookmakers who openly carried on their illegal activities. R.S. Lennie, an investigator appointed by the Police Commission, found the police force generally consisted of a fine body of men but was undermanned, underpaid, and demoralized. He blamed Mayor

The Point Grey campus of the University of British Columbia lay beyond the city limits and the end of the street railway line.

Construction work on the University of British Columbia's Point Grey campus stopped with the outbreak of World War I. In 1922, students, angered by the crowded conditions in the shacks, tents and other makeshift quarters on the Vancouver General Hospital grounds, launched a publicity campaign to pressure the provincial government to complete the Point Grey buildings. The culmination of Varsity Week was the "Great Trek" to Point Grey where students, with class banners, stood in the skeleton of the Science Building. The campaign succeeded; in September 1925 the University moved to its new campus.

Taylor for insisting that Vancouver be an "open town" and for instructing the police to concentrate on murderers and hold-up men to the neglect of the disorderly houses and gambling joints. Shortly after the release of Lennie's report, W.H. Malkin, an Englishman of Methodist antecedents who had been in the wholesale grocery business in Vancouver since 1895, announced he would run against Mayor Taylor. Malkin, who had the support of the Christian Vigilance League, a group organized by some United Church clergymen, campaigned for a "'new' town, a new spirit and a new outlook." Taylor, denying he ever wanted an "open town," claimed he simply did not want "a Sunday School town." The electors, including residents of the about to be amalgamated municipalities of South Vancouver and Point Grey, narrowly chose Malkin and his promises of law, order, and civic morality.[68]

Two years later, with the Depression well underway, morality was a very minor election issue, and voters clearly preferred the flamboyant Taylor to the businesslike Malkin although their platforms were almost identical. The voters returned the incumbent aldermen and approved nine of the twelve money by-laws put forward by the Malkin administration. Taylor was re-elected again in 1932, but in 1934 Gerry McGeer declared that "crime must be stamped out" and warned that Vancouver was in danger of being "handed over to an underworld group that will soon turn this great Canadian city into a bankrupt carbon copy of the City of Chicago in its most evil days."[69]

First elected in 1935, McGeer quickly established himself as a defender of morality and law. He celebrated his first Sunday as mayor, his forty-seventh birthday with a day of "service, humiliation, and prayer" during which citizens would "pray to the God above to give us a vision of our city as 'a city of peace where order shall not rest on force but on the love of all for the city wherein we dwell.'" Protestant and Catholic church leaders responded enthusiastically with special prayers and sermons. Dozens were turned away from the services that the Mayor and Council attended at Christ Church Cathedral and St. Andrew's-Wesley United Church. A few days earlier, McGeer had suspended a number of police officers, fired Police Chief John Cameron, and appointed W.W. Foster, a distinguished soldier, to replace him. During hearings into the suspensions of the officers, it became clear that the police force was completely demoralized. The legal counsel for the new chief reported:

Commercialized vice and well organized crime thrived under Police protection. Well known criminal groups to the knowledge and with the sanction of Ex-Chief of Police John Cameron, and several other members of the Police Force openly carried on the following criminal activities. White slavery and the operation of brothels, gambling, including slot machines, Chinese lotteries, bookmaking and all forms of card, crap and other table games, illegal sale of liquor, bootlegging joints were operating in almost every block of the downtown area, and the illegal sale of drugs was rampant. As a result of this the conditions that developed, robbery with violence, burglary, and theft became a nightly and daily occurrence.

Cameron was subsequently tried but acquitted on a charge of conspiracy to interfere with the police in their attempts to prosecute keepers of houses of ill fame.[70]

Chief Foster set about to eliminate such evils as gambling joints, slot and pinball machines, and bunco games. So effective was his work that police chiefs in Calgary and Winnipeg complained of the influx of refugee crooks. Foster failed to stamp out prostitution. The police could only suppress its most objectionable features such as street-walking, "window-tapping," and brothels with "a view to keeping the City as orderly and free from the nuisance as possible." Nevertheless, McGeer was sufficiently pleased with Foster's first year that he declared Sunday, January 3, 1936 as a day of "prayer and humiliation" and asked citizens to assemble in churches to thank God "for the removal of commercialized vice and the return of peace and order." The thanksgiving was premature for though some former occupants of the bawdy houses had to seek welfare, they soon resumed business by scattering throughout the city.[71]

One reason for morality's popularity as a political issue was the presence of churches. Though no statistics are available on church attendance in Vancouver, over ninety per cent of the population claimed a formal religious affiliation (Appendix, Table X). Vancouver churchmen, both clerical and lay, actively led such provincial reform movements as the war-time campaign for prohibition and the post-war agitation for laws to prohibit the use of opium and similar narcotics. The churches

In Vancouver, as elsewhere in North America, miniature golf was a popular pastime in the 1920s and 1930s. This course, photographed in 1930, was at the corner of Georgia and Cardero Streets near the **entrance to Stanley Park.**

Stuart Thomson photographed this Japanese baseball team in 1929.

Field lacrosse at Brockton Point, Stanley Park, 1930.

The Terminal City Lawn Bowling Club, 1920.

A popular resort, just north of Vancouver, c. 1920.

An outing to Siwash Rock, Stanley Park.

Members of the Vancouver Natural History Society at their 1929 camp.

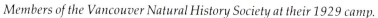

Indian war canoe races were a popular tradition in Burrard Inlet.

The fashionable Spencer's department store.

The elegant dining room of the Hudson's Bay Company.

Nat Bailey's original White Spot Drive-In on South Granville Street in 1930 grew into a chain of popular restaurants and drive-ins.

themselves were a highly visible part of the landscape. In addition to the churches and cathedrals of the traditional Christian denominations, the temples of Eastern religions, and synagogues, Vancouver had the edifices of many sects, often of an evangelical nature. One English visitor counted sixty-five advertisements of different churches and religious organizations in a local paper. "Proselytizing flourishes," he reported, "and any man with manners enough to respond gracefully to the greeting of a fellow-citizen who may be unknown to him will, in the course of a day's stroll, be enlightened as to many methods of climbing the Golden Stair; he will also be impressed by the danger attending the open elevator shaft."[72]

Vancouver was, indeed, a city of contrasts. She remained British Columbia's most important city, but the legislature still controlled her Charter. In the 1920s, she recovered from wartime depression and extended her economic influence eastward into the central prairies, but in the 1930s stagnated economically and had to wrestle with the social and political problems created by the westward migration of the hinterland's unemployed. Vancouver civic leaders periodically feared that "Red Revolutionaries" were about to take over, but the Trades and Labour Council often seemed to have more interests in common with the Board of Trade than with the socialists. Vancouver was pleased to welcome new residents but her citizens were prominent in leading anti-Asian campaigns. Proud of its physical setting, the city established a Town Planning Commission and commissioned an elaborate plan for the future, but Council ignored much of the planners' advice. Vancouver was maturing culturally with the establishment of a university, symphony, and art gallery, but "frontier" crimes of prostitution and gambling remained highly visible problems. Vancouver was very much a place of contrast where the bawdy life style of some of its inhabitants jostled uncomfortably with the aspirations of most citizens for a modern, cultured city.

Although the Lions Gate Bridge opened in November 1938, the British Pacific Properties were still a wilderness on May 29, 1939 when this photograph was taken.

The construction through Stanley Park of the approaches to the Lions Gate Bridge across First Narrows excited much concern about possible desecration of the park. The toll bridge was a private venture built by the Guinness brewing interests to provide access to their luxury subdivision, the British Pacific Properties.

Chapter Four
The Maturing City
1939-1979

Vancouver has lived by the legend of continual growth and feels ill if it is not in a constant state of expansion. The North American disease of proliferation and giantism has become chronic here and seems like normal health. Size, population, business appear as the end and supreme object of civic life. Already Vancouver holds half of British Columbia's people — a top-heavy and dropsical arrangement, but Vancouver never suspects that.[1]

After the first impressions of envy for the charismatic people and the magnificent mountain scenery of Vancouver, the "amour-propre" of the Easterner is restored when he discovers that Vancouver is, in fact, an ugly and undisciplined city that has consumed its available land in a wasteful way and is now threatened with all kinds of difficulties. Perhaps it is the only city in Canada for which a no-growth policy really seems appropriate.[2]

With the outbreak of war in 1939, Vancouver, along with the rest of British Columbia, began to enjoy a period of prosperity that has lasted, with minor interruptions, through the 1970s. Successive civic governments enjoyed the growth stimulated by hinterland expansion and the Pacific Rim demand for Western Canadian resources. Immigrants from elsewhere in Canada and from overseas poured into the city, adding to the housing problem but making the city truly cosmopolitan. In the mid-1960s, private entrepreneurs began a massive redevelopment of the downtown commercial area, but by the late 1960s and early 1970s, Vancouver residents questioned the wisdom of growth. They changed the city's course slightly but did not abandon the growth ethic. The physical boundaries of river, inlet and bay meant that much of that growth spilled over into nearby municipalities.

ECONOMIC GROWTH AND METROPOLITAN RELATIONSHIPS

Vancouver's outstanding asset, her harbour or front door, is a major generator of local revenue. A 1976 study attributed ten per cent of the jobs in Greater Vancouver to port activity. A few years earlier, the port manager estimated that every ton of cargo handled put $10 into the local economy in the form of longshoremen's wages, pilotage and inspection fees, ship repairs and provisions, and crew spending.[3] Since 1936, the National Harbours Board (NHB), a federal agency, has administered the port of Burrard Inlet and has had a significant but not exclusive role in developing it. The extension of the NHB's area of jurisdiction to include the waterfront south to the international border in 1966 reflected Vancouver's emergence in 1963 as the leading Canadian port in terms of tonnage and a shift in exports from a concentration on grain and forest products to a wide variety of minerals including Alberta sulphur and Saskatchewan potash loaded from such specialized facilities as the Pacific Coast Bulk Terminals at Port Moody (1960) and Crow's Nest Pass coal shipped to Japanese steel mills from the Kaiser Resources superport at Roberts Bank (1970). Although coal was the leading export by tonnage in the 1970s, the unique facilities designed for its handling meant it provided relatively few jobs.

Grain and lumber remained important exports. After recovering from the wartime and immediate post-war shipping shortage, the grain trade quickly returned to pre-war levels and greatly expanded when new markets were found in Asia. Indeed, in 1961, huge shipments to China made Vancouver the world's greatest grain shipping centre. This necessitated the expansion of grain elevator capacity, especially by the Saskatchewan

On March 6, 1940 at the Port Coquitlam yards of the CPR, Leonard Frank photographed these thirty-two cars of lumber consigned to the British Controller of Timber Supplies by the H.R. MacMillan Export Company for war purposes.

The federal government's rationing restrictions and price controls inconvenienced consumers but did keep prices down as this 1944 display in one of Woodward's windows demonstrates.

Hayes Bus Manufacturing Company, 1941.

Though Vancouver was distant from any battle scene, the city was prepared for possible air attacks.

Soldiers, sailors and airmen in uniform were a common sight in Vancouver during World War II as all three services had large bases in the city or nearby.

V-J Day, 1945 was the occasion for an impromptu celebration.

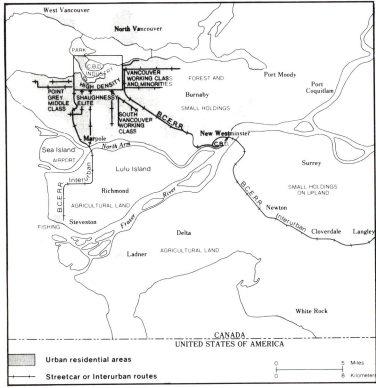

7 Lower Mainland, 1945

Map legend:
- Urban residential areas
- Streetcar or Interurban routes

0 — 5 Miles
0 — 8 Kilometers

several northern bush line operations. After the war, the Canadian government designated the airline as Canada's flag carrier to China, Hong Kong, Japan, Australasia, and South America. Although not all these routes — the one to China is a notable example — have been developed, CP Air has made its Vancouver base an interchange between its Asian, European, and Canadian routes. In 1949 when the airline moved its headquarters from Montreal to the old Boeing Aircraft plant on Vancouver's Sea Island, it employed 1,000 people; in 1969, it moved to a new 870,000 square foot operating centre and employed roughly 3,000 people in Greater Vancouver.[6]

During the War, the federal government had managed the city-owned airport and the RCAF and aircraft manufacturers expanded it extensively. When the city resumed control in 1947, Ottawa agreed to contribute to capital expenditures and subsidize administrative costs. By the late 1950s, when the growth of air traffic overtaxed terminals and runways, the Department of Transport offered to buy the airport and give Vancouver a new terminal. City ratepayers, proud of owning their own airport, twice rejected the sale. Then, in June 1961, after a vigorous public debate between Mayor Thomas Alsbury, who believed the airport was not really a civic responsibility, and Alderman Halford Wilson, long a champion of a civic airport, ratepayers overwhelmingly approved the airport's sale for $2,750,000. The Department of Transport immediately set out to fulfill its promise to improve the airport and, in October 1968, opened a new $32 million terminal building to serve international and domestic carriers, including such locally based regional operators as Pacific Western Airlines.

Major highway building projects, including the Trans-Canada Highway, and the completion of the Pacific Great Eastern Railway to Prince George and on to the Peace River improved Vancouver's access to the prospering Interior and Alberta. In the 1960s the Peace River began to boom with the construction of large scale hydro-electric projects and the expansion of the oil and natural gas industry. These developments, reported the Vancouver Board of Trade, "are creating new business opportunities for those interested in secondary manufactures, sale of industrial supplies and consumer goods, construction, tourist accommodation and transportation as well as forming a healthy base to the economy of the whole Province."[7] The Peace River

and Alberta Wheat Pools (Appendix, Table XIII). Increasing quantities and new forms of exports of wood products also led to the construction of specialized wharves such as North Vancouver's Seaboard Terminal, possibly the world's largest forest products terminal,[4] for shipping packaged lumber and the Fraser-Surrey Docks for exporting wood chips. In addition, the NHB completed its Centennial Pier in British Columbia's 1958 centennial year to handle general cargo. In the mid-1970s, it built the Vanterm and Lynnterm facilities to serve container traffic and general cargo respectively.[5]

The Vancouver headquarters of Canadian Pacific Airlines also reflects the importance of the Pacific Rim. CP Air, a subsidiary of the CPR, began in 1941-42 as the consolidation of

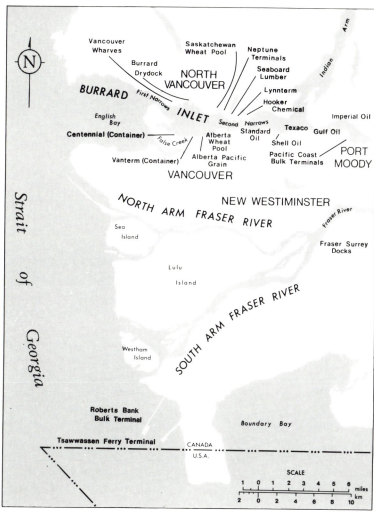

8 The Port of Vancouver

qualities as the manufactured one. As headquarters for B.C. Electric, which the W.A.C. Bennett government took over in 1961, and for Westcoast Transmission, Vancouver performed head office functions for important components of the Peace River economy.

Most oil and gas companies operated on the Alberta side of the Peace River and had their main Canadian offices in Calgary or Edmonton. The discovery of large deposits of oil in Alberta and construction of the Trans-Mountain Pipeline to Burnaby (1953) made British Columbia independent of foreign oil suppliers and led to the expansion and modernization of the Burrard Inlet refineries. The Alberta oil boom, however, reduced Vancouver's role as a financial metropolis. The Vancouver Stock Exchange had recognized this possibility soon after the Leduc discoveries of 1947[8] and their fears appeared likely to become a reality in the late 1970s when even firms not directly involved in the oil and gas industry were moving their head offices from Vancouver to Calgary.[9] Alberta's wealth and ability to draw business away from British Columbia was clearly demonstrated by the Alberta government's purchase of Pacific Western Airlines in 1974 and the subsequent moving of its head office and operations headquarters from Vancouver to Calgary and Edmonton respectively.

Despite the competition from Alberta, Vancouver maintained its role as a western Canadian financial centre. Although still subordinate to Toronto and Montreal, the aggressive competition posed by the Vancouver-based Bank of British Columbia (established 1969) influenced the larger chartered banks to give their regional officials greater discretionary powers in granting loans at least on speculative ventures.[10] Provincial credit unions also strengthened Vancouver's financial position by establishing the headquarters of their central banker, the B.C. Central Credit Union, in the city in 1970.[11] Yet there was still a speculative air about Vancouver financial institutions. Although individual Vancouver residents displayed an interest in forming locally-based trust companies this trend suffered a set-back when investors in Commonwealth Trust (established 1963) lost much capital, and public attention focussed on a long, complex trial of its principals. The Vancouver Stock Exchange, still the third largest in Canada, had such a reputation for speculation that Alex MacDonald, the NDP MLA for Vancouver East, referred to it as

provides Vancouver with much of its electricity and natural gas. The introduction of natural gas, piped to Vancouver by Westcoast Transmission Company, allowed B.C. Electric to demolish its ugly storage cylinders adjacent to the Georgia Viaduct and, incidentally, eliminated a common means of suicide and accidental death as the natural product lacked the same asphyxiating

"a gambling casino" dominated by "investor confusion, trickery and bilking." Highly speculative "penny stocks" listed on its curb exchange often fluctuated wildly. Provincial government intervention in the 1970s led to a tightening of listing regulations and the Exchange again concentrated on its business of providing a forum for trading in the shares of British Columbia companies, especially mining ventures.[12]

Most companies whose shares are traded on the Exchange have head offices in Vancouver. The headquarters of some of the smaller, more speculative ventures may be in a filing cabinet of a lawyer's office, but others, representing major industries, are visible reminders of Vancouver's dominance of the provincial hinterland. Both foreign-owned forestry firms such as Crown Zellerbach, Rayonier Canada, and Weldwood and the locally-owned giants, MacMillan Bloedel and B.C. Forest Products, have large offices in Vancouver. MacMillan Bloedel has over 1,000 head office employees; the others employ between 150 and 300 people each.[13] Similarly, major mining corporations, notably Cominco, a CPR subsidiary with zinc and lead mines and smelters in the West Kootenay and mines at points as distant as Australia and Greenland, have head offices in Vancouver.

The executives of these firms have formed Vancouver's "Establishment." They founded the Employers Council of British Columbia, "the grand council of the B.C. corporate will"; they meet at prestigious clubs, particularly the Vancouver Club and the Shaughnessy Golf and Country Club; they support such cultural organizations as the Vancouver Symphony Society; they favour the Non-Partisan Association in civic politics; and their families tend to intermarry.[14] A few of the elite such as C.N. Woodward and Forrest Rogers belong to pioneer business families; some entrepreneurs such as J.G. Prentice of Canadian Forest Products and Peter Paul Saunders of Versatile Cornat Corporation, an industrial company in a variety of manufacturing and service activities, are European immigrants; others, such as Calvert Knudsen of MacMillan Bloedel, are senior executives imported from the U.S.

The various executives control the hinterland "through the supply of coordinating services and information and the calculation, evaluation and ratification of long range plans and investment strategies."[15] Hinterland development created new opportunities for supporting industries such as the production of chemicals for the pulp and paper industry. Vancouver's importance as a corporate headquarters and the city's continuing attractiveness for tourists stimulated hotel construction in the late 1960s and early 1970s and explain the modest increase in the number of Vancouver residents employed in service industries (Appendix, Tables XI and XIV).

Since major provincial employers are concentrated in Vancouver, it has been logical for major provincial labour unions to have central offices in the city. Major industries also have central bargaining associations. Both Forest Industrial Relations and Construction Labour Relations, for example, have provincial headquarters in Vancouver. This separation of union leaders and employers from the actual work sites has occasioned wild cat strikes in distant places.[16]

Within Vancouver, civic outside workers, construction workers, longshoremen, lumberworkers, bus drivers, newspaper printers, and others have struck from time to time for an assortment of reasons, usually to demand higher wages. The practices of non-striking unions honouring picket lines and of lock-outs by employers have often increased the impact of labour disputes. While the withdrawal of services has often inconvenienced the public and waterfront labour disputes have threatened the port's future prospects, neither militant labour leaders nor grieving workers challenged authority in the same way as did the strikers of 1917-19 or those of the 1930s, nor did employers express the same paranoid fears. On the waterfront, for example, the port manager and the local president of the Longshoremen's and Warehousemen's Union have been known to meet weekly and to share pride in the high productivity of Vancouver's waterfront workers. Blue collar workers, of course, have gradually become less significant in the city's economy. Since 1961, industrial employment within Vancouver has been declining at an average rate of 1.3 per cent per year partly as a consequence of civic efforts to convert False Creek from an industrial area to a mixture of residential, commercial, and recreational uses.[17]

Faced with a limited supply of industrial land, the city eventually discouraged the location of new manufacturing industries within its limits and even pushed some old industries off False Creek. This contrasts sharply with the attitudes in the 1940s when city businessmen actively sought new manufacturing industries. Within days of the declaration of World War II, the Vancouver Board of Trade sought shipbuilding and munitions contracts.[18] They were remarkably successful, and indeed, some manufacturers became so proficient they shipped parts to eastern Canada. War industry provided much new employment in Vancouver, and at peak production, the shipyards employed 25,000 men and women; Boeing's air craft plant, about 5,000; Dominion Bridge, about 2,000. The war workers who joined the wildly enthusiastic celebration of V-J Day in August 1945 quickly turned their cheer to gloom as lay-offs followed the war's end. As in the rest of Canada, economic growth soon took up the slack. Because Vancouver war workers had become highly skilled tradespeople, they were able to find jobs in new industries such as a steel rolling mill that produced practically all the reinforcing and light structural steel used in the province and in specialized factories producing wire rope, logging equipment, and other steel products.[19]

The city actively recruited industries through an Industrial Commissioner hired to provide information for prospective industries and publicize industrial sites especially in the eastern part of the city between Broadway and the Grandview Highway. To ensure Vancouver's competitive position, Mayor Gerry McGeer and his successors continued the fight for freight rate reductions. The city also appointed representatives of the Board of Trade, the Vancouver and District Trades and Labour Council, the railways, the Town Planning Commission and other interested bodies to act as an Industrial Development Commission advising Council on long range policy "to secure the greatest possible industrial development."[20] The Commission eventually questioned the wisdom of seeking new industry when there seemed to be no more than 1,000 acres of suitable vacant industrial land within the city. By the mid-1950s ratepayers were unwilling to spend the money necessary to assemble industrial lands.

Nevertheless, the persistence of old industries, especially lumber processing, gave Vancouver a unique emphasis on first-stage resource processing among North American cities of comparable size.[21] Despite the gradual dispersal of logging away from the Vancouver area, the city remained the dominant centre for sawmilling. Sawmill operators had heavy capital investment in plant and were within easy access of the Georgia Strait pulp mills that converted their waste chips into paper products. In addition, the introduction of new equipment such as self-dumping log barges permitted logs to be transported economically from distant coastal points to city mills.[22] The larger mills on the Fraser River's North Arm could adapt to changing techniques, but the smaller ones on False Creek, many family-owned and operated, were less able to change. A number went out of business during the 1950s and 1960s; some, after disastrous fires. Fires also encouraged larger firms to move. After a five alarm blaze destroyed its Spruce Division in July 1960, B.C Forest Products moved its head office to downtown Vancouver and did not rebuild its mill. Thus, when the city and the CPR, the major landowners, decided False Creek would be more valuable for residential than industrial purposes, few sawmills and related industries were left.[23]

False Creek and its future have always been controversial. In the 1940s and 1950s, civic politicians viewed it as a barrier to easy communications within the city and debated whether to build new bridges or to fill it in. The 1960s debate over False Creek nicely illustrates the conflict between those who continued to see Vancouver's economic future in heavy industry and those who emphasized the city's livability. In 1967 the Park Board and city planners suggested using False Creek for residences and parks. Alderman Edward Sweeney (NPA), whose family owned a cooperage on False Creek, persuaded City Council that this was a "crackpot idea" and convinced them that the area should remain an industrial site.[24] The turning point came in November 1969 when Council split over the question of giving Canadian Hydrocarbons of Calgary a five-year extension on the lease for the site of its newly purchased Vancouver Iron and Engineering Works. VIEW, as it was ironically known, covered eleven acres with dilapidated sheds that would not have been out of place in a woodcut illustrating the ugliness of the Industrial Revolution. Mayor Tom Campbell argued that to deny the lease extension would make the VIEW site into "a dead monument to the obstructionists on City Council."[25] In opposition, TEAM (The Electors Action Movement) aldermen such as Walter Hardwick, an urban geographer, declared that extending the lease would jeopardize the prospect

By 1960, saw mills were moving out from False Creek. After B.C. Forest Products lost its head office and mill in the city's first five alarm fire, July 3, 1960, the company moved its head office to the West End and used the insurance money to expand its operations elsewhere rather than rebuild. Log booms, once a familiar sight, soon ceased to occupy most of False Creek.

of redeveloping False Creek. Faced with hostile public opinion, the Calgary firm cancelled its plans to re-open the VIEW plant which had been closed since the bankruptcy of its previous owners a year earlier. A few months later, City Council formally voted to use the site for housing and parks and asked the National Harbours Board not to renew long-term industrial leases on nearby Granville Island. Today, False Creek with its medium density housing in a park-like setting and Granville Island with its outdoor markets, art school and theatres symbolize Vancouver's emergence as a post-industrial city. Meanwhile the fate of the CPR's plans to redevelop False Creek's north side remains uncertain, and the yards remain, a strong reminder of Vancouver's *raison d'être*. The harbour is an even better reminder for it is one of Vancouver's major advantages in facing the challenge from Edmonton and, especially, from Calgary for metropolitan hegemony in western Canada. The other advantage is the continuing development of the resources of the British Columbia hinterland. Like the Alberta cities, Vancouver has increasingly become a service and head office centre. High rise office towers have replaced smoke belching from the beehive burners of False Creek sawmills as the chief barrier to the view of the North Shore mountains. Yet, Vancouver continues to depend on the provincial hinterland's resources to remain the leading city of western Canada.

POPULATION GROWTH AND ETHNIC RELATIONSHIPS

Reflecting the wartime boom and immediate post-war prosperity and immigration, Vancouver's population grew by 25.2 per cent between 1941 and 1951 (Appendix, Table I). Thereafter, it grew slowly until 1976 when it actually declined for the first time since the Depression. All the other municipalities in the Greater Vancouver Regional District had a higher rate of population growth than Vancouver between 1951 and 1971. Whereas sixty-two per cent of the population of greater Vancouver lived in the city proper in 1951, only forty-three per cent resided there in 1971 even though the total population had increased by seventy-three per cent (Appendix Table II).

Rapidly rising real estate values in the early 1970s accentuated the trend, apparent since 1951, of young families moving to the suburbs. School enrolment statistics demonstrate the phenomenon. In 1966, Vancouver had its peak Grade 1 registration with 6,676 children starting school; six years later, there were only 5,873 students in Grade 6. Corresponding to the decline in the proportion of young families was an increase in the proportion of young adults and elderly people (Appendix, Table VI).[26]

The continued growth of Vancouver proper can be partly explained by the tendency of post-war immigrants, especially Italians, Jews, and Asians to settle in the city itself rather than in surrounding areas. Because Vancouver already had sizeable Asian and British communities, the continental European immigrants added the most new colour to the city. Pre-war refugees such as the Koerner family from Czechoslovakia and the Bentleys from Austria created large forest products firms and became generous patrons of such cultural events as the Vancouver International Festival. Other central and southern Europeans made such a distinct imprint with their European style delicatessens, pastry shops, cafes, and stores that Robson Street informally became known as Robsonstrasse. Some of the smaller immigrant groups were most visible through the construction of churches and community halls to serve their own needs; some of the larger groups such as the Italians built impressive cultural centres. Others established small ethnic neighbourhoods such as the Greeks in Kitsilano where specialized shops and restaurants as well as a church and community centre attract city-wide attention with the celebration of national or religious festivals. Part of east Vancouver became a "Little Italy" with a broad range of Italian-owned and operated stores and services as well as the usual specialty grocery stores and restaurants.[27]

Asians continued to be the largest "non-WASP" ethnic group, but the composition of the Asian community was much different in the 1970s than it had been before the War. In 1940, the Japanese were the largest Asian group with approximately 8,600 residents, many of whom were children; there were about 6,500 Chinese, mostly adult males; and a handful of East Indians. The Japanese and Chinese were still largely confined to "Little Tokyo" and Chinatown. Indeed, when a young Chinese couple sought to buy a lot in West Point Grey, "a better class" residential district, unhappy neighbours asked City Council to restrict Orientals to certain parts of the city. Aldermen doubted the city's power to pass such a by-law but unanimously asked the planning committee to prepare "Can't Live Here" legislation.[28] Nothing came of the incident but it demonstrated the persistence of anti-Chinese sentiment despite the cessation of Chinese immigration in 1923 and the development of sympathy for China in the course of its war with Japan.

The Japanese were the chief victims of the wartime hysteria that also briefly affected the German and Austrian communities in the spring of 1940 when reports of fifth column activity in Holland and Norway shocked Vancouver. When Japan struck Pearl Harbor in December 1941, Vancouver residents initially heeded the advice of their newspapers and of Mayor J.W. Cornett to keep calm. Then, as Japan's army and navy rapidly advanced in Asia and as the federal government appeared to be doing little to protect coastal British Columbia against a Japanese attack from outside or within, it was easy for experienced anti-Asian agitators such as Alderman Halford Wilson to exploit old fears. By mid-February 1942, the Mackenzie King government, urged on by Ian Mackenzie, M.P. for Vancouver Centre and Minister of Pensions and National Health, used the alleged danger of anti-Japanese riots in Vancouver and other coastal centres to justify a decision that all Japanese should be removed from the coast. The first stage of the process increased the Japanese population of Vancouver as Japanese from outside places were assembled at Exhibition Park pending their removal to the ghost towns or new camps of the Interior or to Prairie farms. By fall 1942, only a few Japanese either too ill to be moved or married to white persons remained in the city. As the Japanese departed, "the cleaning shops, and the corner grocery stores fell into other hands. . . By such small indications did the average citizen recognize the consummation of the edict of our Government. . . ." Some Japanese managed to sell their homes and businesses before they left, and those unwilling or unable to do so had their property administered by the Custodian of Enemy Property who sold most of the Japanese properties and chattels including household effects. By June 1945, 426 properties had been sold at prices averaging 86.3 per cent of their assessed value.[29] Although the Japanese Canadians committed no disloyal acts, only in 1949 did the authorities allow them to return to the coast without special permits. Most, however, had made new homes for themselves in the Interior valleys or east of the Rockies, and only a few returned to Vancouver.

During the War, the situation of the Chinese and East Indians changed. Both China and India were loyal allies and India gained independence in 1947. Moreover, British Columbia and Canadians generally exhibited less racial prejudice after the War than before. Restrictive covenants in residential areas and discriminatory laws that kept Asians out of certain occupations were lifted. Asians were also enfranchised; in 1957, Vancouver Centre elected Douglas Jung, a Chinese-Canadian lawyer, as its Member of Parliament. In subsequent years, other members of the Chinese and East Indian communities were elected to City Council and the School Board. Increasing racial toleration also permitted gradual modifications in immigration laws to permit more Asians to enter Canada.

The influx of Asian and other immigrants did create some tensions. By the mid-1970s the School Board complained of the financial burden of providing special classes in English as a second language. It reported in 1979 that nearly forty per cent of the elementary students and twenty-eight per cent of secondary students did not speak English as a first language. Approximately forty-three per cent of these pupils were of Chinese origin; Italians and East Indians were the next largest groups. In 1973, the police department found it desirable to introduce a form of team policing in South Vancouver, the area of highest East Indian concentration, to prevent racial conflict. At the same time, the Sunset Community Centre developed a programme to encourage interaction between East Indians and the host society. Mayor Art Phillips, however, angered human rights supporters (but won praise from the Vancouver *Sun*) for suggesting that a continued high influx of non-white immigrants would lead to racial conflict. Phillips later clarified his argument as he declared the problem was "primarily a spatial question not a racial one," and that immigrants had imposed great pressures on land and housing prices. Moreover, he noted that immigrants had helped make Vancouver "an exciting cosmopolitan city." No one quarrelled with the latter argument.[30]

In becoming a cosmopolitan city, Vancouver ceased to be composed overwhelmingly of people of British origin. Whereas from the turn of the century to 1951, the British group had consistently accounted for approximately three-quarters of the population, by 1971 it represented only slightly more than half

NOTICE TO ALL JAPANESE PERSONS AND PERSONS OF JAPANESE RACIAL ORIGIN

TAKE NOTICE that under Orders Nos. 21, 22, 23 and 24 of the British Columbia Security Commission, the following areas were made prohibited areas to all persons of the Japanese race:—

LULU ISLAND (including Steveston)
SEA ISLAND
EBURNE
MARPOLE
DISTRICT OF QUEENSBOROUGH
CITY OF NEW WESTMINSTER

SAPPERTON
BURQUITLAM
PORT MOODY
IOCO
PORT COQUITLAM
MAILLARDVILLE
FRASER MILLS

AND FURTHER TAKE NOTICE that any person of the Japanese race found within any of the said prohibited areas without a written permit from the British Columbia Security Commission or the Royal Canadian Mounted Police shall be liable to the penalties provided under Order in Council P.C. 1665.

AUSTIN C. TAYLOR,
Chairman,
British Columbia Security Commission

Japanese forcibly evacuated from coastal points outside Vancouver by the federal government were temporarily housed at the Hastings Park Exhibition Grounds. Upper left: Soldiers stuffing mattresses for use by Japanese internees; lower left: Japanese in the communal dining hall at Hastings Park; upper right: notice of prohibited areas; lower right: Japanese children evacuated by city police.

and seemed to be continuing to decline (Appendix, Table IX). Although some neighbourhoods exhibit particular ethnic characteristics, nothing comparable to a ghetto has developed, though Chinatown, of course, remains. Moreover, Canadian immigration laws have excluded immigrants without marketable skills so that new residents readily found employment without displacing those longer established.

THE URBAN LANDSCAPE

Someone who left Vancouver in 1940 and did not return until the mid-1960s would have had little difficulty in finding his way about. True, there were many new homes on the fringes of the city, the West End was becoming noted for its high rise apartments, there had been some slum clearance, but downtown had changed little and industry still dominated False Creek. Had he returned in the late 1970s he would have had to look at the mountains to reassure himself he was in Vancouver and not some other North American metropolis. Even finding the mountains might not be easy for new downtown office towers often blocked the view. Another landmark, False Creek, had changed as multiple unit housing has replaced industry on its south shore. Indeed, Vancouver, once known for the dominance of single family homes, now had nearly as many apartments as single family dwellings.[31] Whereas families of modest means could once have expected to own a home on its own lot within the city, soaring real estate values in the late 1970s meant that only the relatively affluent could afford even a small bungalow anywhere in the city. What did distinguish Vancouver from other North American cities was its lack of internal freeways.

Housing

Housing was the main building activity in the city in the 1940s. The wartime influx of servicemen, munitions workers, and their families exacerbated the "deplorable shortage of housing accommodation" and the "slum conditions of the worst kind" observed in 1937. Because the federal National Housing Act (1938) required municipalities to agree not to charge more than one per cent taxation on the total cost, Vancouver was unable to take advantage of this offer of $1,350,000 for the construction of low rental housing before it expired early in 1940. By that summer Vancouver had a vacancy rate of less than one per cent whereas five per cent was considered normal. The shortage of accommodation was particularly acute for those unable to afford high rents. Many soldiers' families lived in squalid conditions; welfare officials blamed the housing shortage for child delinquency, sickness, and marital problems.[32]

To ease the situation, the federal Wartime Housing Authority built emergency housing near the North Vancouver shipyards and the Sea Island aircraft plant. The construction of over 2,000 new houses, mainly by private builders on previously serviced city land, made 1941 a "banner year" for construction but did not significantly ease the shortage of homes for low income earners. The crisis, however, stimulated the formation of a Post-War Housing Committee including representatives of the business community, the builders, the Trades and Labour Council, and social agencies to plan for a time when resources for house building would again be available. Meanwhile, the conversion of large, older homes into apartments and housekeeping rooms continued with the federal government's assistance and the creation of basement suites proliferated despite zoning by-law strictures against them.

Peace aggravated the housing shortage as many soldiers and civilians who came to Vancouver because of the War decided to stay. Still others followed after the federal government lifted its ban on individuals moving to congested areas and occupying homes without a permit. The return of veterans from overseas, the formation of new families, and the "baby boom" taxed the city's housing supply. To cope with the desperate situation, the "old" Hotel Vancouver became a hostel for veterans and their families, several veterans tried to seize the vacant Little Mountain army barracks to provide shelter for their families, and City Council considered an abortive scheme to import approximately 1,600 wartime houses from the naval base at Bremerton, Washington.

Shortages of essential building materials and conflicts between Ottawa and the city over financing low and moderate cost housing and providing serviced land seriously delayed resolution of the housing shortage. But eventually, a number of projects were completed. A few small scale developments such as family style apartment blocks on West Fourth Avenue filled

These bungalows at 57th and Arbutus in southwestern Vancouver are a good example of the modest family homes constructed throughout greater Vancouver in the 1940s.

The B.C. Electric's chrome-trimmed model kitchen of 1945 featured many appliances that housewives could only dream about during the war and one recent innovation, the automatic washing machine.

in the landscape, but most government-sponsored schemes were completely new subdivisions on vacant or near vacant land near the city limits. All the veterans' homes, apartments or single family residences, were built from a limited variety of architectural designs and their duplicates could be found in many Canadian cities.

The first large development, Renfrew Heights in the city's northeastern section, was conceived in 1945. The city provided land at less than market price and accepted special taxing arrangements, and the Central Mortage and Housing Authority (CMHA) provided all services including sewers, water mains, and roads. When these moderate rental homes were completed in 1948, priority was given to families residing in the "old" Hotel Vancouver. As the Renfrew Heights project was finished, CMHA announced the Fraserview project in south Vancouver. Instead of the 600 Renfrew Heights homes with 96 variations on eight basic styles, Fraserview had 1,100 homes with 238 variations on 34 basic styles. Instead of emphasizing it as a veterans' project by naming streets after battles, military heroes, and wartime place names as in Renfrew Heights, the city recognized Fraserview's proximity to the municipal golf course by naming its streets after famous Canadian golf courses. In both subdivisions, planners created self-contained neighbourhoods and took advantage of steep slopes to lay out attractively curved street patterns even though some existing homes and farms had to be dislocated to make Fraserview a "workingman's Shaughnessy Heights."[33] In both subdivisions, houses were allocated on a priority system based on the number of dependents and in both, rents, though not subsidized, were moderate. Fraserview's opening in September 1950 marked the beginning of the end of the housing shortage for veterans.

Most new homes were built by private builders who scattered them throughout the city on vacant lots in existing neighbourhoods or on previously undeveloped land in the southern and eastern sections. These private homes represented a variety of styles limited only by architects' imaginations and the pocketbooks of their owners. Private builders continued to be active within the city throughout the 1950s, but by the decade's end most land within city limits was fully occupied. Champlain Heights, the last large tract of city-owned land, opened in 1960 as a planned residential development with a variety of housing, including cooperative schemes, for a wide array of income levels and its own shopping centre. One small luxury development was built adjacent to the "new" Shaughnessy Golf Course on land along Marine Drive leased from the Musqueam Indian band. These spacious, expensive homes contrasted sharply with conditions on the reserve below the bluffs. Revenue from land leases, however, permitted the Musqueam band to replace some of the most dilapidated dwellings with new homes, to build a hall and initiate other community services.[34]

Pressure on the city's limited land resources resulted in the transformation of some older areas and in suburbanization. In some cases, change within the city occurred almost without notice; in another case, it was dramatic, and in a third, extremely controversial.

A good example of quiet change occurred in the old single family, largely working class Marpole district. That community was bifurcated by the construction of the Oak Street Bridge and its approaches in the late 1950s; the real transformation occurred when new zoning regulations passed in the early 1960s allowed construction of multiple dwellings. Within a few years, three and four storey frame apartments had replaced many single family homes in this area which was easily accessible by car or bus to downtown.

A more dramatic change in physical appearance, however, occurred in the West End. Depression and the War had accelerated the West End's deterioration into a densely populated area of transients living mainly in rooming houses. Then, in the early 1950s about ninety new apartment blocks were built. Most of these two storey-and-a-penthouse buildings were unimaginative, even "downright ugly," and occupied almost the whole of their sites. By 1956, the City Planning Department, critical of this development's unattractiveness and the serious underuse of land within walking distance of downtown stores and offices and such superb recreational facilities as Stanley Park and English Bay, recommended major rezoning to permit construction of highrise buildings. When the first zoning regulations for yard requirements, vertical light angles, and window views produced stereotyped buildings, they were changed to provide a "bonus system" permitting owners who provided additional open space and off-street parking and who developed large sites to build larger and taller buildings. Such rezoning, improvements

The opening of Fraserview subdivision in 1950 marked the beginning of the end of the immediate post war housing shortage. This aerial view shows the gently curving streets and the nearby Fraserview Golf Course to good advantage. The golf course was built as a make-work project in the 1930s.

There was still vacant land in south Vancouver when bus service began on Cambie Street to 49th Avenue in 1952.

in highrise construction techniques, and a population bulge among young adults and the over-50 age group provided the circumstances that made the construction crane a prominent feature of the West End's skyline especially around its perimeter close to Stanley Park and overlooking English Bay. Except for 1960-61 when there was a nation-wide recession, over 1,000 suites were built each year from 1958 to 1971. By the latter year, 97.3 per cent of all dwelling units in the West End were apartments or flats. The West End had become "the largest high density highrise apartment area in Canada." Although the area remained remarkable for the transience of its residents, it maintained its own neighbourhoods and social surveys revealed that residents generally regarded the West End as a successful urban environment.[35]

While many private developers undertook redevelopment of the West End, public authorities redeveloped Strathcona as a slum clearance project. Despite its dilapidated appearance, Strathcona was a relatively stable communty and residents balked at the prospect of having their neighbourhood completely overturned. Civic officials, church leaders, social scientists, town planners, and the press from the 1940s on warned of the urgent need to clear Strathcona's slums to prevent the spread of blight and social problems. The worst districts in the city were along the waterfront and industrial area adjacent to Kitsilano,[36] but the area receiving the greatest attention was Strathcona. With federal and provincial financing, a team of University of British Columbia social scientists under Dr. Leonard Marsh completed a Demonstration Housing Survey in 1947. They described Strathcona as a clear example of how the lack of earlier planning hastened the deterioration of older neighbourhoods:

> Laid out when it was thought this might be a good residential district, it reflects in miniature the optimism of those days, the abundance of land, but also the rapid changes and haphazard development which have characterized many other parts of Vancouver. Other districts were opened up; those who could afford to, moved to the south and the west. Small scale industries began their invasion, street cars were withdrawn, though the tracks still remain, and the process of decay thus started is now the outstanding feature of the area. Because the houses were almost

universally built of wood, for many of which twenty years would have been a fair span of life, the deterioration at many points is now extreme. The absence of a housing and slum clearance program, and the pressure of the present critical shortage have intensified the overcrowding and the inadequacy which had already become apparent in the thirties.[37]

The survey team observed that Strathcona was not "an unqualified slum area or necessarily the worst" though it was close to the central business district, the waterfront, the "blight-core of False Creek," and had such unattractive features as the gas works, a slaughter house, and the city dump. Nevertheless, good basic utilities, including sidewalks, open spaces, and a variety of community buildings made it worth rehabilitating. In 1950, Dr. Marsh outlined a $15 million dollar project consisting of low rental apartments and row housing to provide better accommodation for the area's 7,000 people, "to demonstrate the importance of *building* neighbourhoods," and "to strike at the heart of the city blight by a bold method of urban regeneration." Even though Marsh's scheme called for senior governments to pay most redevelopment costs, City Council was reluctant to take on any burden that might raise the taxes of existing home owners in order to provide homes for others.[38] The city confined its assistance to low cost housing to a promise to pay 12.5 per cent of the operating losses of a federal-provincial plan to develop 200 acres at Riley Park, Little Mountain.

Meanwhile, Strathcona continued to deteriorate. A federally funded survey completed by the Planning Department in 1957 recommended comprehensive redevelopment of the inner city, including Strathcona, as part of a twenty year plan. The area still had some characteristics of a neighbourhood, but the report suggested demolishing entire blocks and relocating approximately 10,700 people in public housing funded by the three levels of government. Following a common Canadian practice of the time, the bulldozers came in, individuals were displaced, and new homes were built for some of them in the nearby large projects, MacLean Park, Skeena Terrace, and Raymur.

In undertaking these massive projects, the city ignored the Chinese community's complaints that redevelopment would disrupt the lives of many elderly Chinese men and endanger the

The West End in transition. By 1971, luxurious high rises were replacing the houses of the West End.

Chinatown economy. In 1968, the community, fresh from its success in stopping plans to bisect Chinatown with a freeway, was roused by the city's announcement that it was about to clear additional blocks and move a further 3,000 people. At an October 1968 meeting sponsored by the Strathcona Area Council, a voluntary group composed of representatives of social agencies, local organizations, and ethnic associations, a number of Chinese residents opposed renewal and expressed their wish to remain in the area. Subsequently, they organized the Strathcona Property Owners and Tenants Association (SPOTA). The senior governments accepted SPOTA's suggestion that the neighbourhood be preserved and rehabilitated with government funds. By refusing to provide funds for redevelopment, they forced the city to agree. Thus, Strathcona became an important experiment in rehabilitating private property and public facilities with public funds provided to individual owners through a combined grant and loan scheme and in citizenship participation in the planning process. Moreover, the Strathcona project allowed an old community to retain "some sense of stability and security."[39]

While there were changes within the city, the lack of land, improved highway facilities, and soaring real estate values in the early 1970s accelerated an established trend towards suburban growth. When B.C. Hydro increased its suburban bus service extensively in the early 1970s, it was responding to the existence of densely settled suburban areas and traffic jams. Vancouver's suburbs were created with the help of the automobile, not mass transit. Except for the old suburb of Burnaby, large scale expansion into nearby municipalities was largely governed by the construction of bridges, the Deas Island tunnel, freeways, and the lifting of tolls on several bridges and the tunnel. The Lions Gate Bridge, constructed by Guinness interests in 1938, was the key to the settlement of the western part of North Vancouver and West Vancouver, especially the Guinness' luxurious mountain-side subdivision, the British Properties. Rapid population growth in North Vancouver's eastern part coincided with construction of a new Second Narrows Bridge (1956-60) and the Upper Levels Highway. Similarly, completion of the Oak Street Bridge in 1957 inaugurated Richmond's rapid growth; the opening of the Deas Island Tunnel and Highway 499 (1959) made commuting to downtown Vancouver from

Delta, Surrey, and White Rock feasible. The Highway 401 freeway from Vancouver's eastern border through Burnaby and Coquitlam, across the Port Mann Bridge (1964) to Surrey prompted the proliferation of residential subdivisions in these municipalities and even further east in the Fraser Valley. The same availability of convenient road access and relatively cheap land away from traffic congestion also led some industries to move to the suburban municipalities, especially to such industrial parks as Lake City in Burnaby, Annacis Island in the Fraser River near New Westminster, and Newton in Surrey.

The growth of the suburban municipalities led the provincial government to create the Greater Vancouver Regional District (see below, p.157) and encouraged private developers to construct a number of suburban shopping centres which usually included branches of one or more of Vancouver's three major department stores as well as smaller shops, often chain stores. The original centre, Park Royal, was opened in 1950 as one of the first two shopping centres in Canada. The second large centre, Oakridge, on the city's southern slope opened in 1959. The shopping centres of the 1960s and 1970s, however, were all in suburban municipalities: Brentwood in Burnaby (1961); Richmond Square (1965); Guildford and Surrey Place, both in Surrey (1966 and 1972 respectively); Lougheed Mall between Burnaby and Coquitlam (1969); Lansdowne Park in Richmond (1977) and Coquitlam Mall (1979). The last two malls are so large that they have included several major department stores from the beginning while some older centres have undergone two and even three major expansions. Suburbia and its shopping centres had replaced the farms, the woodlands, and the small holdings that had been characteristic of much of the Lower Mainland before World War II.

Downtown

The proliferation of suburban shopping centres threatened the future of downtown. The department stores had "hedged their bets" by going into the suburbs, but many small stores had difficulties. The shopping centres did not cause downtown's decline, but their appearance was a helpful catalyst in bringing about long-needed change.

Downtown Vancouver changed little during the Depression

and War. By 1945 it clearly needed modernization, especially relief for the traffic congestion that had been evident for some years. Early in 1946 over one hundred businessmen organized the Downtown Business Association to promote and preserve the economic, commercial, and social welfare of the central business district. Their first recommendation was a parking survey. Although the establishment of the Downtown Parking Corporation, the introduction of parking meters, and the BCER's gradual replacement of streetcars by trolley and gas buses during the post-war decade eased traffic problems, downtown remained congested. Some businessmen even suggested building a proposed new post office and civic centre outside the downtown core but most preferred to have such projects sited to "anchor business downtown. . . where the big taxes are collected."[40]

The civic centre, an idea put forward in the 1929 Bartholemew Report, was championed by Mayor Gerry McGeer who envisioned constructing a library and auditorium building as a twin for his City Hall. Despite the debate over its location, the civic centre was a luxury that the taxpayers refused to support. In the 1940s and 1950s, City Council concentrated on replacing and extending such essential services as roads, sidewalks, street lighting, schools, and sewers. In 1946, a third of Vancouver's homes still lacked sewer connections. Fortunately, the Greater Vancouver Water Board had the water supply well in hand, although the city's pride in her pure water had been injured in 1942 when the federal government threatened to use the War Measures Act if Greater Vancouver did not chlorinate its water supply to bring it up to international health standards.[41]

The most important new civic project of the early 1950s was the eight lane Granville Street Bridge (1954). By improving access to downtown it symbolized the belief that if traffic problems were solved, downtown's rejuvenation would automatically follow. Instead, the area remained seedy. Many of the frame houses on the commercial core's periphery were over fifty years old and rapidly deteriorating. Eaton's purchased the prime Georgia and Granville site of the old Hotel Vancouver for a new department store but discouraged other developers by using it as a parking lot for some years. The most exciting retailing development, as mentioned earlier, was the opening of one of Canada's first shopping centres, West Vancouver's Park Royal, in September 1950. Apart from the striking glass house built by B.C. Electric on Burrard Street (1957), the Burrard Building (1956) and some low-rise office blocks in the West End overlooking the Inlet, little new office space was built downtown. In the mid-1950s some of the more dilapidated housing north of Georgia and east of Richards was demolished to make way for the new Post Office (1958) and a civic auditorium, the Queen Elizabeth Theatre (1959).

That the major new buildings of the 1950s can be individually listed indicates the dearth of construction activity. The obvious lack of new building, the continued appearance of new suburban shopping centres, the presence of empty stores downtown, warnings of city planners that downtown was becoming a "virtual business slum", a decline in the tax base, and reports of inner city deterioration in the United States aroused political concern about downtown's future. In December 1962, W.G. Rathie, an accountant, won the mayor's chair with the slogan, "Let's Get Vancouver Moving."

Although the city had no overall plan for downtown development, Rathie quickly went to work. He commissioned a Seattle real estate consultant to make an economic base study and sought developers in eastern Canada, Britain, and Europe. His timing was excellent. Large scale capital investment was coming into the province as the forest, mining, and hydro-electric power industries were expanding; developers were already beginning to look at Vancouver. Past history suggested that capital inflows into the hinterland were "followed in a few months by new office construction in the core." By the mid-1960s, locally based firms such as MacMillan Bloedel and Westcoast Transmission were erecting their own head office buildings. The MacMillan Bloedel building was remarkable for what its architect, Arthur Erickson, called a "Doric Facade"; the Westcoast Building, for its unique structural system which, with the exception of an inner core, saw it built from the top down. Investors from Britain, the United States, Hong Kong, and eastern Canada were also willing to provide the capital for massive general office blocks and underground shopping malls modelled on Montreal's Place Ville Marie. Some of the developers who built the towers collectively known as the Bentall Centre were local firms; others such as the Trizec Corporation, which developed the Royal Centre in association with the Royal Bank, were based in eastern

Canada. By 1978, however, it was estimated that half of Vancouver's prime office and apartment space was owned by Hong Kong interests who maintained a low profile.[42]

The most controversial of the downtown complexes was Pacific Centre. After studying planning department reports and inviting developers to submit proposals for redeveloping Block 42, the north-west corner of Georgia and Granville, City Council in 1965 decided to favour a consortium of Cemp Investments (a Bronfman family firm), the Toronto-Dominion Bank, and Eaton's, the owners of the adjacent Block 52. The many small shopkeepers in Block 42 complained they would be dispossessed when their older and rather unattractive buildings were demolished. Council promised to do "everything reasonably possible" to help them during reconstruction but used its expropriation powers to help assemble the land. Council agreed with the Board of Trade that a development of "such magnitude" would "transform downtown Vancouver" and become "a symbol of confidence for the citizens of Vancouver in the City's future growth and development." Pacific Centre did become a symbol of confidence. Between 1966 and 1973, the rentable office space in downtown Vancouver almost doubled.[43]

Paradoxically, on its completion, Pacific Centre also became a symbol of redevelopment's negative effects. The complex, including Eaton's store, a thirty storey Toronto-Dominion Bank building, an eighteen storey IBM building, and the Four Seasons Hotel, is linked by an underground shopping mall with the Hudson's Bay department store and the Bank of Nova Scotia Tower in Vancouver Centre. Critics blamed its designers for creating wind tunnels, erecting "towers of gloom and darkness" with black anodized exteriors, and destroying surface pedestrian traffic. Nothing could be done about the wind tunnels, but public pressure led the city to order that the last component tower, the Four Seasons Hotel, be lighter in colour. In an attempt to restore street level activity, the city adopted a Minneapolis plan and turned Granville Street into a pedestrian mall with widened sidewalks and a narrowed street open only to buses, taxis, and emergency vehicles. The underground shops, however, retained their popularity and Granville Mall appeared to be a planner's mistake.[44]

After seeing the new towers such as those of Pacific Centre, Vancouver residents began to wonder if they wanted New York-like canyons or a view of their mountains. Such concern about the preservation of Vancouver's natural beauty led the NDP provincial government to turn a proposed fifty-five storey provincial office tower into a low level complex with an ice skating rink, restaurants, and park-like surroundings designed to draw pedestrians to its amenities. Similar public concern effectively killed the Harbour Park or Four Seasons proposal, a multi-million dollar scheme to build fourteen high rise apartment buildings, a marina, and commercial buildings on the waterfront near the entrance to Stanley Park.[45] Vancouver residents also feared the effects of Project 200 on their view. This $200 million project, devised in 1965 by Grosvenor-Laing, British developers, and Marathon Realty, the real estate arm of the CPR, was to include thirty-six high-rises and smaller buildings for offices, stores, and apartments erected on a deck over the CPR tracks. When the city decided not to build a waterfront expressway as an approach to a proposed third crossing of Burrard Inlet, the developers reduced their plan to one office tower — Granville Square — and a CPR telecommunications centre.

When the developers of Project 200 formally abandoned their plans in March 1973 they cited as one reason, the transformation of Gastown. Named after "Gassy Jack" Deighton, the voluble hotelkeeper of the 1860s and 1870s, Gastown had once been the city's commercial centre. Later, it became a wholesale and warehouse district, but, after the War, new wholesale districts along the Grandview Highway and in suburban industrial parks drew many firms away from downtown. Despite the presence of two major retail stores adjacent to the area, Woodward's and the Army and Navy, a discount department store opened in the 1930s, pedestrian traffic declined after the BCER ceased interurban operations and closed its depot at Hastings and Carrall and after the North Vancouver ferry service ended in 1958. From the perspective of the late 1970s, the discontinuance of light rapid transit and a system of moving people across the Inlet without new bridges seems tragic indeed. The interurbans were the victims of the popularity of the automobile which reduced passenger business and created congestion on downtown streets where the BCER lacked a separate right of way. The ferries became redundant when the new Second Narrows Bridge opened. In the short run, however,

Using the principles employed in suspension bridges, Vancouver architects Rhone and Iredale and engineer Bogue Babicki designed the Westcoast Transmission Building which, after the central core was completed, was constructed from the top down. Westcoast operates a pipeline bringing natural gas from the Peace River district to the lower Fraser Valley.

the greatest impact of the end of interurban and ferry service occurred in the area around the BCER depot and the ferry slip. By 1965 a city planner remarked that the lasting impression of the Gastown area was of people, "especially old men," many of whom had lived in the area's cheap hotels and rooming houses for years.[46]

Beginning in the late 1950s, some individual merchants tried to "clean up" the area. Property owners established a Townsite Committee in 1962 and drew the City Planning Department's attention to the desirability of preserving the facades of architectually significant buildings as had been done in Norwich, England and San Francisco.[47] Then, in 1966, Larry Killam, a developer who had seen the success of Toronto's Yorkville, began to buy and restore old buildings. The real impetus for Gastown's transformation came two years later when the Community Arts Council, already anxious to preserve historic architecture, responded to the prospect of Project 200 demolishing the area and sponsored a walking tour of forty-six historic buildings and sites. Over six hundred people, including Mayor Tom Campbell, participated in the walk. Their enthusiasm was contagious. Within weeks, property values in Gastown jumped as developers realized the area's potential for small shops, restaurants, and offices. Over the next three years, people, especially young ones, set up boutiques selling their own crafts or imported trinkets and clothing. Many of these ventures failed, but Gastown remained. The city allocated a million dollars for cobblestoning and beautifying Maple Tree Square and for street improvements; the promoters of Project 200 announced plans to redevelop Gaslight Square as a commercial complex; and the provincial government designated Gastown and its neighbour, Chinatown, historic areas thus controlling demolition and allowing shops to remain open on Sunday to serve tourists. But by the late 1970s the Gastown boom was fading. Area shops faced stiff competition for pedestrian traffic from Pacific Centre and other underground shopping malls, the Robson Street area, and Granville Island Market.

While the city's commercial and residential space was being altered, Vancouver residents continued to discuss freeways and debate a third crossing of Burrard Inlet — either a bridge or a tunnel — "with all the fervour of a Second Coming." The 1957 Five Year Plan set aside $3.5 million to acquire land for an expressway on the model of those in many American cities, Toronto, and Montreal, and link it with the four lane Trans-Canada Highway then being built through Burnaby. Over the next decade, the subject of freeways, their routes, financing, and relationship to a new Burrard Inlet crossing was extensively studied. Between 1954 and 1970, a "carousel" of forty-seven published and at least forty confidential studies of transportation problems was prepared at a cost of at least $10 million. One indication of the vigour of public interest was a Council-sponsored discussion of the crossing in 1972. This meeting, held in a high school auditorium, attracted no fewer than sixty delegations bearing briefs, but degenerated into a "despicable" display by Council before finally adjourning at 1:35 a.m.[48]

One of the few concrete results of these plans was the decision of ratepayers to replace the aging Georgia Viaduct. City Council instructed its engineering consultant to design the new viaduct so that it could serve as a link for east-west, north-south, and waterfront freeways. When Council accepted the engineer's advice to link the freeways via Carrall Street through the heart of Chinatown, it faced massive opposition. Though Vancouver citizens were generally apathetic about civic politics, they were quick to respond to specific issues. The protest against the freeway is a classic illustration of Vancouver's brand of participatory democracy. Not only did the Chinese community want to protect its neighbourhood, but businessmen, academics, developers, architects, the Board of Trade, the press, radio stations, the Visitors and Convention Bureau, the Community Arts Council and other public interest groups also protested. Because of such widespread protest and crowded and angry public meetings, City Council changed its mind. It went ahead with building the new Georgia Viaduct, but early in 1968 abandoned the plan to build the Carrall Street connector and effectively ended all freeway planning. Opposition to the freeway had, in fact, become a rallying point for civic reformers who challenged NPA control of City Hall. Without a freeway, the third crossing made little sense. The federal government delayed making a final decision on granting assistance; the NDP provincial government in 1974 reallocated funds set aside for the third crossing to rapid transit including construction of two "sea buses" or passenger ferries to transport people from downtown

September 27, 1963

"Let's see, there were the elections of '63, '66, '69, '72, '75, and three more promised for this one . . . "

North Vancouver to the CPR station at the foot of Granville Street.

In the forty years after the beginning of World War II, Vancouver's physical appearance changed greatly. Old areas — the West End, Downtown, and False Creek — were almost completely transformed and Strathcona underwent extensive redevelopment and rehabilitation. On the city's boundaries and in the adjacent municipalities, residential subdivisions replaced bushland and small farms. Yet these important changes should not obscure the continuity of the urban landscape. The mountains and ocean still provided a backdrop; the street grid pattern remained largely undisturbed as Vancouver residents spurned the North American passion for freeways; and, apart from some infilling, some apartment building and rejuvenation in areas such as Kitsilano, most residential neighbourhoods remained more or less intact. Relative constancy was only slightly less apparent in such established east side areas as Hastings and South Vancouver, traditionally the home of the working classes, than in such west side districts as Point Grey and Kerrisdale, long favoured by the business and professional classes. Amidst dramatic changes on its landscape, Vancouver had quietly retained much stability.

CIVIC POLITICS AND GOVERNMENT

From its founding in 1937, the Non-Partisan Association (NPA) dominated City Hall, electing many of its mayoralty candidates and, with rare exception, a solid majority of aldermen and members of the School and Parks Boards. As the Vancouver *Sun* once remarked, "a Non-Partisan endorsation is as good as a kiss of victory." Because Vancouver no longer has wards and qualifications for candidacy are minimal, voters are frequently presented with the names of dozens of candidates. In 1968, for example, 87 candidates sought 27 offices; in 1972, 125; in 1978, 117. By selecting and advertising a slate through voting-guide postcards and newspaper advertisements, the NPA simplified voting for Vancouver electors. Independent candidates were many, and rival political organizations appeared from time to time, but only non-NPA candidates with strong personal followings got elected. Thus when Laura Jamieson of the CCF, Thomas Alsbury of the Civic Voters Association, Fred Hume, an

Major Groups in Civic Politics, 1937-1980[a]

[In order of appearance]

Commonwealth Co-operative Federation (CCF)	1937-61[b]
Non-Partisan Association (NPA)	1937-
Civic Reform Party	1947-50
Civic Improvement Group	c. 1947
Civic Voters Association (CVA)	1957-62
Civic Action Association (CAA)	1964-66[c]
Citizens for the Improvement of Vancouver	c. 1966
The Electors Action Movement (TEAM)	1968-
Committee of Progressive Electors (COPE)	1968-
New Democratic Party (NDP)	1970-74

a. Terminal dates are, in some cases, approximate as some groups simply faded away.
b. The CCF became the NDP in 1961. The NDP has had an ambivalent attitude towards direct participation in civic politics.
c. The CAA merged with the NPA which then formally became known as the Civic Non-Partisan Party.

Independent, and Harry Rankin of the left-wing Committee of Progressive Electors (COPE) got elected they had no effective coattails. So firm was the NPA's control of the city that when both Alsbury and Evelyn Caldwell of the Civic Voters Association (CVA) were elected to Council in 1957, newspaper headlines proclaimed that the NPA "grip" on the city had been broken.[49] Not until 1972 did The Electors Action Movement (TEAM) interrupt NPA domination of City Council.

When the indefatigable Gerry McGeer ran as an NPA candidate in 1946, he jokingly described the NPA approach to party politics, at least insofar as it applied to him:

> The Liberals call me rebel
> The Tories call me red
> The Communists call me the devil
> And the CCF wishes me dead.

A politician such as McGeer, nominally a Liberal but often a thorn in the side of Liberal governments, could find a comfortable home in the NPA whose only formal platform was its original

"Mr. Chairman—fellow civic-minded citizens . . ."

The Vancouver Sun. December 5, 1951.

"What d'you mean, it's all over . . . I'm only up to my second plebiscite."

December 10, 1964

goal of keeping "party" politics out of City Hall and of being "the first line of defence in civic affairs against the socialists and communists."[50] In fact the only party seeking to control civic government at the time of the NPA's formation was the CCF. On the surface, the Vancouver situation seems very much like the confrontation that occurred in Winnipeg between the Citizen's League and the labour movement. Vancouver, however, lacked the polarization that was a legacy of the Winnipeg General Strike. Moreover despite the participation of the CCF/NDP in civic politics, the presence of various socialist candidates over the years, and the perennial re-election of Alderman Harry Rankin, the "left wing" has not been a serious factor in civic politics since Dr. Telford's election in 1938.

Although the NPA lacks a formal policy or ideology, four principles do recur in NPA mayoralty platforms: improvements to basic services such as streets, bridges and sewers; additions to civic amenities such as civic centre and sports arena schemes; encouragement to private developers; and firmer administration of law and order. In dealing with the first two issues, which usually required borrowing money, Council depended on the good will of sixty per cent of the ratepayers who chose to vote on the particular by-law. The ratepayers generally approved borrowing funds for the basic engineering projects presented in a series of Five Year Plans but generally rejected comprehensive schemes that provided funds for redevelopment or such luxuries as a coliseum. A rare exception to the latter principle was the 1952 passage of a by-law providing $750,000 towards construction of a 36,000 seat stadium for the 1954 British Empire Games.

Since encouraging private developers did not normally require direct expenditure of public funds, Council could act without reference to the citizens except at the biennial elections.[51] Voters enthusiastically endorsed William Rathie and his promise to "Get Vancouver Moving" in 1962, but gave him fair warning of their reluctance to give direct assistance to private developers when they rejected a proposal to assist Stafford Smythe of the Toronto Maple Leafs to build a 17,500 seat downtown coliseum. Nevertheless, in 1966, Rathie urged voters to re-elect him and support his plans for the private redevelopment of Block 42/52 as a stimulus to downtown development that would make Vancouver a match for Montreal. Rathie's chief opponent, Tom Campbell, recognizing the popularity of downtown development

did not attack redevelopment but convinced voters that he could secure a better deal and provide more public participation in planning. As Mayor, Campbell secured NPA endorsement in 1968 and 1970 and got a better deal but otherwise continued the growth and development policies that had become his predecessors' hallmarks.

Campbell's 1970 campaign is the best example of an appeal based on law and order. Although "cleaning up crime" and more effective police work had been cries of mayoralty candidates since Vancouver's earliest days, Campbell's firm stand against the "hippies" and his suggestion that the War Measures Act — imposed in October 1970 during the Quebec Crisis — could be used against the Vancouver Libertarian Front, the Youth International Party ("yippies"), the Maoists, the drug pushers, and American draft dodgers was faintly reminiscent of Gerry McGeer's position on the unruly unemployed. Campbell praised the police and offered to get them any needed special equipment including guns, helmets, and riot sticks. His opponents accused him of being a danger to civil order, but he was the voters' choice as he "rode back into office on a riot stick."[52]

The NPA's domination helps explain public apathy to civic elections. So too, does the usually dull campaign procedure. Door-to-door canvassing, lawn signs, mass rallies and public opinion polls by TEAM and COPE in 1968 were a refreshing change but only increased the turn out to forty-four per cent. During the war, Mayor J.W. Cornett had decided that elaborate electioneering was inappropriate. He held no public meetings but relied on radio speeches and newspaper advertisements. Post-war candidates, notably Fred Hume, followed a similar policy. Indeed, when public meetings were held, candidates frequently outnumbered voters. Often the newspapers carried little election news but the popularity of radio "hot line" shows in the 1960s and 1970s gave candidates a wider forum than documentary evidence indicates. Some candidates also used television to get their names before the public. Both Art Phillips in 1972 and Jack Volrich in 1976 appeared in television commercials the summer before their elections. Nevertheless, voter apathy persisted. In 1976, about thirty-five per cent of the electorate cast ballots, a percentage close to the average figure over a number of years.[53]

The dullness of many campaigns gave incumbents and those

Mayor Tom Campbell swings on a wrecker's ball in this publicity shot marking the commencement of demolition on the downtown Block 42 site.

MAYORS OF VANCOUVER, 1939-1980

1939-40	Dr. J. Lyle Telford (CCF)
1941-46	J.W. Cornett (Independent)
1947	G.G. McGeer* (NPA)
1948	Charles Jones* (NPA)
1949-50	C.E. Thompson (NPA)
1951-58	F.J. Hume (Ind., NPA)
1959-62	A.T. Alsbury (CVA, NPA)
1963-66	W.G. Rathie (NPA)
1967-72	T.J. Campbell (Ind., NPA)
1973-76	Art Phillips (TEAM)
1977-	Jack Volrich (TEAM, Independent)

*Died in office

who ran as part of the NPA slate a decided advantage in seeking Council and School or Park Board seats. Because the mayor had a high profile, slate-making was less important to the office, and personalities rather than affiliations or policies were often important issues. Thus, independents and non-NPA nominees could become mayor. The NPA, however, had an uncanny knack of turning such mayors into NPA candidates.[54] In 1950, Fred Hume, former mayor of New Westminster and a prominent electrical contractor and sportsman, defeated Charles Thompson, the NPA incumbent. Two years later, the NPA did not endorse a mayoralty candidate and Hume won again. In 1954, Hume was the NPA choice and he remained as NPA mayor until 1958.

As mayor, Hume took pride in drawing attention to the city through such means as hosting the British Empire Games and in building the Granville Street Bridge, "the widest bridge on the continent." Yet, as the *Sun* noted, after eight years of his administration, sewage polluted the bathing beaches, the smog problem was worsening, the city lacked a chronic hospital, the police had been under four years of emergency administration, and the city had allowed the provincial government to trample on it. Nevertheless, for eight years Vancouver voters endorsed Hume who long maintained his popularity by avoiding "doing anything that might have even faintly unpleasant side effects." As the friendlier *Province* observed, Hume could not help liking

people.[55]

The man who defeated Hume was Thomas Alsbury, a high school principal and onetime CCF supporter. Alsbury won as the CVA candidate but when he sought re-election two years later, was the NPA choice. When Alsbury retired in 1962, another NPA man, William Rathie, an accountant, won the election and retained the mayor's office until 1966 when T.J. "Tom" Campbell, a young apartment developer then running as an independent, beat him. Subsequently, Campbell too secured NPA endorsment.

Although the NPA almost collapsed at the time of Campbell's retirement in 1972, it gradually rebuilt its organization, capitalized on dissension within TEAM which had replaced it, and by 1978 had a clear majority on all elected bodies. The NPA also demonstrated that it had not forgotten its old absorptive talents; its successful mayoralty candidate in 1978, Jack Volrich, a lawyer, had been first elected mayor in 1976 as the TEAM nominee.[56]

TEAM was the only group to challenge the NPA effectively. Unlike NPA officers who tended to be over 50, employed in a managerial capacity, and supporters of the Social Credit, Liberal, or Conservative parties, TEAM leaders were usually under 40, included a high proportion of university trained professionals, and favoured the Liberal party or the NDP at the provincial and federal levels.[57] The "great freeway debate" of 1967 had encouraged many people to "put their efforts into getting the spirit of the city awakened and move the city in the right direction" particularly in social and environmental matters. TEAM believed it was "the city's job to initiate and act" rather than to *react* as they accused the NPA of doing. In fall 1967, Bill Bellman, a radio broadcaster, and Ed Lawson of the Teamsters Union began organizing weekly luncheon meetings of business and professional people including several University of British Columbia faculty members to discuss the city's future. In February 1968, Bellman and Lawson became co-chairmen of TEAM. By December 1968 TEAM had about 900 members but its immediate electoral success was minimal. Gradually, TEAM built up support for itself and capitalized on increasing distrust of development to score a landslide victory in 1972 when its candidates won 22 of 27 positions. TEAM, however, did not really introduce dramatic changes. During the 1974 campaign,

Mayor Art Phillips claimed that TEAM "scrapped the old NPA policy of growth for growth's sake which led to black towers and concrete. . . . Now downtown development must enhance our natural setting." The most visible results were the Granville Mall and the erection of traffic barriers on certain West End streets. Another TEAM legacy was the False Creek housing project it developed in association with Marathon Realty to provide subsidized units for low income earners and the handicapped as well as luxury condominiums.[58]

TEAM also failed to institute its plan for major electoral reform, namely the ward system. Although TEAM had advocated wards in 1968, by the time the movement had political power, its members were divided among those who wanted a full ward system, those who favoured a partial ward plan, and those who wanted to retain the *status quo* of no wards at all. The voters, in any case, were not particularly interested. Only 21.9 per cent of them voted and they opposed change. Five years later, in 1978, the city responded to continuing pressure from ward system advocates and held another plebiscite. Despite the attempts of opponents to equate wards with corruption, the electors narrowly approved a ward system. At the same time, they re-elected Mayor Volrich and six NPA aldermen who opposed wards. In spite of city council decision to accept the outcome of the vote whatever it was, Mayor Volrich announced that a change could not be justified but that Council would appoint an independent commission to study the merits and implications of both the at-large and ward systems. The introduction of the ward system would be an interesting exercise since Vancouver residents are often more aroused by neighbourhood issues such as the proposed Chinatown Freeway or Marathon Realty's plan to build a large shopping centre in the Arbutus area (an incident which led Jack Volrich into civic politics) than they are by city-wide matters.[59]

TEAM had also promised to strengthen the policy-making function of elected representatives. In 1976 one of their aldermen, Fritz Bowers, a professor of engineering, resigned from Council to accept the position of City Manager, a position created in 1974 as a response to the increasing size and complexity of civic government. Walter Hardwick, a TEAM alderman, has explained how in the immediate post-war years, Vancouver adopted "a full corporate model of government":

The senior administrators, by necessity in part, adopted a dual role of administration and policy initiator and advisor. City Council in turn acted as if they were the owner, the directors of a company, or the trustees of the public wealth. The senior administrators drew their information and values about the urban scene from the bureaucracy and, when necessary, from experts outside the system, usually experts from the engineering or financial section. Given the preoccupation of the population at large with the material up-grading of the city and a common wisdom that growth was "good" the system worked remarkably well.[60]

The bureaucracy, headed since 1955 by a two man Board of Administration, though conservative in its policies, was not ignorant of change. In the mid-1960s, a number of senior city officials, particularly architects, planners, and engineers, realized that while they were altering the city's physical shape, they were often unaware of the social impact of such changes. In response, the Board of Administration urged creation of a Social Planning Department. When formed in 1968, the Department broke the city down into local areas and endeavoured to coordinate social services in the District. It soon decided, however, that its staff, who were trained in a multiplicity of disciplines, would be more effective in attacking city-wide problems such as services for the elderly and immigrants rather than concentrating on neighbourhoods.[61] The Community Resources Boards, coordinated by the Vancouver Resources Board, an agency established by the NDP provincial government in 1975, partly revived the idea of social services being administered on a neighbourhood basis, but the Social Credit provincial government elected later in 1975, effectively ended these Boards.

The creation of another level of government, the Greater Vancouver Regional District (GVRD), in 1967 confirmed that Vancouver was no longer just a city surrounded by rural municipalities but rather the core of an urbanized Lower Mainland. The need for metropolitan cooperation had long been recognized in the existence of metropolitan boards concerned with water, sewerage, drainage, and public health. In 1948, the Lower Mainland municipalities formed a Regional Planning Board for the lower Fraser Valley. Then, in 1957, the provincial Department of Municipal Affairs passed necessary legislation and initiated discussions designed to lead to the formation of a metropolitan area, but these plans came to naught. Eight years later, the provincial government passed legislation dividing the province into twenty-eight regional districts. The immediate concern was improvement of the administration of health care and hospital services, but this function was quickly extended to cover many services including those previously handled by special purpose boards. In 1967, the province created the GVRD including municipalities east to Coquitlam and Surrey, south to the United States border, and north to Lion's Bay. As the largest entity in a system generally based on representation by population, Vancouver got five of the twenty-two directors' seats and twenty-two of the sixty-one votes. Since 1973 GVRD members have been elected at the regular civic elections. The Board has gradually taken over most of the functions of the earlier special boards and has added such responsibilities as capital financing, planning, building regulations, housing, and air pollution control.[62] It is in planning and managing growth for "The Livable Region," that the GVRD may make its greatest impact. In 1978, growth was proceeding more slowly than anticipated. Amidst world-wide questioning of the wisdom of "zero growth," some Vancouver commentators doubted the merits of non-growth and decentralizing policies. Indeed, in his successful campaign for re-election, Mayor Volrich stressed the need for a "more positive attitude toward growth and development".[63]

In creating the GVRD, the provincial government demonstrated it was still master of the municipalities, including Vancouver. The city, however, can no longer complain of inadequate representation in that government. Whether the provincial government was that of the Coalition (1941-52), Social Credit (1952-72; 1975-), or NDP (1972-75), Vancouver has usually been well represented in the Cabinet. One post, that of Attorney-General, has been a virtual Vancouver monopoly, although Robert Bonner, a Vancouver lawyer, briefly sought political refuge in "safe" Socred ridings in the Interior. The W.A.C. Bennett government has been perceived as favouring the hinterland over Vancouver, but at times, Bennett had as many as four Vancouver MLAs in his cabinet. Vancouver, of course, joined the rest of the province in electing Social Credit candidates. In 1952, the city elected only three Social Credit

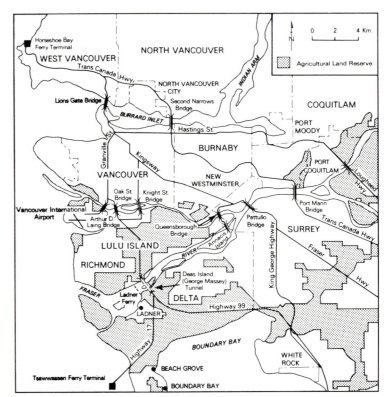

9 Greater Vancouver Region, 1978

MLAs, but the next year, the CCF saved only one of its Vancouver East seats in a Social Credit sweep that eliminated Liberals and Conservatives from Vancouver constituencies. Social Credit, however, never regained that overwhelming control of the Vancouver seats. The city's east side resumed its role as a CCF/NDP stronghold; the NDP victories in ten of Vancouver's twelve seats in 1972 was an aberration reflecting, more dramatically than in some other parts of the province, discontent with the twenty-year-old W.A.C. Bennett government. The only seats to elude the NDP were the two seats in Point Grey the Liberals had held since the mid-1960s. When the province returned to Social Credit in 1975, however, those seats became Social Credit as the incumbents Patrick McGeer (a nephew of

Gerry McGeer) and Garde Gardom crossed the floor of the Legislature. Both were appointed to the Cabinet when William Bennett (W.A.C. Bennett's son) formed the new Social Credit government.

As suggested above, Vancouver gradually became very well represented in the provincial government. In 1962 the city had nineteen per cent of the seats and thirty per cent of the province's population. Several redistributions and rapid growth outside city limits reversed the imbalance. By 1971, Vancouver had twenty-two per cent of the seats but only twenty per cent of the people. Three separate commissions on redistribution commented on this. In his 1966 report, H.F. Angus observed:

> In the northern half of the Province and in the Kootenays the demand for disproportionate representation in the Legislative Assembly appeared to be inspired in part by fear of the dominance of the Province by the Lower Mainland, and especially by Vancouver. The extraordinary belief seemed to exist that the people of the Lower Mainland were economic parasites, producing little wealth themselves, and intent on exploiting the people who live in the "under-developed" areas.[64]

The 1978 Commission recommended reducing Vancouver's representation by one member.

Although the federal government really plays the largest role of any government in affecting the lives of Canadians, Ottawa often seemed remote. Nevertheless, federal elections were sometimes interesting and Vancouver tended to follow national election patterns. If the Liberals did well nationally, they usually did well in Vancouver; if the Conservatives were successful as in 1957, 1958, and 1979, they did very well in Vancouver. The traditional exception was the largely working class constituency, Vancouver East, a CCF/NDP stronghold from its creation in the early 1930s until Art Lee (1974-79) briefly held it for the Liberals. In 1979, the NDP regained the seat and added the adjacent Vancouver-Kingsway constituency it had sometimes held in the past. The city's west side re-elected Conservative MPs, although from May 1979 to February 1980, Art Phillips of Vancouver Centre had the distinction of being the only Liberal MP west of Winnipeg. Whether the disappearance of Liberal MPs in the elections of 1979 and 1980 is merely an aberration or the beginning of a new trend is not clear.

SOCIAL AND CULTURAL DEVELOPMENT

Though Vancouver was definitely a metropolitan centre, it retained a frontier roughness. It was seldom the leading Canadian metropolitan centre in crime statistics, but its offences per capita were well above the national average. Two traditional crimes — violations of provincial liquor laws and gambling — declined in significance but did not disappear when relaxation of liquor laws reduced the opportunities for bootleggers and the creation of government lotteries satisfied the gambling instincts of some. Before the laws were changed, gambling provided two major police scandals. In 1947, a new Police Commission, including Mayor McGeer, who seemed to be repeating history, suspended the chief and several city police force officers and undertook wholesale promotions, demotions, and transfers within the department. A subsequent investigation produced evidence of "negligence and laxity in law enforcement and open defiance of the police by racketeers." The new chief, Walter Mulligan, complained that gambling places had been running "wide open." Eight years later, a Toronto tabloid, *Flash*, charged there was corruption in Vancouver's Police Department. A few days later, the Police Commission suspended Chief Mulligan "at his own request" and the Attorney-General appointed a Royal Commission to investigate. Many allegations of widespread corruption were made during the hearings and local newspapers reporting the inquiry often read like scandal sheets themselves. In the end, R.H. Tupper, the Royal Commissioner, cleared all high ranking officers with the exception of Mulligan who, he reported, had conspired in 1949 to accept bribes.[65]

As a port, Vancouver has long been a centre for prostitution and the illegal drug trade. The police cleared prostitutes out of one downtown neighbourhood only to have them reappear in another. By 1978, several court decisions hampered the Police Department's ability to lay charges. The ladies of the night — approximately 800 of them — worked openly. Their favourite haunts included Davie Street and Georgia near Hornby close to many of the city's major hotels and to the Court House itself.[66]

The illegal drug trade and the presence in the city of many drug addicts was a much greater social and police problem. To

Children at the Chinese New Year Festival in Chinatown.

The Chinese New Year is a major tourist attraction.

Children at play in a downtown schoolyard.

support their habit, many addicts, particularly of heroin, resorted to theft and robbery. In the early 1970s, the Vancouver public, like the public elsewhere in the western world, was also seriously concerned about the increasing use of marijuana and other "soft" drugs and of hallucinogens such as LSD especially by young people. Vancouver, as Canada's west coast haven, seemed to have more than its share of users of these drugs as "hippies" and other young wanderers drifted westward across North America. A counterculture grew up in Vancouver which espoused a "gentle lifestyle" based on communal living, natural foods, music, flowers, and poetry. Political issues centred on environmental concerns. Kitsilano saw another evolution as the centre of this counterculture, and craft shops, natural food stores and restaurants, and jazz clubs along with the international headquarters of Greenpeace revived the ailing commercial stretch along Fourth Avenue. The large houses in "Kits" were ideal for communal living and relatively inexpensive in the early seventies, but like such areas in other cities, Kitsilano has become *chic* and real estate prices have escalated as developers have moved in.

The public could tolerate that district and Gastown as colourful additions to the city, but civic authorities would not permit open defiance of the law. During summer 1970 the federal government had set up temporary hostels for travelling youth. At the beginning of October, the government wanted to close the hostel in old barracks at Jericho Beach, but the approximately 300 residents refused to leave. After considerable buck-passing between the city and the federal government, 150 R.C.M.P. evicted them. When the young people congregated on a nearby city street, city police warned them about unlawful assembly and then sent in the riot squad. In the subsequent melee, twenty-five young people and six policemen were injured. The incident might have soon been forgotten were it not for Mayor Campbell's remark that the War Measures Act applied to British Columbia and for the Gastown Riot the following August when city police, both uniformed and under-cover, and including four on horseback, broke up the yippie's "Grasstown Smoke-In and Street Jamboree." Apparent brutality by a few overzealous policemen angered many citizens who had little sympathy for the drug culture.[67]

Vancouver also acquired a reputation for riotous behaviour during such activities as the Grey Cup football game and its related "festivities." Indeed, some sports reporters claimed to have kept two sets of statistics for games in Vancouver: one on the game itself, the other on the number of arrests for drunkenness and related offences.[68]

Despite the boorish image created by some, most Vancouver sports fans were proud of such facilities as Empire Stadium, built for the 1954 British Empire Games and for some years the largest stadium in Canada. The stadium enabled the city to secure a professional franchise in the Canadian Football League and Vancouverites enjoyed being part of the "big time." Thanks to effective promotion, going to football games became a popular pastime for those who could afford it, even though the B.C. Lions didn't "roar in '54" or for some time thereafter. About 3,500 residents held shares in the team and for some years had considerable decision-making power. Such democracy may be desirable in government, but it does not win football games. Only when power was entrusted to a small executive group did the team briefly become successful when it won the Grey Cup in 1964.

Professional football's popularity waned slightly as the team returned to its losing ways and as the opening of the Pacific Coliseum at the Pacific National Exhibition grounds in 1968 made professional ice hockey the fashionable spectator sport. Although the Vancouver Canucks were in last place in the minor Western Hockey League, they drew large crowds especially since season ticket holders hoped they would get first chance at tickets when Vancouver acquired a National Hockey League franchise. As in the earlier campaign to get a professional football franchise, Vancouver's quest for a NHL team put civic pride at stake. At last, in 1970, Vancouver got an NHL team, albeit one initially owned by a Minnesota investment firm rather than local interests. The financial success of the Canucks led local promoters to bring a World Hockey Association team to Vancouver. The Vancouver Blazers failed, but the city retained its reputation as a supporter of professional sports. Given that tradition, the presence of many European immigrants, and a winning team, the Vancouver Whitecaps of the North American Soccer League were an almost instant success.[69]

At the same time, the city has maintained and expanded a longstanding program of community recreation. The Vancouver

Vancouver is a rich blend of many ethnic groups.

Children from the Musqueam Indian Reserve, 1958. The reserve, adjacent to the University Endowment Lands, has benefited in recent years from revenues on land leased for the Shaugnessy Golf Course and a luxury subdivision.

Aquatic Centre on English Bay which replaced the old Crystal pool houses an Olympic-sized indoor pool; a new 'Kits' Beach pool serves hundreds of bathers at a time. Neighbourhood park tennis courts sport all-weather surfaces, and adventure playgrounds (some designed by internationally acclaimed Vancouver landscape architect Cornelia Oberlander) have sprung up across the city. Thousands of joggers have joined the legendary walkers on the seawall in Stanley Park and on the many other water-side paths in a city where outdoor activity for young and old is almost a religion.

Vancouver has continued to experience an active cultural life. Since its formation in 1946, the Community Arts Council, composed of individuals and groups interested in the arts, has initiated many cultural programmes and lobbied government for financial support for the arts and for better city planning. The Council is the direct outgrowth of a unique 1946 survey of the arts sponsored by the Junior League. The survey team was amazed by the number of groups spontaneously organized to promote various forms of the arts. Those with literary interests, for example, could choose to be members of the Burns Fellowship, the Dickens Fellowship, or the Shakespeare Society; those interested in the visual arts might easily visit the Art Gallery and see either touring shows or the works of local artists; music lovers could listen to the regular concerts of the Vancouver Symphony Orchestra or the summer time operettas of Theatre Under the Stars (TUTS) in Stanley Park. Vancouver's uncertain summer weather and competition from the Vancouver International Festival, an extensive summer programme of symphony concerts, solo performances, dance, films, operas, plays, and even jazz concerts, contributed to TUTS' demise. The first Festival coincided with the provincial centennial of 1958; the second, with the opening of the Queen Elizabeth Theatre. Though it secured assistance from corporations, private individuals, and the three levels of government, the Festival itself failed financially and was discontinued in 1967.

Despite this failure and the competition for leisure hours from local television stations — CBUT (Canadian Broadcasting Corporation, 1953), CHAN (CTV, 1960) and CKVU (Independent, 1974) and the CBC's French language station, CBUFT (1976) — as well as American channels brought in by cable from Bellingham, Seattle, and Tacoma, Vancouver continued to support many cultural activities. Indeed, in 1973, the Vancouver Symphony Orchestra complained that the Queen Elizabeth Theatre was overbooked at certain seasons with special events ranging from nursing school graduations to jazz performances and touring rock shows. The rock shows, however, more frequently appeared in one of the large buildings on the Exhibition grounds or at Empire Stadium. Another extensive user of the Queen Elizabeth Theatre was the Vancouver Opera Association. Organized in 1959, the Association survived financial difficulties and the reluctance of Vancouver audiences to venture very far from traditionally popular operas and was able to sell ninety-six per cent of its tickets in 1978-79. To provide alternative accommodation for the Symphony, its friends successfully lobbied federal and provincial governments and private individuals for donations and sold lottery tickets to buy the old Orpheum Theatre and remodel it as a home for the Symphony. Similar public enthusiasm raised funds "To Take the Art Gallery To Court" in hopes the old Court House on Georgia Street became available as a new home for the Art Gallery.[70]

Vancouver continued to enjoy a variety of amateur theatrical productions, some visiting companies and performers, including those engaged by local impresarios such as Hugh Pickett and David Y.H. Lui and, since the 1960s, such resident professional companies as the Playhouse Theatre and the Arts Club. One of the most innovative theatres has been the Vancouver East Cultural Centre, opened in 1973 in an old church. On most nights of the year, Vancouver theatre-goers may choose from several live performances in theatres in various parts of the city and its suburbs.

Many of the plays produced in Vancouver were also written by local playwrights. Similarly, the city has been home to many writers of fiction and non-fiction alike. Works illustrating the delights of the city seem to be unusually common while poetry is the most popular creative form. It has been suggested "that if you were to toss a pebble into a crowd in Vancouver, it would hit a poet."[71] It might be more likely to strike a publisher of poetry. Vancouver, since the 1940s, has been home to a succession of little magazines some, but not all, based at the University of British Columbia and Simon Fraser University. Several small literary presses operate in Vancouver, such as Talonbooks and blewointment press.

As their numbers grew, various ethnic groups created their own shopping areas and restaurants in greater Vancouver. This Italian restaurant is located on Commercial Street.

The wide Granville Street bridge, opened in 1954, led to a downtown that had altered little since the early 1930s.

The artistic talents of Vancouver residents have also been manifest in popular music. Several singers such as Juliette, a CBC star; Terry Jacks whose "Seasons in the Sun" was one of the world's best selling single records; and the rock group Bachman-Turner Overdrive resided in Vancouver. In addition, many Vancouver performers have been recorded locally. By 1976, the city had fifteen recording studios including the Little Mountain Sound Company, "the TV and radio jingle capital of Canada."[72] In recent years, Vancouver studios have attracted performers and producers from the United States, creating yet another new "industry."

One explanation of Vancouver's artistic activity put forward in 1957 is still valid. In describing Vancouver's artistic climate, Neal Harlow, Librarian of the University of British Columbia, wrote of:

> its special character, a product of newness, westernness, and wilderness. A century of physical development has modified rawness and immaturity. Immigration, communication, and the impress of an international port have alleviated the penalties of separation from other great centres. There is a freshness and vigour in creation and a lively concern that artistic activity and appreciation should develop together.[73]

Such favourable comments are not untypical of observations Vancouver residents make about their community. Indeed, outsiders often remark on Vancouver residents' smugness about the extent of the city's growth and the beauty of the city's natural setting; they even warn that unchecked growth may ultimately lead to the city's ruin. Occasionally, Vancouver residents have listened. In retrospect, however, the popularity of limited growth from the mid-1960s through the mid-1970s was probably an aberration rather than the beginning of a trend away from traditional aspirations for greatness and material wealth. Too many men have come to Vancouver, made money, bettered their condition, enjoyed "tinsel and glitter," and created a city more cosmopolitan than Mayor Taylor dared imagine, to allow an easy abandonment of the growth ethic. Moreover, although Vancouver is almost a century old, it still retains a sense of youth.

The narrowness of the peninsula on which Vancouver sits has meant that only by redeveloping land for more effective uses has the city been able to expand in recent years. The almost complete physical transformation of such areas as downtown, Strathcona, the West End and False Creek contribute to the impression of newness. Thus, what might have been a handicap had become an asset.

Nature of course, has been kind to Vancouver. Although skyscrapers — many of them handsome buildings in their own right — impair some views and residential subdivisions creep up the North Shore mountains towards the timber slashes that advertise the proximity of ski resorts, the mountains still overlook the city and its busy harbour. In spite of itself, Vancouver has largely resolved the conundrum of reconciling its continuing aspirations for greatness and material wealth with pride in natural beauty. By sea and by land, Vancouver has indeed prospered midst a spectacular setting.

Appendix
Statistical Tables

TABLE I
Population Growth in Vancouver,
1891-1971

Year	Population	Numerical Change	Per Cent Change
1891	13,709	—	—
1901 a.	27,010	13,301	97.0
1901 b.	28,530	14,821	108.1
1911 a.	100,401	73,391	271.7
1911 c.	120,847	92,317	323.6
1921 a.	117,217	16,812	16.7
1921 c.	163,220	42,373	35.1
1931	246,593	83,373	51.0
1941	275,353	28,760	11.7
1951	344,833	69,480	25.2
1961	384,522	39,689	11.5
1971	426,256	41,734	10.8

a. City only
b. City and South Vancouver
c. City, South Vancouver, and Point Grey
Source: *Censuses of Canada, 1891-1971.*

TABLE II
Vancouver City as a Proportion of Greater Vancouver,
1901-1971

Year	Vancouver	Greater Vancouver[a]	Vancouver as % of Greater Vancouver
1901	27,010	35,394	76.3
1911	120,847[b]	142,215	85.0
1921	163,220[b]	220,503	74.0
1931	246,593	334,389	73.7
1941	275,353	388,687	70.8
1951	344,833	554,188	62.2
1961	384,522	769,006	50.0
1971	426,256	985,689	43.2

a. Greater Vancouver includes the municipalities listed in Table III.
b. Figures adjusted to include South Vancouver and Point Grey.
Source: *Censuses of Canada, 1901-1971.*

TABLE IIa.
Population of Vancouver as a Percentage of the Population of
British Columbia, 1891-1971

Year	Vancouver	British Columbia	Vancouver as % of British Columbia
1891	13,709	98,173	14
1901	27,010	178,657	15
1911	120,847	392,480	31
1921	163,220	524,582	31
1931	246,593	694,263	36
1941	275,353	817,861	33
1951	344,833	1,165,210	30
	(591,960)*		(47)
1961	384,522	1,629,082	24
	(790,165)*		(48)
1971	426,256	2,184,621	20
	(1,028,335) #		(47)

* Metropolitan Area as defined by the census.
# Greater Vancouver Regional District
Source: *Censuses of Canada, 1891-1971.*

TABLE III
Population Growth in Vancouver and Nearby Municipalities,
1901-1971

Municipality	1901[a]	1911[a]	1921	1931	1941	1951	1961	1971
Burnaby	—	—	12,883	25,564	30,328	58,376	100,517	125,660
Coquitlam	—	—	2,374	4,871	7,949	15,697	29,052	53,073
Delta	—	—	2,839	3,709	4,287	6,701	14,597	45,860
Indian Reserves	—	—	1,017	899	443	821	1,150	1,599
New Westminster	6,499	13,199	14,495	17,524	21,967	28,638	33,654	42,835
North Vancouver City	365	8,169	7,652	8,510	8,914	15,687	23,656	31,847
North Vancouver District	—	—	2,950	4,788	5,931	14,469	38,971	57,861
Point Grey	—	4,320	13,736					
Richmond	—	—	4,825	8,182	10,370	19,186	43,323	62,121
South Vancouver	1,520	16,126	32,267	—	—	—	—	—
Surrey	—	—	5,814	8,388	14,840	33,670	70,838	98,601
University Endowment Lands	—	—	—	575	636	2,120	3,272	3,536
Vancouver	27,010	100,401	117,217	246,593	275,353	344,833	384,522	426,256
West Vancouver	—	—	2,434	4,786	7,669	13,990	25,454	36,440

a. In 1901 and 1911, some of the municipalities in existence but having only small populations were not listed separately in the census.
Source: *Censuses of Canada, 1901-1971.*

TABLE IV
Population Growth in Major Western Cities, 1901-1971

Year	Winnipeg	Regina	Saskatoon	Calgary	Edmonton	Vancouver
1901	42,340	2,249	113	4,392	4,176	27,010
1911	136,035	30,213	12,004	43,704	24,900	100,401
1921	179,087	34,432	25,739	63,305	58,821	163,200
1931	218,785	53,209	43,291	83,761	79,187	246,593
1941	221,960	58,245	43,027	88,904	93,817	275,353
1951	235,710	71,319	53,268	129,060	159,631	344,833
1956	255,093	89,755	72,858	181,780	226,002	368,444
1961	265,429	112,141	95,526	249,641	281,027	384,522
1966	257,005	131,127	115,892	330,575	376,925	410,375
1971	246,270	139,469	126,449	403,319	438,152	426,256

Source: *Censuses of Canada, 1901-1971.*

TABLE V
Number of Males per 100 Females in Vancouver, 1891-1971

Year	Ratio
1891	187.58
1901	144.83
1911	149.92
1921	110.26
1931	114.21
1941	102.80
1951	94.83
1961	97
1971	95

Source: *Censuses of Canada, 1891-1971.*

TABLE VI
Age Composition of Vancouver's Population, 1921-1971

Year	0-14	15-44	45-64	65+	Total Population
1921	29,087 (24.8%)	62,776 (53.5%)	21,462 (18.3%)	3,752 (3.2%)	117,217[a]
1931	54,203 (21.9%)	120,354 (48.8%)	59,112 (24.0%)	12,373 (5.0%)	246,593[a]
1941	48,048 (17.4%)	130,632 (47.4%)	72,666 (26.4%)	24,007 (8.7%)	275,353
1951	72,191 (20.9%)	151,210 (43.8%)	77,226 (22.3%)	44,206 (12.8%)	344,823
1961	89,869 (23.4%)	152,244 (39.6%)	89,167 (23.2%)	53,242 (13.8%)	384,522
1971	83,205 (19.5%)	185,105 (43.4%)	100,410 (23.5%)	57,525 (13.5%)	426,255

a. Includes unknown.

Source: *Censuses of Canada, 1921-1971.*

TABLE VII
Birthplace of Vancouver's Canadian-Born Population, 1911-1961

Birthplace	1911 No.	%	1921 No.	%	1931 No.	%	1941 No.	%	1951 No.	%	1961 No.	%
Maritimes	5,698	12.8	6,900	8.7	8,033	6.3	7,416	4.4	8,903	3.8	8,011	3.2
Quebec	2,170	4.9	3,000	3.8	3,650	2.8	3,819	2.3	5,148	2.2	5,380	2.1
Ontario	16,663	37.8	21,200	26.6	23,809	18.6	22,920	13.7	25,153	10.8	21,723	8.7
Prairies	3,925	8.9	9,100	11.4	21,763	17.0	39,953	23.9	71,550	30.7	67,579	26.8
B.C. and Other	15,522	35.4	39,720	49.6	71,141	55.3	92,986	55.6	121,837	52.3	148,994	59.1
Total Canadian-Born	43,978	43.8	79,920	49.0	128,396	52.1	167,084	60.7	232,591	67.5	251,687	65.4
Total	100,401		163,220		246,573		275,353		344,833		384,522	

Source: Norbert MacDonald, "Population Growth and Change in Seattle and Vancouver, 1880-1960," *Pacific Historical Review,* Vol. 39 (1970), p. 305.

TABLE VIII
Birthplace of Vancouver's Foreign-Born Population, 1911-1971

Birthplace	1911 No.	%	1921 No.	%	1931 No.	%	1941 No.	%	1951 No.	%	1961 No.	%	1971 No.	%
England & Wales	18,414	18.3	32,140	19.7	46,151	18.7	44,432	16.1	44,287	12.8	37,410	9.7	45,310	10.6
Scotland	9,650	9.6	14,900	9.1	21,613	8.8	20,080	7.3	19,265	5.9	16,551	4.3	—	—
Ireland	2,625	2.6	4,260	2.6	5,573	2.2	5,166	1.9	3,564	1.0	3,097	—	1,720	—
Scandinavia	1,888	1.8	2,121	1.3	6,107	2.5	5,276	1.9	5,301	1.5	6,628	1.7	—	—
Germany	733	—	264	—	893	—	956	—	1,386	—	8,618	2.2	8,230	1.9
Other Western Europe	266	—	379	—	441	—	416	—	—	—	—	—	6,720	1.6
Eastern Europe	1,106	1.1	1,305	—	3,129	1.2	4,674	1.7	—	—	10,441	2.7	14,035	3.3
Italy	1,922	1.9	1,110	—	1,478	—	1,416	—	1,834	—	7,402	1.9	10,160	2.4
Other Southern Europe	226	—	310	—	293	—	—	—	—	—	—	—	8,940	2.1
United States	10,401	10.3	10,500	6.4	10,870	4.4	10,833	3.9	11,213	3.2	9,484	2.4	10,240	2.4
China	3,364	3.3	8,100	4.9	11,533	4.7	5,427	2.0	6,378	1.8	10,512	2.7	14,985	3.5
Japan	1,841	1.8	4,150	2.5	4,133	1.7	3,331	1.2	—	—	—	—	8,300	1.9
Other or Unknown	3,987	3.9	3,861	2.4	5,983	2.4	6,252	2.3	19,014	4.9	22,692	5.9	11,800	2.8
Total Foreign-born	56,423	56.2	83,300	51.0	118,197	47.9	108,259	39.3	112,242	32.5	132,835	34.5	146,715	34.4
Total	100,401		163,220		246,593		275,353		344,833		384,522		426,265	

Notes: Percentages are not given when less than 1.0.
In 1951 and 1961, the census contracted the number of its categories and lumped some in with "others or unknown."

Source: *Censuses of Canada, 1911-1971.*

TABLE IX
Ethnic Origins of Vancouver's Population, 1901-1971

Ethnic Group	1901 No.	%	1911 No.	%	1921 No.	%	1931 No.	%	1941 No.	%	1951 No.	%	1961 No.	%	1971 No.	%
Asian	2,840	10.5	6,085	6.1	11,006	9.4	21,868	8.9	16,138	5.9	10,256	3.0	19,915	5.2	35,685	8.4
British Isles	20,328	75.3	73,996	73.7	79,458	76.8	190,132	77.1	190,132	77.1	212,817	77.3	230,234	59.9	225,995	53.0
French	598	2.2	1,798	1.8	2,252	1.9	4,480	1.8	6,303	2.3	9,899	2.9	12,113	3.2	14,330	3.4
German	871	3.2	2,826	2.8	1,117	1.0	4,371	1.0	4,958	1.8	12,774	3.7	26,561	6.9	32,515	7.6
Italian	203	—	2,256	2.2	1,590	1.4	3,330	1.3	3,644	1.3	5,095	1.5	12,941	3.4	19,020	4.5
Jewish	205	—	973	1.0	1,270	1.1	2,407	—	2,812	1.0	4,029	1.2	4,145	1.1	7,995	1.9
Netherlands	68	—	296	—	738	—	1,936	—	3,308	1.2	6,290	1.8	9,311	2.4	7,670	1.8
Polish	—	—	60	—	174	—	1,222	—	2,659	—	5,334	1.5	7,117	1.9	6,315	1.5
Russian	66	—	240	—	357	—	1,435	—	2,596	—	3,929	1.1	4,840	1.3	3,085	—
Scandinavian	452	1.7	2,545	2.5	2,660	2.3	8,447	3.4	10,472	3.8	16,320	4.7	18,782	4.9	15,465	3.6
Ukrainian	—	—	—	—	107	—	512	—	1,913	—	7,226	2.1	9,247	2.4	12,105	2.8
Other European	98	—	1,215	1.2	1,678	1.4	5,615	2.3	7,039	2.6	10,912	3.2	22,624	5.9	10,920	2.6
Other & Unknown	1,281	4.7	8,111	8.1	659	—	838	—	694	—	8,231	2.4	6,692	1.7	35,190	8.3

Sources: *Censuses of Canada, 1901-1971.*

TABLE X
Major Religious Affiliations of Vancouver's Population, 1891-1971

Religion	1891 No.	%	1901 No.	%	1911 No.	%	1921 No.	%	1931 No.	%	1941 No.	%
Anglican	3,754	27.4	7,063	26.1	26,321	26.2	35,137	30.0	71,359	28.9	84,947	30.9
Baptist	696	5.1	1,553	5.7	6,088	6.1	5,473	4.6	10,578	4.3	12,663	4.6
Buddhist	—	—	—	—	1,935	1.9	2,794	2.4	6,018	2.4	5,171	1.9
Confucian	—	—	—	—	2,929	2.9	5,916	5.0	9,711	3.9	5,529	2.0
Greek Orthodox	—	—	2	—	425	—	541	—	1,341	—	1,783	—
Jewish	83	—	202	—	967	1.0	1,248	1.1	2,372	1.0	2,742	1.0
Lutheran	299	2.2	446	1.6	3,001	3.0	2,036	1.7	8,903	3.6	10,151	3.7
Methodist	2,215	16.2	3,785	14.0	14,155	14.1	14,968	12.8	106[a]	—	15	—
Pentecostal	—	—	—	—	2	—	58	—	846	—	1,326	—
Presbyterian	3,369	24.6	6,505	24.1	26,409	26.3	31,595	26.9	35,366	14.3	39,637	14.4
Roman Catholic	552	11.3	3,064	11.3	10,271	10.2	10,842	9.3	23,635	9.6	43,133	12.5
United Church	—	—	—	—	—	—	—	—	61,213	24.8	69,246	25.1
Other or None	1,741	12.7	4,390	16.2	18,169	18.1	6,609	5.6	15,085	6.1	12,830	4.7
Total	13,709	—	27,010	—	100,401	—	117,217	—	246,593	—	275,353	—

Religion	1951 No.	%	1961 No.	%	1971 No.	%
Anglican	94,168	27.3	82,015	21.3	66,845	15.7
Baptist	14,324	4.2	14,071	3.7	13,320	3.1
Buddhist & Confucian	2,302	—	—	—	—	—
Greek Orthodox	4,052	1.2	5,832	1.5	7,645	1.8
Jewish	5,015	1.5	6,344	1.6	6,910	1.6
Lutheran	15,376	4.5	24,485	6.3	21,670	5.1
Pentecostal	2,608	—	3,463	1.0	5,050	1.1
Presbyterian	35,321	10.2	27,746	7.2	23,025	5.4
Roman Catholic	43,133	12.5	63,351	16.4	87,415	20.5
Ukrainian Catholic	1,988	—	2,220	—	3,095	—
United Church	101,804	29.5	106,789	27.8	80,665	18.9
Other or None	24,742	7.2	48,206	12.5	110,585	25.9
Total	344,833	—	384,522	—	426,270	—

a. Almost all Methodists and Congregationalists (of whom there were very few in Vancouver) and some Presbyterians joined the newly formed United Church of Canada in 1925.

Source: *Censuses of Canada, 1891-1971.*

TABLE XI
The Labour Force of Greater Vancouver by Industry, 1921-1971

Industry	1921[a]	1931	1941	1951	1961	1971
Primary: agriculture, forestry fishing, mining	4.86%	6.57%	5.75%	3.76%	3.27%	2.41%
Manufacturing						
Construction	16.99	13.66	18.53	25.56	19.50	18.02
Transportation &	8.31	7.84	7.17	7.13	6.75	6.92
Communication	12.34	9.98	9.63	12.49	11.85	11.38
Trade						
Finance, insurance, real estate	17.62	13.12	13.46	21.12	20.32	19.82
Service (including	3.96	2.02	1.67	4.78	5.40	6.52
government)	28.18	21.48	23.58	25.76	29.98	34.10
Clerical	n/a	10.75	11.84	n/a	n/a	n/a
Other	7.69	14.34	7.96	1.35	2.88	0.08
Total Labour Force	53,090	136,301	138,562	210,358	294,759	425,960

a. 1921 figures are not strictly comparable because the census used a slightly different system of classification and because they refer to the city only.

Source: *Censuses of Canada, 1921-1971.*

TABLE XII
Value of Building Permits Issued in Vancouver, 1902-1978

Year	Value of Permits	Year	Value of Permits	Year	Value of Permits
1902	$ 833,607.00	1928	$ 12,777,293.00	1954	$ 45,285,787.00
1903	1,426,148.00	1929	21,572,727.00	1955	55,446,193.00
1904	1,986,590.00	1930	14,645,206.00	1956	64,679,148.00
1905	2,653,000.00	1931	10,066,425.00	1957	56,499,913.00
1906	4,308,410.00	1932	2,854,206.00	1958	56,433,775.00
1907	5,632,744.00	1933	1,564,541.00	1959	58,869,832.00
1908	5,950,893.00	1934	1,418,822.00	1960	36,847,190.00
1909	7,258,565.00	1935	3,892,665.00	1961	38,848,449.00
1910	13,150,365.00	1936	4,641,545.00	1962	44,852,461.00
1911	17,652,642.00	1937	6,760,880.00	1963	52,544,433.00
1912	19,388,322.00	1938	8,224,300.00	1964	79,037,630.00
1913	10,423,197.00	1939	6,253,796.00	1965	84,351,749.00
1914	4,484,476.00	1940	8,053,725.00	1966	68,801,850.00
1915	1,593,379.00	1941	9,216,520.00	1967	100,154,600.00
1916	2,412,889.00	1942	5,996,015.00	1968	109,658,419.00
1917	768,255.00	1943	4,663,734.00	1969	114,423,702.00
1918	1,440,384.00	1944	12,601,818.00	1970	71,296,808.00
1919	2,271,411.00	1945	16,843,897.00	1971	136,680,538.00
1920	3,709,873.00	1946	28,136,963.00	1972	131,373,502.00
1921	3,145,132.00	1947	21,877,675.00	1973	180,785,220.00
1922	8,661,695.00	1948	37,242,817.00	1974	134,675,267.00
1923	6,277,574.00	1949	33,041,252.00	1975	185,019,687.00
1924	6,230,774.00	1950	34,999,669.00	1976	236,357,663.00
1925	7,963,575.00	1951	23,942,309.00	1977	232,537,058.00
1926	15,501,262.00	1952	28,387,737.00	1978	233,534,985.00
1927	10,687,167.00	1953	50,748,757.00		

Sources: 1902-1936, City of Vancouver, Annual Report; 1937-1978, City of Vancouver, Department of Permits and Licenses, monthly reports.

TABLE XIII
Grain Shipments from Vancouver, 1921-1971[a]

Year	Bushels	Year	Bushels
1921	1,251,070	1947	53,733,502
1922	14,463,883	1948	42,375,830
1923	24,663,017	1949	76,391,093
1924	53,240,516	1950	53,558,871
1925	34,868,192	1951	87,231,376
1926	45,229,906	1952	122,505,635
1927	43,602,210	1953	108,009,206
1928	97,561,716	1954	102,851,406
1929	73,984,114	1955	84,654,601
1930	63,437,312	1956	123,667,097
1931	70,841,445	1957	140,921,784
1932	105,006,925	1958	137,532,166
1933	68,828,024	1959	148,531,179
1934	51,757,614	1960	129,478,222
1935	46,265,612	1961	162,606,166
1936	64,812,823	1962	158,474,175
1937	23,749,368	1963	179,503,551
1938	26,884,700	1964	204,013,205
1939	33,677,610	1965	169,205,721
1940	8,783,092	1966	203,499,755
1941	5,565,309	1967	173,973,736
1942	10,286,460	1968	189,528,114
1943	19,504,771	1969	162,292,838
1945	40,613,096	1970	215,712,297
1946	65,997,393	1971	274,660,050

Sources: 1921-1935, Vancouver Harbour Commission, *Annual Report*; 1936-1971, National Harbours Board, *Annual Report*.

a. NHB figures include a small portion of grain shipped by rail. In most years, non-water-borne shipments accounted for less than two per cent of the total exports.

TABLE XIV
The Growth of Manufacturing in Vancouver, 1891-1971

Year	Population	Number of Firms	Number of Employees	Payroll $(000)	Value of Products $(000)
1891	13,709	94[a]	1,084	565	1,895
1901	27,010	71	2,151	1,346	4,990
1911	100,401	130	8,866	4,020	15,070
1921	117,217	441	10,438	12,446	65,036
1931	246,593	681	14,209	17,095	72,999
1941	275,353	864	25,233	34,133	162,983
1951	344,833	1,255	34,376	96,222	461,594
1961	384,522	1,143	30,989	141,169	509,666[b]
1971	426,256	2,029	49,121	378,599	2,167,753

a. In 1891 all shops and factories were included; after 1901, only those with five or more employees.
b. In 1952, the value of factory shipments replaced the gross value of products. (See *Canada Year Book, 1965*, p. 658.)

Source: *Censuses of Canada, 1891-1911; Canada Year Book, 1921-1971.*

Notes

Abbreviations

BCER   British Columbia Electric Railway
BCHQ   *British Columbia Historical Quarterly*
BCS   *BC Studies*
CAR   *Canadian Annual Review*
CCC   City Clerk's Correspondence
CHR   *Canadian Historical Review*
CMJ   *Canadian Municipal Journal*
D. Hist.   Directorate of History, Department of National Defence, Ottawa
PABC   Provincial Archives of British Columbia
PAC   Public Archives of Canada
UBC   University of British Columbia Library, Special Collections
UHR   *Urban History Review*
VCA   Vancouver City Archives
VDNA   *Vancouver Daily-News Advertiser*

INTRODUCTION

[1] July mean temperature is 17.4° C; January mean temperature, 2.4° C. On average, there are 161 days of precipitation and the total is 1,068.1 cm of which 52.3 cm are snow. Based upon airport records, these figures tend to underestimate rainfall and overestimate moderation of the climate. Most parts of Vancouver are closer to the mountains and farther away from the sea's moderating influence than the airport. Source: *Canada Year Book, 1976-77* (Ottawa, Minister of Industry, Trade and Commerce, 1977), p.42.

[2] Charles E. Borden, "Cultural History of the Fraser-Delta Region: An Outline," *BCS*, No. 6-7 (Fall-Winter 1970), pp. 97, 101; Rolf Knight, *Indians at Work: An Informal History of Native Indian Labour in British Columbia, 1858-1930* (Vancouver, 1978), *passim.*

[3] George Vancouver, *A Voyage of Discovery to the North Pacific Ocean and Round the World* (London, 1801), Vol. 2, p. 303.

[4] F.W. Howay, "Early Settlement on Burrard Inlet," *BCHQ*, Vol. I (April 1937), pp. 103-104.

[5] F.W. Howay, "Early Shipping in Burrard Inlet, 1863-1870," *BCHQ*, Vol. I (January 1937), pp. 3-20.

[6] W. Kaye Lamb, "The Pioneer Days of the Trans-Pacific Service, 1887-1891," *BCHQ*, Vol. I (July 1937), pp. 143-169.

[7] William Van Horne to William Smithe, 14 June 1884, in British Columbia, *Sessional Papers*, 1885, p. 129.

[8] Van Horne to Smithe, 9 September 1884, PABC, Premier's Correspondence, 1883-86; Crown Grant, 13 February 1886, PABC, File C/C, 30.7, C16.

[9] John Robson to his brother, 15 February 1886, PABC, John Robson, Correspondence, File H/D, R57, R573.

[10] Norbert MacDonald, "Vancouver in the Nineteenth Century," *UHR*, No. 1-75 (June 1975), p. 52.

[11] The relevant documents are in British Columbia, *Sessional Papers*, 1886.

[12] Vancouver *Herald*, 15 January and 19 February 1886; Richard H. Alexander *et al.* to the Legislative Assembly of British Columbia, (c.15 February 1886), PABC, File CC70, V27.

[13] Victoria *Daily Colonist*, 20 March 1886.

[14] R.H. Alexander, "Reminiscences of the Early Days of British Columbia," Canadian Club, Vancouver, *Addresses and Proceedings*, 1910-11, p. 16; J.M. Spinks et al. to Speaker and Members of the House of Assembly, n.d. [c. February-March, 1886], PABC, File CC70, V27.

[15] Victoria *Daily Times*, 6 May 1886; *Colonist*, 1 May 1886; *Mainland Guardian* (New Westminster), 5 May 1886.

[16] *Times*, 6 May 1886; Vancouver *Daily Advertiser*, 25 and 26 May 1886; Vancouver *Herald*, 28 May 1886.

[17] Superintendent H.B. Roycraft, Provincial Police, to John Robson, 17 June 1886, PABC, Provincial Secretary's Correspondence, Series A2, Vol. 28. Recollections of the fire may be found in various publications prepared by J.S. Matthews including the *Vancouver Historical Journal*, no. 1 (January 1958). The transient nature of the population helps explain the lack of precise casualty figures.

[18]Vancouver *Advertiser*, 29 June 1886 cited in D.A. McGregor, "The Marvel of Vancouver," *British Columbia Magazine*, Vol. 7 (June 1911), p. 467.

CHAPTER ONE

[1]R.G. McKay to editor, *VDNA*, 4 March 1890.

[2]*News*, 29 March 1887.

[3]M. Picken, comp., *City of Vancouver, Terminus of the Canadian Pacific Railway: British Columbia Hand Book* (Vancouver, 1887), p. 33.

[4]G.W.S. Brooks, "Edgar Crow Baker: An Entrepreneur in Early British Columbia," *BCS*, No. 31 (Autumn 1976), pp. 23-43.

[5]*VDNA*, 27 May 1887 and 30 December 1890; Toronto *Globe*, 31 October 1890. (The *Globe* advertisement specifically illustrated the rise: 1886, $50; 1887, $70; 1888, $150; 1889, $250; 1890, $300; 1891, $500); *World*, Souvenir Edition, June 1896.

[6]*VDNA*, 1 March and 30 July 1890; *News*, 10 September 1886.

[7]R.A.J. McDonald, "Business Leaders in Early Vancouver, 1886-1914," Ph.D. thesis, University of British Columbia, 1977, pp. 55, 66-67.

[8]*VDNA*, 18 June 1887.

[9]Among outside proposals were offers from Portland's *West Shore* and the Toronto *Globe*. Real estate agents provided sufficient advertising to enable the *Globe* to publish four pages of Vancouver material on 31 October 1891.

[10]Vancouver City Council, Minute Book, 25 August, 8 September, and 24 February 1890.

[11]*VDNA*, 5 October 1887, 1 January 1889, 6 March 1890. See also Ramsay Cook and Robert Craig Brown, *Canada, 1896-1921: A Nation Transformed* (Toronto, 1974), p. 86.

[12]*VDNA*, 20 August 1887, 12 January and 30 March 1897; David Oppenheimer, *The Mineral Resources of British Columbia* (Vancouver, 1889). See also S.S. Fowler, "Early Smelters in British Columbia," *BCHQ*, Vol. 3 (July 1939), pp. 18-30.

[13]Bell and Miller to David Oppenheimer, 11 July 1891, VCA, CCC, Vol. 4.

[14]J.M. Browning, Vancouver land commissioner, became president and Harry Abbott, a director.

[15]*VDNA*, 2 March 1890 and 20 January 1891.

[16]M.I. Rogers, *B.C. Sugar* (Vancouver, 1958); McDonald, "Business Leaders," p. 93.

[17]*News*, 19 August 1886; *VDNA*, 2 May 1891.

[18]*VDNA*, 11 July 1890; *World*, 20 June 1896; W. Kaye Lamb, "The Pioneer Days of the Trans-Pacific Service," *BCHQ*, Vol. 1 (July 1937), pp. 143-164 and "Empress to the Orient," *BCHQ*, Vol. 4 (January 1940), pp. 29-56 and (April 1940), pp. 79-110; J.H. Hamilton, "The All-Red Route, 1893-1958: A History of the Trans-Pacific Mail Service between British Columbia, Australia and New Zealand," *BCHQ*, Vol. 20 (January-April 1956), pp. 1-126.

[19]Vancouver City Council Minute Book, 4 and 11 August 1890; United States Consul in Vancouver, Despatches, 21 October 1891 (Microfilm in PABC).

[20]*VDNA*, 25 March 1888. The vote was 125 to 8 (*VDNA*, 24 May 1888).

[21]Vancouver City Council, Minute Book, 24 May 1892. The provincial government opened a combined railway and traffic bridge across the Fraser River at New Westminster in 1904 at a cost of slightly more than $1 million.

[22]*World*, 17 March 1891; Nelson *Miner*, 16 February 1895 quoted in Isobel M. Bescoby, "Some Social Aspects of the Canadian Mining Advance into the Cariboo and Kootenay," M.A. thesis, University of British Columbia, 1935, p. 56; Patricia E. Roy, "Railways, Politicians and the Development of the City of Vancouver as a Metropolitan Centre," M.A. thesis, University of Toronto, 1963, Chapter II.

[23]*World*, 10 July 1891, 25 and 26 September 1893; S.E. Ruzicka, "The Decline of Victoria as a Metropolitan Centre, 1885-1901," M.A. thesis, University of Victoria, 1973; H.T. Logan, *Tuum Est: A History of the University of British Columbia* (Vancouver, 1958), pp. 3-12.

[24]Robert A.J. McDonald, "Victoria, Vancouver, and the Economic Development of British Columbia, 1886-1914," in Alan F.J. Artibise, ed., *Town and City: Aspects of Western Canadian Urban Development* (forthcoming, 1980.)

[25]In 1891, males formed 65.2 per cent of the population. If the Chinese, who were almost exclusively male, are eliminated from the calculations, the figure is 63.2 per cent. The census showed 2,522 married men but only 1,928 married women; E.D. McLaren *et al.* to Mayor and Aldermen, 17 January 1896, VCA, CCC, Vol. 11; Vancouver City Council, Minute Book, 6 February 1894.

[26]Norbert MacDonald, "The Canadian Pacific Railway and Vancouver's Development to 1900," *BCS*, No. 35 (Autumn 1977), p. 26.

[27]For a history of British Columbia attitudes to the Chinese see W. Peter Ward, *White Canada Forever* (Montreal, 1978), pp. 3-76.

[28]Vancouver *Morning News*, 2 June 1886; Patricia E. Roy, "The Preservation of the Peace in Vancouver: The Aftermath of the Anti-Chinese Riot of 1887," *BCS*, No. 31 (Autumn 1976), pp. 44-59.

[29]Harland Bartholomew and Associates, *A Plan for the City of Vancouver* (Vancouver, 1928), p. 24; Vancouver *Sunday Province*, 24 July 1927.

[30]Campbell Sweney, Diary, April 1892, VCA; Marjorie Allan, comp., *The History of Christ Church Cathedral* (Vancouver, 1959), p.6.

[31]*VDNA*, 20 October 1888.

[32]*VDNA*, 8 November 1888 and 19 March 1890.

[33]*Williams' British Columbia Directory*, 1891, p. 122; McDonald, "Business Leaders," p. 264; *VDNA*, 6 February 1889; Vancouver *Telegram*, 29

October and 15 November 1890.

[34]*VDNA*, 6 February and 21 March 1889; Harrison Thomas, Medical Health Officer to Mayor and Council, December 1896, VCA, CCC, Vol. 10.

[35]McDonald, "Business Leaders," pp. 261-263; W.F. Salsbury *et al.* to Vancouver City Council, 18 September 1895, VCA, Unaccessioned Public Records; Johnson & Farrell to F.S. Barnard, 11 November 1895, UBC, BCER Papers, Box 334. The street railway offered the passes for $25 each.

[36]*VDNA*, 30 July 1890 and 31 July 1891.

[37]*VDNA*, 1 January 1891.

[38]*VDNA*, 10 and 16 August 1887; Harrison Thomas to Mayor and Council, 28 May 1893, VCA, CCC, Vol. 7; Margaret W. Andrews, "Medical Services in Vancouver, 1886-1920: A Study in the Interplay of Attitudes, Medical Knowledge, and Administrative Structures," Ph.D. thesis, University of British Columbia, 1979.

[39]Report to Chairman of Board of Health [1888], VCA, CCC, Vol. 1; W. Downie to T.F. McGuigan, 11 September 1893, VCA, CCC, Vol. 6; A. M. Robertson, Medical Health Officer, to Chairman, Board of Health, 29 June 1888, VCA, CCC, Vol. 1; G. Huntley, Inspector, to Health Committee, VCA, CCC, Vol. 4.

[40]*VDNA*, 14 May 1889; *News*, 4 March 1887; G. Huntley to Health Committee, 24 March 1891, VCA, CCC, Vol, 4; Vancouver Board of Trade, Annual Report, 1897-98.

[41]*World*, 20 June 1896; A.H. Sinclair, "Municipal Monopolies and Their Management," (1891), rpt. in Paul Rutherford, ed., *Saving the Canadian City: The First Phase, 1880-1920* (Toronto, 1974), p. 36.

[42]Vancouver City Council, Minute Book, 6 September 1886 and 21 March 1887; *Advertiser*, 22 January 1887; *VDNA*, 26 and 27 May and 5 June 1887. The Hill Family Papers in VCA contain considerable material on the Coquitlam Water Works Company; H.B. Smith, "Vancouver Waterworks," *Transactions*, Canadian Society of Civil Engineers, Read on 5 December 1899.

[43]*News*, 27 November 1887; *VDNA*, 1 January 1888; Douglas Sladen *On the Cars and Off* (London, 1895), p. 371.

[44]H.T. Ceperley to J.C. Keith, 23 September 1890, UBC, Vancouver Street Railway, Letter Book, 1889-92; Report of Vancouver Electric Railway and Lighting Company, 2 February 1891, UBC, Vancouver Electric Railway and Lighting Company Statements, 1891-93.

[45]*News*, 12 April 1887.

[46]*VDNA*, 30 September 1888; *News*, 11 December 1886; *World*, 24 March 1891; MacDonald, "The Canadian Pacific Railway," p. 22.

[47]*World*, 17 March 1891. At the height of the controversy, Oppenheimer refused to attend the board meeting of the Vancouver City Foundry and Machine Works of which both he and Carter-Cotton were directors unless Carter-Cotton proved his allegations against Oppenheimer's handling of certain aspects of the city engineer case or apologized.

[48]*VDNA*, 8 May, 15 June, and 18 August 1889; 27 July and 1 October 1890.

[49]*VDNA*, 26 February and 21 October 1890. In 1895, the city reduced the assessment on improvements by fifty per cent.

[50]Canada, Royal Commission on the Liquor Traffic, Minutes of Evidence (Ottawa, 1894), Vol. III, pp. 610-612; *VDNA*, 19 February and 22 June 1888; Vancouver City Council, Minute Book, 5 March 1888; Vancouver *Daily World, Illustrated Souvenir Publication,* 1896, p. 6.

[51]Vancouver City Council, Minute Book, 28 November 1887 and 25 July 1892; Ethel Wilson, "Young Vancouver Seen Through the Eyes of Youth," *Habitat,* Vol. X (1967), p. 139; Frederick D. Thompson, *In the Track of the Sun* (London, 1893), p. 15.

[52]James M. Sandison, ed., *Schools of Old Vancouver* (Vancouver, 1971); K.A. Waites, *The First Fifty Years: Vancouver High Schools* (Vancouver, 1940), p. 21.

[53]Gwen Hayball, "A History of the Vancouver Public Library, 1869-1900," *B.C. Historical News,* Vol. 10 (April 1977); Henry Pybus, "The Museum of Vancouver, British Columbia," *The Museum's Journal,* Vol. 25 (July 1925), rpt. in Art, Historical and Scientific Association of Vancouver, *Museum Notes,* Vol. 1 (February 1926), p. 8; "The Art, Historical and Scientific Association of Vancouver, B.C.," *Museum Notes,* Vol. 1 (June 1926), pp. 3ff.

[54]*World*, 5 January 1891.

[55]*News*, 11 August 1888; G.A. Cran and Norman Hacking, *Annals of the Royal Vancouver Yacht Club, 1903-1965* (Vancouver, Royal Vancouver Yacht Club, 1965).

[56]William C. McKee, "The History of the Vancouver Park System, 1886-1929," M.A. thesis, University of Victoria, 1976 and "The Vancouver Park System, 1886-1929: A Product of Local Businessmen," *UHR,* 3-78 (February 1979), pp. 33-49.

CHAPTER TWO

[1]L.D. Taylor, 31 August 1910, Address to the Union of Canadian Municipalities, Toronto, *CMJ*, (October 1910), p. 415.

[2]L.D. McCann cautiously states that "metropolitan status had been decisively won by the eve of World War I" but his evidence indicates that this was true by 1901. "Urban Growth in a Staple Economy: The Emergence of Vancouver as a Regional Metropolis, 1886-1914," in L.J. Evenden, ed., *Vancouver: A Western Metropolis* (Victoria, 1978), p. 34.

[3]Robert Adam, "Vancouver and Her Trade with East Asia," M.A. thesis, University of Victoria, 1980, Chapter II.

[4]McDonald, "Business Leaders," p. 45.

[5]Margaret A. Ormsby, *British Columbia: A History* (Toronto, 1958), p. 336.

[6]Vancouver Board of Trade, Annual Report, 1897-98, p. 13; L. Edwin Dudley to William R. Day, 27 January 1898, United States Consular Reports, Despatches from Vancouver; Dudley to Day, 6 December 1897, *ibid.* Edgar Crow Baker, "Diary," 1 July 1898 quoted in G.W.S. Brooks, "Edgar Crow Baker: An Entrepreneur in Early British Columbia," M.A. Thesis, University of British Columbia, 1976, p. 316.

[7]See Norbert MacDonald, "Seattle, Vancouver and the Klondike," *CHR*, Vol. 49 (September 1968), pp. 234-246 and Roy, "Railways, Politicians and the Development of the City of Vancouver," Chapter III.

[8]McDonald, "Business Leaders," *passim.*

[9]"Vancouver Information and Tourist Association,"*British Columbia Magazine,* Vol. 7 (1911); McDonald, "Business Leaders," pp. 102-104.

[10]See H.K. Ralston, "The 1900 Strike of Fraser River Sockeye Salmon Fishermen," M.A. thesis, University of British Columbia, 1965.

[11]*A.Y.P. Year Book of Vancouver* (Vancouver, 1909), p. 45 quoted in McDonald, "Business Leaders," p. 77; F.W. Howay and E.O.S. Scholefield, *British Columbia* (Winnipeg, 1914), Vol. IV, p. 726; Vancouver Board of Trade, Monthly Meeting Minute Book, 4 March 1913, VCA, Add. Mss. 300; McDonald, "Business Leaders," pp. 77-79, and 175.

[12]John K. Martin, "The Industrial Growth of Vancouver: Its Significance," *Man-to-Man Magazine*, Vol. VI (September 1910), p. 650; D.M. Churchill, "False Creek Development," M.A. thesis, University of British Columbia, 1953, p. 56; T.D. Regehr, *Canadian Northern Railway* (Toronto, 1976), pp. 326-333.

[13]Martin, "Industrial Growth," p. 651; McDonald, "Business Leaders," pp. 84-85.

[14]W.H. Malkin, President, Vancouver Board of Trade, *Annual Report*, 1902-03, pp. 12-13.

[15]H.M. Tapley, Acting Secretary, Vancouver Trade Expansion Committee, Circular Letter, 3 July 1911, PABC, Add. Mss. 18, Vol. II; *Province*, 4 January 1913; Alan Wilson, *John Northway: A Blue Serge Canadian* (Toronto, 1956), p. 105; G.E. Mills and D.W. Holdsworth, "The B.C. Mills Prefabricated System: The Emergence of Ready-Made Buildings in Western Canada," *Occasional Papers in Archaeology and History*, No. 14 (Ottawa, 1975), p. 151.

[16]*Province*, 28 June 1912, 6 November and 3 December 1909; Vancouver Board of Trade, Monthly Meeting Book, 2 December 1909, VCA, Add. Mss. 300.

[17]*Province*, 29 June 1907; William Skene, Secretary, Vancouver Board of Trade to Premier Richard McBride, 31 December 1906, PABC, Premier's Official Correspondence, Box 26. Juvenile court records seldom mentioned ethnic backgrounds. See Diane L. Matters, "A Chance to Make Good: Juvenile Males and the Law in Vancouver, B.C., 1910-1915," M.A. thesis, University of B.C., 1978, p. 85.

[18]Vancouver Board of Trade, Monthly Meeting Minute Book, 5 September 1911, VCA, Add. Mss. 300; Dorothy Blakey Smith, "Early Memories of Vancouver," Vancouver Historical Society, *Newsletter*, Vol. 13 (November 1973), pp. 3-6; *VDNA*, 7 February 1912; *Times* (London), 10 October 1908; McDonald, "Business Leaders," p. 185.

[19]*VDNA*, 7 February 1912; "Opening Doors: Vancouver's East End," *Sound Heritage*, Vol. VIII (1979), p. 30.

[20]Howay and Scholefield, *British Columbia*, Vol. III, p. 1114.

[21]*Province*, 10 January 1910; F.R. Glover to R.H. Sperling, 2 October 1909, and R.H. Sperling to Michael Urwin, 28 January 1913, UBC, BCER Papers; Patricia E. Roy, "The British Columbia Electric Railway and Its Street Railway Employees: Paternalism in Labour Relations," *BCS*, No. 16 (Winter 1972-73), pp. 7-8. Professionals also complained about Americans taking jobs. When Vancouver City Council proposed to hire a firm of American consulting engineers, the Vancouver branch of the Canadian Society of Civil Engineers protested (*Province*, 8 November 1910).

[22]This account is based on Paul Phillips, *No Power Greater: A Century of Labour in British Columbia* (Vancouver, 1967), pp. 39-41 and Canada, Royal Commission on Industrial Disputes in the Province of British Columbia, *Report*, (Ottawa, 1903). For the context of the "free speech" dispute see A. Ross McCormack, *Reformers, Rebels and Revolutionaries: The Western Radical Movement, 1899-1909* (Toronto, 1977), pp. 106-107.

[23]Ken Adachi, *The Enemy That Never Was* (Toronto, 1976), p. 131.

[24]*World*, 12 February 1910.

[25]Mayor A. Bethune to Wilfrid Laurier, 14 September 1907, PAC, Laurier Papers, #129142; *CAR*, 1907, p. 383.

[26]*CAR*, 1907, p. 385. This account is drawn mainly from H. Sugimoto, "The Vancouver Riots of 1907: A Canadian Episode," in H. Conroy and T.S. Miyakawa, eds. *East Across the Pacific* (Santa Barbara, 1972), pp. 92-126.

[27]*World*, 18 January 1908; George H. Cowan, "Geo. H. Cowan's Position on the Asiatic Question," Speech at Vancouver, 3 October 1908.

[28]Chief Constable R.J. Chamberlain to Chairman, Board of Police Commissioners, 8 February 1909, VCA, CCC, Vol. 27.

[29]"Diary of Beatrice Webb, 26 June-7 August 1911," Vol. 29 quoted in George Feaver, "The Webbs in Canada: Fabian Pilgrims on the Canadian Frontier," *CHR*, Vol. LVIII (September 1977), p. 268; R.E. Vernede, *The Fair Dominion* (London, 1911), p. 259; McDonald, "Business Leaders," p. 100.

[30]"Vancouver, A City of Beautiful Homes," *British Columbia Magazine*, Vol. 7 (December 1911), pp. 1313-1315; Deryck W. Holdsworth, "House and Home in Vancouver: Images of West Coast Urbanism, 1886-1929," in G.A. Stelter and A.F.J. Artibise, eds., *The Canadian City: Essays in Urban History* (Toronto, 1977), pp. 186-211.

[31]Patricia E. Roy, "The British Columbia Electric Railway, 1897-1929: A British Company in British Columbia," Ph.D. thesis, University of

British Columbia, 1970, Chapters II and III.

[32]*Province*, 21 September and 4 May 1907.

[33]*Province*, 27 April 1907.

[34]*VDNA*, 6 January 1912; Twenty-seven residents of Hastings Townsite to Mayor and Council, 27 March 1911, VCA, CCC, Vol. 33.

[35]In 1905, the BCER began operating the railway as an electrified interurban line under a long term lease from the CPR.

[36]This account is based mainly on A.H. Lewis, *South Vancouver: Past and Present* (Vancouver, [1920]).

[37]"The Making of South Vancouver," *British Columbia Magazine*, Vol. 7 (June 1911), pp. 642-643.

[38]Lewis, *South Vancouver*, pp. 12-18; Bartholomew, *A Plan for the City of Vancouver*, p. 309.

[39]R.H. Sperling to Binder, 2 November 1906 and 23 March 1907, UBC, BCER Papers, Letters from the General Manager; Bartholomew, *Plan*, p. 297; "Potential Suburbs of Vancouver: Point Grey," *Man-to-Man Magazine*, Vol. VI (November 1910), pp. 968-969.

[40]Roy, "The British Columbia Electric Railway," pp. 97-103.

[41]The first banks to establish branches in Vancouver were the Bank of Montreal, the Bank of British Columbia, and the Bank of British North America. Between 1895 and 1900, the Imperial Bank of Canada, the Merchants Bank of Halifax (after 1901, the Royal Bank of Canada), Molson's Bank, and the Canadian Bank of Commerce opened Vancouver branches. In 1901, the Bank of Commerce bought out the Bank of British Columbia. The incorporators of the Bank of Vancouver included three prominent Vancouver businessmen: W.H. Malkin, R.P. McLennan, and H.T. Ceperley as well as three Victoria capitalists and a Cranbrook lawyer. On the Dominion Trust Building see Harold Kalman and John Roaf, *Exploring Vancouver 2* (Vancouver, 1978), p. 94.

[42]Henry Howard, *Canada: The Western Cities: Their Borrowings and Their Assets* (London, 1914), pp. 46-50; *VDNA*, 5 January 1912; Vancouver Board of Trade, *Annual Report*, 1912; Margaret W. Andrews, "Medical Services in Vancouver, 1886-1920: A Study in the Interplay of Attitudes, Medical Knowledge, and Administrative Structures," Ph.D. thesis, University of British Columbia, 1979, pp. 38-39.

[43]Testimony before British Columbia, Royal Commission on the Milk Supply in British Columbia, 1913. The death rate decreased steadily from 13 per 1,000 in 1907 to 9.5 per 1,000 in 1913. Both figures compare favourably with statistics from Toronto and Winnipeg. In Toronto, the rates were 15.5 and 14.0 respectively; in Winnipeg, 15.6 and 11.9. Vancouver Medical Health Officer to Health Committee, 2 February 1914, VCA, CCC, Vol. 52; Michael J. Piva, *The Condition of the Working Class in Toronto* (Ottawa, 1979), p. 114; Alan F.J. Artibise, *Winnipeg: A Social History of Urban Growth, 1874-1914* (Montreal, 1975), p. 224.

[44]*World* 5 January 1909; *Province*, 12 January 1912.

[45]L.D. Taylor to City Council, 25 September 1911, VCA, CCC, Vol. 35;

[46]*CMJ*, October 1912, pp. 388-89.

[46]*The Single Tax Review*, May-June 1911, p. 13; *World*, 14 February 1910; *Province*, 10 January 1910.

[47]*Province*, 9 November 1910; McDonald, "Business Leaders," pp. 285-305.

[48]See diagram, *Province*, 4 January 1911; *Province*, 14 January 1911; *VDNA*, 11 January 1911; *Province*, 31 December 1910.

[49]L.D. Taylor and William McQueen to Speaker and Members of the Legislative Assembly, 30 December 1911, Legislative Library, Clerk of the House Papers, 1912; J.G. Hay, City Solicitor, to City Clerk, 28 February 1912, VCA, CCC, Vol. 42; British Columbia, Royal Commission on Municipal Government, Evidence and Documents, 1912, p. 62.

[50]*VDNA*, 1 January 1911.

[51]*Province*, 9 November 1912.

[52]Unsigned, undated memorandum, PABC, Premier's Official Correspondence, 1911, File 137; *Province*, 20 February 1913. In early 1913, Point Grey faced a seccession movement as a number of Shaughnessy residents asked the legislature to create a separate district. Their grievances were resolved by provincial legislation ensuring that only single family homes and such necessary auxiliary buildings as stables and garages could be built in Shaughnessy.

[53]Diane L. Matters, "The Development of Public Welfare Institutions in Vancouver, 1910-1920," B.A. essay, University of Victoria, 1973, pp. 58-59; McKee, "The Vancouver Park System," pp. 45-47.

[54]Nancy Howell and Maxwell L. Howell, *Sports and Games in Canadian Life* (Toronto, 1969), *passim*; McDonald, "Business Leaders," p. 274.

[55]Colin Browne, *Motion Picture Production in British Columbia: 1898-1940* (Victoria, 1979), p. 10.

[56]Ross Johnson, "No Compromise—No Political Trading: The Marxian Socialist Tradition in British Columbia," Ph.D. thesis, University of British Columbia, 1975, p. 236; McDonald, "Business Leaders," pp. 254-255.

[57]Holdsworth, "House and Home in Vancouver," p. 199; Mrs. R.H. Tupper, *The History of the Georgian Club,* (Vancouver, 1961).

[58]Matters, "Development of Public Welfare Institutions," pp. 55-56; Star Rosenthal, "Union Maids: Organized Women Workers in Vancouver, 1900-1915," *BCS*, No. 41 (Spring 1979), pp. 36-55.

[59]T.F. Langlois to Premier McBride, 16 February 1904, PABC, Premier's Official Correspondence, Box 23, File 350. See McDonald, "Business Leaders," pp. 298-299 for an analysis of businessmen as moral reformers.

[60]A list of the houses may be found in VCA, CCC, Vol. 25; Chamberlain to Board of Police Commissioners, 8 February 1909, VCA, CCC, Vol. 27; *VDNA*, 28 August 1912.

[61]J.J. Banfield to Mr. Justice Gregory, 17 May 1911, VCA, CCC, Vol. 25.

[62]R.G. MacBeth, *Recent Canada West Letters* (Brantford, 1911), p. 43.

[63]*VDNA*, 12 January and 16 April 1912.

[64]John Taylor, "The Urban West: Public Welfare and a Theory of Urban Development," in A.R. McCormack and Ian MacPherson, eds., *Cities in the West* (Ottawa, 1975), pp. 286-313; Marilyn J. Harrison, "The Social Influences of the United Church of Canada in British Columbia, 1930-1948," M.A. thesis, University of British Columbia, 1975, p. 23; Diane L. Matters, "Public Welfare Vancouver Style, 1910-1920," *Journal of Canadian Studies*, Vol. 14 (Spring 1979), pp. 3-15; *Province*, 23 December 1907.

CHAPTER THREE

[1]A.J. Tomlin to R.B. Bennett, 23 October 1933, PAC, R.B. Bennett Papers, #353960-1

[2]*Province*, 28 August 1914.

[3]C.H. Daniels, *A Narrative History of the Terminal City Club* (Vancouver, 1936), p. 35.

[4]*CAR*, 1913, pp. 272-273; H. Cathcart, Deputy Minister of Lands, Memo for T.D. Pattullo, 21 August 1939, PABC, T.D. Pattullo Papers, Vol. 66; *CAR*, 1916, p. 772; Roy, "Railways, Politicians and the Development of the City of Vancouver," p. 231, n. 15; Bartholomew, *A Plan for the City of Vancouver*, p. 202. A brief sketch of the Reserve's history appears in *Province*, 17 April 1946.

[5]Jonathan Rogers, Presidential Address, Vancouver Board of Trade, 15 March 1916, Vancouver Board of Trade, Monthly Meeting Minute Book; Vancouver Board of Trade, Meeting, 12 October 1915, Minute Book. Both in VCA, Add. Mss. 300.

[6]W.E. Payne to W. McQueen, 20 April 1923, VCA, CCC, Vol. 72; Leah Stevens, "Rise of the Port of Vancouver, British Columbia," *Economic Geography*, Vol. 12 (January 1936), pp. 61-70.

[7]G.G. McGeer to Mayor and Aldermen, 2 November 1929, VCA, CCC, Vol. 127.

[8]L.D. Taylor to City Council, 21 March 1925, VCA, CCC, Vol. 114; Vancouver, *Industrial Survey*, 1927 p. 6; Vancouver Board of Trade, *Industrial Survey of Vancouver and Its Adjacent Territory* [Vancouver, 1929].

[9]This account is largely based on William Templeton, "Vancouver Airport and Seaplane Harbour — The First Sixteen Years," VCA, Typescript, 1947; William Templeton to Harbour, Utilities and Airport Committee, 6 January 1941, VCA CCC, Vol. 247.

[10]In June 1911, some three to four thousand members of the Building Trades Council struck to support the carpenters' demand for a closed shop. Some other unions donated to a strike fund and some businessmen, fearing violence, took steps to protect their property. A general strike, however, did not develop.

[11]Phillips, *No Power Greater*, pp. 68-70.

[12]The Metal Trades Council, for example, planned to strike to support BCER workers and before the BCER dispute was settled, the Trades and Labour Council considered a general strike to support the letter carriers.

[13]Phillips, *No Power Greater*, p. 72. See also David J. Bercuson, *Fools and Wise Men: The Rise and Fall of the One Big Union* (Toronto, 1978), p. 106; Ross McCormack, *Reformers, Rebels and Revolutionaries: The Western Canadian Radical Movement, 1899-1919* (Toronto, 1977), p. 146; Stuart Jamieson, *Times of Trouble: Labour Unrest and Industrial Conflict in Canada, 1900-66* (Ottawa, 1968), p. 166; Dorothy Steeves, *The Compassionate Rebel: Ernest E. Winch and His Times* (Vancouver, 1960), p. 38.

[14]The phrase is S.J. Crowe's, Liberal-Unionist M.P. for Vancouver-Burrard, *Province*, 2 August 1918.

[15]*Province*, 3 August 1918.

[16]*Province*, 6 August 1918; George Kidd to Manager of B.C. Telephone Company *et al.*, 29 November 1918, UBC, BCER Papers, Box 104. Royal North West Mounted Police agents regularly reported on Socialist meetings and military authorities planned to reactivate returned soldiers and ship such equipment as an armoured car and machine guns to Vancouver in case of trouble. The army insisted that on "no account" were soldiers to be used as strike breakers or as guards for strike breakers but would be present "to preserve law and order and protect life and property." Adjutant-General to General Officer Commanding, 24-29 May 1919, D. Hist., 322.09 (D806).

[17]*Province*, 29 May 1919; G.G. McGeer to John Oliver, 23 May 1919, PABC, Premier's Official Correspondence, 1915-20, File "McG."; G.O.C. to S.M.C. (Ottawa), 5 June 1919, D. Hist., 322.09 (D806) and W.G. Murrin to R. Bartlett, 7 July 1919, UBC, BCER Papers, Letters from the General Manager; *Report of the Activities of the Vancouver Citizen's League* (Vancouver, 1919), p.12.

[18]*Report of the Activities of the Vancouver Citizen's League*, p. 6; Bercuson, *Fools and Wise Men*, pp. 130-131; Patricia E. Roy, "Regulating the British Columbia Electric Railway: The First Public Utilities Commission in British Columbia," *BCS*, No. 11 (Fall 1970), pp. 6-9; R.P. Clark to G.O.C., 24 June 1919, D. Hist., 322.09 (D806).

[19]Phillips, *No Power Greater*, pp. 83-93; City of Vancouver, *Industrial Survey*, p. 49.

[20]*Province*, 28 May and 15 June 1935.

[21]This account of the strike is drawn mainly from R.C. McCandless, "Vancouver's 'Red Menace' of 1935: The Waterfront Situation," *BCS*, No. 22 (Summer 1974), pp. 56-70 and from Phillips, *No Power Greater*, pp. 103-104. G.G. McGeer, Speech on CKWX, 14 June 1935, copy in VCA, Mayor's Correspondence, Vol. 10.

[22]*VDNA*, 20 November 1914; J.H. McVety to J.D. McNiven, 6 December 1929, PABC, Premier's Official Correspondence; H.W. Cooper, Memo, 19 January 1931, VCA, CCC, Vol. 155.

[23]Statistics prepared by Leonard D. Marsh, Director of Social Research at McGill University, quoted in *Province*, 25 March 1935.

[24]*Province*, 5 and 6 December 1929; Alderman W.C. Atherton to Relief and Employment Committee, 5 December 1929, VCA, CCC, Vol. 136.

[25]J.W. Cooper to Alderman W.C. Atherton, 3 September 1931, VCA, CCC, Vol. 155; *Province*, 4 March 1932; Brig. J. Sutherland Brown to Secretary, Department of National Defence, 2 May 1932, PAC, DND Records, Vol. 2576; Statement of Mayor L.D. Taylor, 19 December 1932, VCA, Mayor's Correspondence, Vol. 8; C.M. Stewart, Unemployed Block Council #1, South Fraser District to Mayor and Aldermen, 20 December 1932, VCA, CCC, Vol. 168. For details of the Relief Camp Workers' Union and its activities see Ronald Liversedge, *Recollections of the On to Ottawa Trek*, (Toronto, 1973).

[26]Liversedge, *Recollections*, p. 62.

[27]*Province*, 24 and 29 April 1935; G.G. McGeer to Attorney General Gordon Sloan, 10 May 1935, VCA, Mayor's Correspondence, Vol. 13.

[28]Steve Brodie, *Bloody Sunday* (Vancouver, 1974); *Province*, 1 June 1938; W.L.M. King, "Diary," 17 June 1938, PAC, King Papers.

[29]Proceedings of Conference Between the Honorable T.D. Pattullo and a Delegation from the Canadian Commonwealth Federation [*sic*], 20 June 1938, PABC, Add. Mss. 3, Vol. 73.

[30]See Tables IV, VII, and X in Norbert MacDonald, "Population Growth and Change in Seattle and Vancouver, 1880-1960," *Pacific Historical Review*, Vol. 39 (August 1970), pp. 297-321. In 1911, 44.3 per cent of the Canadian-born population had been born in the four western provinces; in 1941, that figure was 79.5 per cent.

[31]Freda Walhouse, "The Influence of Minority Ethnic Groups on the Cultural Geography of Vancouver," M.A. thesis, University of British Columbia, 1961; *Sun*, 18 September 1970, magazine; VDNA, 11 July 1915 quoted in Matters, "The Development of Public Welfare Institutions in Vancouver, 1910-1920," p. 17; VDNA, 7 February 1912.

[32]See Patricia E. Roy, "Protecting Their Pocketbooks and Preserving Their Race: White Merchants and Oriental Competition," in A.R. McCormack and Ian MacPherson, eds., *Cities in the West* (Ottawa, 1975), pp. 116-138.

[33]Quoted in Harold Kalman, *Exploring Vancouver 2* (Vancouver, 1978), p.117.

[34]Vancouver Town Planning Commission, *Preliminary Report Upon Economic Background and Population* (Vancouver, 1944), pp. 22-29; *Industrial Survey*, 1929, p. 37; Dominion Bureau of Statistics, Seventh Census of Canada, 1931, Bulletin No. XL (Ottawa, 1934), p. 2.

[35]*Province*, 6 October 1928 and 21 February 1905; Thomas Adams, "Town and Rural Planning in British Columbia," *CMJ*, Vol. XV (January 1919), pp. 24-26.

[36]VDNA, 23 February 1912. For a discussion of earlier efforts to beautify Vancouver see William C. McKee, "The Vancouver Parks Board."

[37]This paragraph is based mainly on J.A. Walker, "Town Planning in Vancouver," *The Municipal Review of Canada*, June 1935, pp. 5-10.

[38]W. McQueen to J.D. Williams, City Solicitor, 31 July 1926, VCA, Vancouver Town Planning Commission Records, Vol. 5; W.E. Bland to Mayor L.D. Taylor, 29 November 1928, VCA, CCC, Vol. 124; Walter Van Nus, "Towards the City Efficient: The Theory and Practice of Zoning, 1919-1939," in Alan F.J. Artibise and Gilbert A. Stelter, eds., *The Usable Urban Past* (Toronto, 1979), p. 229; John Weaver, "The Property Industry and Land Use Controls: The Vancouver Experience, 1910-1945," *Plan Canada*, Vol. 19 (September-December 1979), pp. 211-225.

[39]Town Planning Commission, *Preliminary Report*, p. 9; V.S. Pendakur, *Cities, Citizens and Freeways* (Vancouver, 1972), pp. 4-5.

[40]*Province*, 1 November 1936; G.H. Dorrell to D.E. McTaggart, Corporation Counsel, [January 1939], VCA, Town Planning Commssion Records, Vol. 2.

[41]*Province*, 5 November 1926 and 26 November 1935; Vancouver Town Planning Commission, Report to City Council, Vancouver, B.C. on the Zoning Survey of Ward One, 31 December 1934, VCA, CCC, Vol. 193. The city replaced site area restrictions with a minimum floor area of 400 square feet per building and allowed two storey buildings on the 33 foot lots that were becoming common as the original 66 foot lots were subdivided.

[42]VCA clipping, 16 June 1934.

[43]Walter G. Hardwick, *Vancouver* (Don Mills, 1974), p. 120.

[44]*Province*, 22 June 1927; *Sun*, 18 February 1928.

[45]The other choices, in order, were: Central School, the old City Hall site at Pender and Main, and a proposed civic centre near the north end of the Burrard Street bridge.

[46]*Province*, 20 December 1934 and 5 June 1935. Ronald Kenvyn claims that the CPR, which had extensive holdings of vacant residential land south of False Creek, offered to donate sufficient park land to replace Strathcona Park if the city hall were built on that site and that this tippped the balance in favour of Strathcona Park, *Province*, 11 March 1939.

[47]*Province*, 16 April 1918; Vancouver, Committee on Taxation, Proceedings, 19 November 1920, copy in VCA, Mayor's Correspondence, Vol. 2; City of Vancouver, Report of Joint Committee on Broadening of Municipal Taxation, February 1929, VCA, CCC, Vol. 82.

[48]William McQueen to R.B. Bennett, 31 December 1930, VCA, CCC, Vol. 136; H.W. Cooper, Memo, 19 January 1931, VCA, CCC, Vol. 155. Statistics prepared by Leonard D. Marsh, Director of Social Research, McGill University, quoted in *Province*, 25 March 1935.

[49]A.J. Pilkington, City Treasurer, to Mayor and Council, 27 November 1933, VCA, CCC, Vol. 178; H.F. Hines, Secretary, Vancouver School Board, to Mayor and Council, 25 April 1933, VCA, CCC, Vol.

171; C.W. Thompson, Chief, Vancouver Fire Department, to Fire and Light Committee, 8 May 1933, VCA, CCC, Vol. 177.

[50]G.G. McGeer, *The Conquest of Poverty* (Gardenvale, P.Q., [1935]), pp. 9 and 69; *Province*, 30 January 1935.

[51]*Province*, 6 December 1934; T.C. Bradshaw, *Survey of Financial Conditions*, City of Vancouver, 7 March 1935; C.E. Tisdall *et al.*, *Taxation and Financial Survey of the City of Vancouver*, May 1, 1935; Province, 22 February 1935. Talk of a city manager was not new. In 1923, the Associated Property Owners suggested it as a means of achieving economy and efficiency. Several years later, when the provincial government passed enabling legislation, Vancouver did not use it to appoint a manager because Comptroller A.J. Pilkington was acting as city manager in all but name, George C. Cross, "Democratic Government for Greater Vancouver in the Making," *Municipal News of British Columbia*, April 1926, p. 296. A series of scandals over mismanagement of city funds revived interest in a city manager in 1937, but not until 1974 was a city manager appointed.

[52]T.D. Pattullo to Charles Jones, City Clerk, 14 January 1935, VCA, Mayor's Correspondence, Vol. 10. McGeer had suggested Vancouver would have a deficit of $5,331,594 for 1935; the city budget, introduced in April, predicted a deficit of $845,000; the "Brain Trust" committee, reporting in May, estimated the 1935 deficit at $3,856,745. *Province*, 11 April and 2 May 1935.

[53]Vancouver Federated Ratepayers, 15 May 1935, PABC, T.D. Pattullo Papers, Vol. 55; *Province*, 16 May 1935. See list of subscribers in VCA, Mayor's Correspondence, Vol. 10; McGeer, *The Conquest of Poverty*, p. 3. Charles Woodward to McGeer, 13 June 1935 and McGeer to Pattullo, 13 July 1935, VCA, Mayor's Correspondence, Vol. 10.

[54]Statement, 4 December 1936, VCA, Mayor's Correspondence, Vol. 15; G.C. Miller to Mayor, 4 January 1937, VCA, Mayor's Correspondence, Vol. 15. To reduce the number of tax sale lots, the city allowed delinquent homeowners to clear boulevards and ditches at a rate of 50 cents per hour to be applied to their taxes.

[55]*Province*, 22 February 1935; William McAdam to John Oliver, 20 October 1921, PABC, T.D. Pattullo Papers, Vol. 13; Samuel Fawcett to John Oliver, 18 October 1926, PABC, Pattullo Papers, Vol. 22; W.C. Woodward to John Oliver [25 June 1925] and Oliver to Woodward, 14 August 1935, PABC, Pattullo Papers, Vol. 21. On the eve of calling the 1928 election, Premier J.D. McLean appointed two Vancouver lawyers, Dugald Donaghy and Ian Mackenzie, to his cabinet.

[56]See Ian Parker, "The Provincial Party," *BCS*, No. 8 (Winter 1970-71), pp. 17-28 and "Simon Fraser Tolmie: The Last Conservative Premier of British Columbia," *BCS*, No. 11 (Fall 1971), pp. 21-36.

[57]British Columbia, Statutes, 4 Geo V, c 96, "An Act Relating to Shaughnessy Heights"; "Public Enquiry re Proposed Severance of Shaughnessy Heights, 1914," PABC, Royal Commissions; G. Kidd to M. Urwin, 23 February 1915, UBC, BCER Papers, Letters from the General Manager; Jack Loutet, "Municipal Affairs in British Columbia," *CMJ*, December 1915, p. 436; S.T. Frost, "Municipal Politics Reviewed by Reporter," *Province*, 31 January 1929; Corporation of South Vancouver, Annual Report, 1921, p. 31; H. Bartholomew, *A Plan for Greater Vancouver*, pp. 309-310; F.J. Gillespie to John Hart, 15 May 1919, Legislative Library, Clerk of the House Papers, 1920.

[58]T.D. Pattullo to Mayor W.R. Owen, 15 February 1924, VCA, Mayor's Correspondence, Vol. 3; Louis P. Cain, "Water and Sanitation Services in Vancouver: An Historical Perspective," *BCS*, No. 30 (Summer 1976), pp. 39-40; *Province*, 11 November 1926; J.W. McIntosh, Medical Health Officer, to Mayor and Council, 1936 Annual Report, VCA, CCC, Vol. 199.

[59]This account draws heavily on D.C. Corbett and E.R. Toren, "A Survey of Metropolitan Governments: A Report to the Metropolitan Joint Committee" (Vancouver, 1958), pp. 24-28.

[60]Mayor's Speech, 6 January 1926, VCA, CCC, Vol. 110.

[61]*Province*, 26 October 1926, 11 June 1927; *Sun*, 26 October 1926. The plebiscite was really a public opinion poll. The vote was:

	Amalgamation	County Council	Status Quo
Vancouver	4,162	689	2,339
Point Grey	1,670	613	856
South Vancouver	2,464	114	243

Paton circulated his ideas by mailing a pamphlet, S.E. Beckett, *Report to the Council of the Municipality of Point Grey, British Columbia on Closer Union of Point Grey with Government Authorities over Greater Vancouver* (Point Grey, 1926). In the final Point Grey vote, 2,030 favoured amalgamation; 758 opposed it.

[62]*Province*, 23 November 1928.

[63]W. McQueen to Mayor and Council, 9 January 1920, VCA, CCC, Vol. 78; McQueen to Mayor and Council, 18 June 1923, VCA, CCC, Vol. 92; *Sun*, 17 January 1921.

[64]*Province*, 4 and 12 December 1935; *Sun*, 9 December 1935; F. Howlett to Mayor and Council, 16 December 1935, VCA, CCC, Vol. 199.

[65]A.M. Anderson, one of the successful CCF candidates, resigned shortly after the election because his eligibility for office was questioned. *Province*, 14 December 1936.

[66]*The Vancouver Poetry Society, 1916-1946: A Book of Days* (Toronto, 1946). On music see Dorothy Salisbury, "Music in Vancouver," *Canadian Library Association Bulletin*, Vol. 13 (Fall 1957), pp. 161-164.

[67]W.H. Malkin to Mayor and Aldermen, 22 November 1940, VCA, CCC, Vol. 246; B.C. Art League, Minute Book, *passim*, VCA, Add. Mss.

168.

[68]G.G. McGeer to John Oliver, 15 September 1926, PABC, T.D. Pattullo Papers, Vol. 22; *Province*, 24 November 1926; R.S. Lennie to Mayor and Council, 23 August 1928, VCA, Mayor's Correspondence, Vol. 4; *Province*, 2 October 1928; L.D. Taylor's "Open Letter to the Voters of Vancouver, October 1928," VCA, W.H. Malkin Papers.

[69]*Province*, 11 December 1930; G.G. McGeer, Speech at Hotel Vancouver, 21 November 1934, PABC, McGeer Papers, Vol. 7.

[70]McGeer to Clergy of Vancouver, 6 January 1935, VCA, Mayor's Correspondence, Vol. 12; T.G. McLelan to McGeer, 18 February 1935, *ibid.*

[71]*Province*, 9 January 1935; Memorandum re Certain Vice Conditions in the City of Vancouver by Police Magistrate H.S. Wood, Col. W.W. Foster, and Oscar Orr, City Prosecutor, 5 September 1935, VCA, Mayor's Correspondence, Vol. 12; A.S. Rae, Det-Sgt. i/c Morality Detail to W.W. Foster, 9 May 1939 and W. R. Bone, Administrator, City of Vancouver, Social Service Department to Alderman H.L. Corey, 20 January 1939, VCA, Mayor's Correspondence, Vol. 36.

[72]Charles W. Thompson, *Life is a Jest: The Testimony of a Wanderer* (London, 1924), p. 33.

CHAPTER FOUR

[1]Bruce Hutchison, *The Unknown Country: Canada and Her People* (Toronto, 1942), p. 323.

[2]Humphrey Carver, *Compassionate Landscape* (Toronto, 1975), p. 169.

[3]National Harbours Board, Port of Vancouver, *Impact: The Port of Vancouver and Its Impact on the Economy of the Greater Vancouver Region* (Vancouver, 1976); Captain B.D.L. Johnson, Port Manager, *Province*, 31 May 1966.

[4]Real Estate Board of Greater Vancouver, *Real Estate Trends in Metropolitan Vancouver* (Vancouver, 1978).

[5]The previous two paragraphs are largely based on C.N. Forward, "The Functional Characteristics of the Geographic Port of Vancouver," in L.J. Evenden, ed., *Vancouver: Western Metropolis*, pp. 57-77.

[6]*Province*, 3 March 1949; *Sun*, 6 December 1969.

[7]Vancouver Board of Trade, *Report on Northern British Columbia, Resource Development*, 1965, p. iv.

[8]Vancouver Stock Exchange, Minute Book, 27 January 1948, PABC, Add. Mss. 18.

[9]*Province*, 25 March 1978.

[10]K.G. Denike, "Financial Metropolis of the West," in Evenden, *Vancouver*, p. 47.

[11]Roger Leslie, "History of Industrial Development in Vancouver," in Chuck Davis, ed., *The Vancouver Book* (North Vancouver, 1976), p.343.

[12]*Province*, 25 March 1971; Victoria *Times*, 30 March 1977. The Exchange also sought new listings of outside firms. Some members toured several Pacific nations in 1973.

[13]Roger Hayter, "Forestry in British Columbia: A Resource Base of Vancouver's Dominance," in Evenden, *Vancouver*, p. 108.

[14]Keith Bradbury, "The Establishment," *Sun*, 5 and 6 December 1970.

[15]P.D. McGovern, "Industrial Development in the Vancouver Area," *Economic Geography*, Vol. 37 (1961), p. 200.

[16]Stuart Jamieson, "Regional Factors in Industrial Conflict: The Case of British Columbia," *Canadian Journal of Economics and Political Science*, Vol. 28 (1962), p. 412.

[17]*Port Vancouver News*, Vol. 1 (July 1976); Len Tennant, *Industry in Vancouver: A Report for Discussion* (Vancouver: 1977), p. 53.

[18]Vancouver Board of Trade, Special Minute Book, 18 September 1939, VCA, Add. Mss. 300.

[19]J.C. Ingram, "Industrial Development in British Columbia: Past Present and Future," *The Canadian Mining and Metallurgical Bulletin*, Vol. 51 (September 1958), p. 582.

[20]Statement of Policy and Function of the Industrial Development Commision of the City of Vancouver, [c. August 1949], VCA, RG9A1, Vol. 14.

[21]G.P.T. Steed, "Intrametropolitan Manufacturing: Spatial Distribution and Locational Dynamics in Greater Vancouver," *Canadian Geographer*, Vol. XVII (1973), p. 237.

[22]Walter G. Hardwick, "The Persistence of Vancouver as the Focus for Wood Processing in Coastal British Columbia," *Canadian Geographer*, Vol. IX (1965), pp. 92-96.

[23]Walter G. Hardwick, *Vancouver* (Don Mills, 1974), pp. 96-97; Sue Baptie, comp., *First Growth: The Story of British Columbia Forest Products Limited* (Vancouver, 1975), p. 152.

[24]*Sun*, 18 October 1967.

[25]*Sun*, 15 November 1969. A useful study of the debate over False Creek is F.J. Elligott, "The Planning Decision Making Process of Vancouver's False Creek: A Case Study, 1918-1974," M.A. thesis, University of British Columbia, 1977.

[26]Michele Lioy, *Social Trends in Greater Vancouver: A Study of a North American Metropolis* (Vancouver, 1975), pp. 15, 113; Vancouver School Board, *Annual Report 1971-2*, p. 22.

[27]Lioy, *Social Trends*, pp. 29-32; Marlene Hier, "Ethnicity and Residential Location," M.A. thesis, University of British Columbia, 1973; K.F. Grant, "Food Habits and Food Shopping Patterns of Greek Immigrants in Vancouver," in J.V. Minghi, ed., *Peoples of the Living Land* (Vancouver: 1972), pp. 125-144; *A Chronicle of the Hellenic Community of Vancouver* (Vancouver, [1977]); Donald Gale, "The Impact of Italians on Retail Functions and Facades in Vancouver, 1921-1961," in Minghi, *Peoples*, pp. 107-124.

[28]*Special Committee on Orientals* (Ottawa, 1941), pp. 8-9; *Sun*, 4

February 1941; Vancouver *News-Herald,* 4 February 1941.

[29]British Columbia Security Commission, *Removal of Japanese from Protected Areas,* March 4, 1942 to October 31, 1942, pp. 6-7; *Report of Advisory Committee on Japanese Property in Greater Vancouver* (copy in VCA).

[30]Vancouver School Board, *Annual Report,* 1978, p. 26; *Sun,* 6 and 10 March 1975; Michael G. Campbell, "The Sikhs of Vancouver: A Case Study in Minority-Host Relations," M.A. thesis, University of British Columbia, 1977, pp. 66-69; *Province,* 28 May 1975.

[31]Peter M. George, *The Housing Issue* ([Vancouver], 1973), p. 11.

[32]F.E. Buck *et al.* to Mayor and Council, 15 November 1937, VCA, CCC, Vol. 215; W.R. Bone to Alderman G.C. Miller, 31 December 1941, VCA, CCC, Vol. 247.

[33]*Province,* 16 November 1948.

[34]Hardwick, *Vancouver,* p. 127; *Sun,* 4 November 1970; Barbara Ann Weightman, "The Musqueam Reserve: A Case Study of the Indian Social Milieu in an Urban Environment," Ph.D. thesis, University of Washington, 1972, pp. 33-38.

[35]G.F. Fountain, "Zoning Administration in Canada," *Plan Canada,* Vol. 2 (1961), p. 119. This paragraph draws extensively on George Gray, Vincent Keddie, and Josephine Kwan, "Patterns of Neighbourhood Change — The West End of Vancouver," University of British Columbia, Department of Anthropology and Sociology, Report to the Ministry of State for Urban Affairs, 1976.

[36]In the early 1970s, Kitsilano's residential section underwent extensive change as private developers demolished working class houses that had been converted into low rental suites and replaced them with more expensive apartments and condominiums. See Peter W. Stobie, "Private Inner City Redevelopment in Vancouver: A Case Study of Kitsilano," M.A. thesis, University of British Columbia, 1979.

[37]University of British Columbia, Demonstration Housing Survey, Interim Report, 30 July 1947, Copy in VCA, RG9A1, Vol. 13.

[38]"A Summary of the Report on the Slum Clearance and Urban Rehabilitation Project, 'Strathcona Area,' Vancouver," [c. April 1950]. Copy in VCA, RG9A1, Vol. 13.

[39]S.T. Wong, "Urban Redevelopment and Rehabilitation in the Strathcona Area: A Case Study of an East Vancouver Community," in Evenden, *Vancouver,* p. 267. See also James Lowden, "A Case Study of Community Rehabilitation: The Strathcona Rehabilitation Project," *Plan Canada,* Vol. 13 (1973), pp. 136-140.

[40]*Province,* 24 November 1947.

[41]*Province,* 11 December 1947 and 20 November 1946. For an outline of the chlorination controversy see James Morton, *Capilano: The Story of a River* (Toronto, 1970), Chapter VI.

[42]See Hardwick, *Vancouver,* pp. 60-61; Robert W. Collier, *Contemporary Cathedrals: Large-Scale Developments in Canadian Cities* (Montreal,

1974), p. 48; Donald Gutstein, *Vancouver Ltd.* (Toronto, 1975), pp. 52-54; *Sun,* 25 March 1978.

[43]R. Thompson, City Clerk, to Mrs. W.T. Lane, President, Community Arts Council, 22 March 1965, VCA, Add. Mss. 301, Vol. 12; Vancouver Board of Trade, Report on Proposals for Blocks 42 and 52, 18 May 1966, VCA, Add. Mss. 301, Vol. 18; Hardwick, *Vancouver,* p. 61.

[44]Robert W. Collier, "Downtown: Metropolitan Focus," in Evenden, *Vancouver,* p. 163; Harold Kalman, *Exploring Vancouver 2* (Vancouver, 1978), p. 81; Toronto *Globe,* 24 March 1979.

[45]This account is largely based on Collier, *Contemporary Cathedrals,* pp. 48-67. In 1971, voters refused to buy the whole site but in 1973 approved the purchase of ten acres of it. Legal technicalities later forced the city to buy the whole 13.4 acres. In 1976, Council decided to devote the entire site for public use and to abandon any plans to lease it to developers (*Sun,* 22 September 1976).

[46]City of Vancouver Planning Department, *Downtown East Side* (Vancouver, 1965), p. 21; George, *The Housing Issue,* p. 7.

[47]Preliminary Report of the Townsite Committee on Project 200, 11 July 1966. Copy in VCA, Add. Mss. 301, Vol. 18.

[48]Collier, *Contemporary Cathedrals,* p. 49; V.S. Pendakur, *Cities, Citizens, and Freeways* (Vancouver, 1972), pp. 47, 145ff.

[49]*Sun,* 12 December 1946 and 12 December 1957.

[50]*Province,* 8 October 1948.

[51]Mayoralty candidates have been elected biennially since 1927. Each year until 1966 half the aldermen and members of the School Board and Park Board were elected for a two year term. Beginning in 1966, all positions were contested biennially.

[52]*Sun,* 3 and 10 December 1970.

[53]*Sun,* 4 December 1970 and 18 November 1976. A Vancouver *Province* survey of 500 voters in 1955, a non-mayoralty year, revealed that eighty-three per cent had no interest in the civic election (13 December 1955). In 1970, a *Sun* survey found that one-third of Vancouver residents polled could not name a single alderman (9 November 1970). The lowest turnout was in 1945, a non-mayoralty year when twenty-three per cent voted; the highest, in 1946, when fifty-one per cent voted, City of Vancouver, *Municipal Year Book,* 1979, p. 22.

[54]On at least one occasion, the NPA also absorbed a rival "party" when Civic Action Association merged with it. For official purposes, the NPA became known as the Civic Non-Partisan Association. Fern Miller, "Vancouver Civic Political Parties: Developing a Model of Party-system Change and Stabilization," *BCS,* No. 25 (Spring 1975), p. 16, n. 20.

[55]*Sun,* 4 December 1954, 3 December 1958, and 6 December 1956; *Province,* 6 December 1958.

[56]Joan Anderson, "Vancouver: Back to the Sixties," *City Magazine,* Vol. 4 (April 1979), pp. 8-9.

[57]See Robert Easton and Paul Tennant, "Vancouver Civic Party Leadership: Backgrounds, Attitudes, and Non-civic Party Affiliations," *BCS*, No. 2 (Summer 1969), pp. 19-29.

[58]Pendakur, *Cities*, p. 76; *Province*, 18 November 1974; Gutstein, *Vancouver Ltd.*, pp. 84-87. While in "opposition," TEAM Councillors, with the help of Harry Rankin and some NPA members, modified Project 200 and Marathon Realty's plan to build a large shopping centre adjacent to its west side Arbutus Village residential subdivision and killed the Four Seasons Project.

[59]*Sun*, 25 October 1973; Vancouver *Express*, 20 November 1978.

[60]Mayor's Inaugural Address, 3 January 1973, copy in VCA, Rebecca Watson Papers; Walter G. Hardwick and David F. Hardwick, "Civic Government: Corporate, Consultative or Participatory?" in David Lay, ed., *Community Participation and the Spatial Order of the City* (Vancouver, 1974), p. 91.

[61]This account is based largely on Maurice Egan, "Social Planning in Vancouver," *Plan Canada*, Vol. 17 (June 1977), pp. 118-126. See also Hardwick, *Vancouver, passim*.

[62]In the 1968 civic election, amalgamation with Burnaby was an issue. The TEAM candidate, Alan Emmott, resigned as mayor of Burnaby to run in Vancouver. His defeat effectively ended talk of amalgamation (*Sun*, 24 June 1969).

[63]GVRD Planning Department, *The Livable Region 1976/1986: Proposals to Manage the Growth of Greater Vancouver* (Vancouver, 1975); Randy Glover, "The Repercussions of Non-Growth," *Sun*, 12 April 1978; Vancouver *Express*, 17 November 1978.

[64]British Columbia, *Report of the Commission of Inquiry into Redefinition of Electoral Districts* (Victoria, 1966), p. 16. See also British Columbia, *Report of the Commission of Inquiry into Redefinition of Electoral Districts under the Public Inquiries Act, British Columbia* (Victoria, 1975); British Columbia, Royal Commission on Electoral Reform, 1978, *Interim Report on Redefinition of Electoral Districts* (Victoria, 1978).

[65]*Province*, 25 January, 1 March and 20 March 1947, and 29 February 1956.

[66]*Province*, 30 June 1979.

[67]British Columbia, Royal Commission, *Report on Gastown Inquiry by Thomas A. Dohm*, October 1971.

[68]In addition to the newspapers of the day see Jack Sullivan, *The Grey Cup Story* (Toronto, 1974), pp. 167-168.

[69]For details see Denny Boyd, *The Vancouver Canucks Story* (Toronto, 1973).

[70]*Province*, 30 June 1979.

[71]Charles Lillard, "Daylight in the Swamp: A Guide to the West Coast Renaissance," *Malahat Review*, No. 45 (January 1978), p. 321.

[72]Paul Korn and Dorian de Wolf, "The Recording Industry," in Davis, *The Vancouver Book*, p. 406.

[73]Neal Harlow, "Climate for the Arts," *Vancouver* (Vancouver, 1957), p. 3.

A Note on Sources and Suggestions for Further Reading

Vancouver's history has been well preserved. The obstreperousness of the legendary Major J.S. Matthews, City Archivist (1933-70), made Vancouver aware of the importance of its past long before heritage conservation was fashionable and before the city had forgotten or destroyed much of her documentary history. Whether "The Major" would approve of the hospitable and highly professional archivists who work in the building that bears his name is a moot point. From the researchers' point of view the City of Vancouver Archives has only two problems: such an abundance of well-catalogued resources that it is impossible for any one historian to examine them all and a superb but distracting view of the English Bay beach and the entrance to False Creek. That view, however, does remind the historian that Vancouver has a lively present as well as an exciting past. The Archives' many private manuscript collections are readily accessible through published inventories and thorough finding aids. The heart of the holdings, however, are the official city records, especially the City Clerk's Correspondence and the Mayor's Papers. The former is particularly valuable for the early years for practically every piece of business conducted by the city crossed the Clerk's desk. The Mayor's Papers do not become extensive until the 1930s. City records are generally available through to the mid-1950s.

A second important primary source are the newspapers. Consulting the Vancouver papers for specific topics is relatively easy because the Legislative Library has produced a detailed index to the major Vancouver and Victoria newspapers from 1900 to date. Microfilm copies of the index were made available to the libraries of the three provincial universities a few years ago, but the index is ideally used in Victoria since the Legislative Library is currently re-indexing some earlier years when coverage was spotty and is keeping the index up to date. The Provincial Archives of British Columbia has a similar index for pre-1900 newspapers.

An extensive bibliography of articles, books, and theses relating to Vancouver may be found in A.F.J. Artibise, *Western Canada Since 1870: A Select Bibliography* (Vancouver, 1978), pp. 236-246. The quarterly multidisciplinary journal, *BC Studies* should also be examined. It publishes not only articles on Vancouver but also includes a very extensive bibliography of recent books and articles on British Columbia prepared by Frances Woodward as well as her occasional bibliographies of recent theses relating to British Columbia. The Vancouver

Historical Society's revival of its quarterly, *Vancouver History* (P.O. Box 3071, Vancouver, B.C. V6B 3X6) promises to make available an interesting variety of documents and short articles relating to aspects of city history. The bibliographic notes below are designed to supplement the Artibise volume and to add to this volume's footnotes by drawing attention to recent works and pointing out others that are especially helpful.

Given the wealth of documentation for Vancouver's history it is disappointing that few studies have been made of it. The two general histories, Eric Nicol, *Vancouver* (Toronto, 1970) and Alan Morley, *Vancouver: Milltown to Metropolis* (Vancouver, 1961) are largely anecdotal. In *The Vancouver Book* (Vancouver, 1976) Chuck Davis has edited a rich and varied almanac of Vancouver that includes many short historical sketches of parts of the city's history.

Vancouver is a photogenic city and published collections of photographs abound. However many such as Barry Broadfoot, *et al.*, *The City of Vancouver* (North Vancouver, 1976) reveal more about the fine quality of photography than they do about the city. The city itself has two excellent historical photographic collections. The extensive holdings of the City Archives are second only to those of the Historical Photographs section of the Vancouver Public Library. Good use has been made of these photographs in several collections the best of which is Ann Kloppenborg, *et al.*, *Vancouver's First Century: A City Album 1860-1960* (Vancouver, 1977), a book that grew out of a series of articles published in the *Urban Reader*, a bi-monthly magazine published by the city's Social Planning Department. Norbert MacDonald has also prepared a volume of slides and commentary on Vancouver to 1920 in Canada's Visual History published by the National Film Board and the National Museum of Man, National Museums of Canada.

MacDonald has also published the best scholarly work on Vancouver in the form of several articles written as part of a long-term project comparing the histories of Vancouver and Seattle. In addition to the articles on the Klondike and Population Growth mentioned in the footnotes, the reader should consult two of his articles published in *BC Studies*: "The Canadian Pacific Railway and Vancouver's Development to 1900," No. 35 (Autumn 1977), pp.3-35 and "A Critical Growth Cycle for Vancouver, 1900-1914," No. 17 (Spring 1973), pp. 26-42. The best history thesis on Vancouver is R.A.J. McDonald, "Business Leaders in Early Vancouver, 1886-1914," Ph.D. thesis, University of British Columbia, 1977. As well as analysing Vancouver's business elite, this thesis well describes the economic milieu in which they worked. Two University of British Columbia geographers cover some of the same ground in their theses: John Bottomley, "Ideology, Planning and the Landscape: The Business Community, Urban Reform and the Establishment of Town Planning in Vancouver, British Columbia," Ph.D. thesis, 1977 and Angus E. Robertson, "The Pursuit of Power, and

Privacy: A Study of Vancouver's West End Elite, 1886-1914," M.A. thesis, 1977.

SPECIFIC THEMES

Early Years

The *British Columbia Historical Quarterly (1937-1958)* included many scholarly articles on Burrard Inlet especially by F.W. Howay. Most are listed in the footnotes to the Introduction to this volume. A useful overview is Helen Boutilier's "Vancouver's Earliest Days," Vol. 10 (April 1946), pp. 151-170.

Economic Growth

The contemporary scene is much better served than the historical. Nevertheless, *Vancouver: Western Metropolis*, a collection of essays by geographers edited by L.J. Evenden (Victoria, 1978) includes some historical material, notably L.D. McCann's essay on Vancouver's emergence as a regional metropolis, 1886-1914 while others such as C.N. Forward's study of the port of Vancouver include historical information. On economic rivalries within British Columbia before 1914, R. Cole Harris's, "Locating the University of British Columbia", *BC Studies*, No. 32 (Winter 1976-77), pp. 106-125 reveals much about interurban rivalries within the province. The broad provincial context in which Vancouver existed is best set out in Margaret A. Ormsby, *British Columbia: A History* (Toronto, 1958).

On labour, Paul Phillips, *No Power Greater: A Century of Labour in British Columbia* (Vancouver, 1967) provides a useful overview. However, since it was written over a decade ago, archival holdings of labour records have greatly increased and the approach of labour historians has shifted. The Special Collections Division of the University of British Columbia Library has been particularly active in collecting labour material, and more extensive research may well revise some of Phillips' observations; nevertheless, his book remains a good introduction to the sometimes turbulent history of labour in the province.

Population Growth and Ethnic Relationships

Apart from Norbert MacDonald's fine article comparing population growth in Vancouver and Seattle, there are few historical studies on population growth. In the course of outlining future plans, the Planning Department of the Greater Vancouver Regional District has included historical data in some of its publications but its primary interest is naturally the future, not the past. For the 1960s and 1970s, Michele Lioy's compendium, *Social Trends in Greater Vancouver: A Study of a North American Metropolis* (Vancouver, 1975) is invaluable.

Ethnic groups have been moderately well served by historians.

Although *Strangers Entertained: A History of the Ethnic Groups of British Columbia*, ed. John Norris (Vancouver, 1971) deals with the entire province, it is strongest on Vancouver. Because they have been the most controversial ethnic group, the greatest amount of literature concerns Asians, especially the Japanese. Ken Adachi's *The Enemy That Never Was* (Toronto, 1976) is a detailed and eminently readable history of the Japanese community in Canada, which, prior to 1942, was concentrated in greater Vancouver. For historical purposes, C.H. Young, H.R.Y. Reid, and W.A. Carrothers, *The Japanese-Canadians* (Toronto, 1938) offers good insight into the Japanese community in the 1930s and includes a chapter on the Chinese. The publication of a history of the Chinese in Canada by a multi-disciplinary team based at the University of British Columbia should remedy a serious deficiency in ethnic historiography. Of the other histories of ethnic groups, the best is probably Irene Howard, *Vancouver's Svenskar: A History of the Swedish Community in Vancouver* (Vancouver, 1970). Howard's title, however, is somewhat misleading as the volume deals with the whole province.

Urban Landscape

One of the most enjoyable books on the urban landscape is Harold Kalman's, *Exploring Vancouver 2* (Vancouver, 1978), a well-informed and illustrated architectural tour of Vancouver, its historical and contemporary buildings. The development controversy of the 1960s and 1970s has generated several books by participants and close observers. Warnett Kennedy, *Vancouver Tomorrow: A Search for Greatness* (Vancouver, 1975), V.S. Pendakur, *Cities, Citizens and Freeways* (Vancouver, 1972) and Walter G. Hardwick, *Vancouver* (Don Mills, 1974) are particularly interesting because their authors all served on City Council, though not necessarily at the same time. Hardwick's book, designed as an introduction to Vancouver for geography students, covers a much broader area than the developmental and political controversies. In *Contemporary Cathedrals: Large Scale Developments in Canadian Cities* (Montreal, 1974), Robert W. Collier, a planner, outlines some of the debates in Vancouver while Donald Gutstein's *Vancouver Ltd.* (Toronto, 1975) examines the developers responsible for the changed face of the city.

In a more historical framework, James W. Morton in *The Capilano: The Story of a River* (Toronto, 1970) outlines the development of greater Vancouver's water system. The only other studies of a utility are of the B.C. Electric Railway which provided electricity, gas and public transportation. In addition to the articles cited in the footnotes, see Patricia E. Roy, "The Fine Arts of Lobbying and Persuading: The Case of the B.C. Electric Railway," in David S.Macmillan, ed. *Canadian Business History: Selected Studies 1497-1971* (Toronto, 1972), pp. 125-143 and "Direct Management from Abroad: The Formative Years of the British Columbia Railway," *Business History Review*, Vol. XLVIII (Summer 1973), pp. 239-259.

Civic Politics

In the 1960s and 1970s, civic politics overlapped with development of the urban landscape. On the earlier period, apart from Fern Miller, "Vancouver Civic Political Parties: Developing a Model of Party-System Change and Stablization," *BC Studies*, No. 25 (Spring 1975), pp. 3-31 which outlines the emergence of parties since 1937 and some studies of the Greater Vancouver Regional District very little has been done. Except for a few contemporary magazine and newspaper articles there are, for example, no biographical studies of such colourful mayors as L.D. Taylor or G.G. McGeer or any analysis of City Council before the NPA.

Social and Cultural Developments

The sources for these are widely scattered. Often the most useful are two or three page articles in professional or trade magazines written on the occasion of a group's convention in Vancouver. One of the few published biographies of a Vancouver resident, Elsie Gregory MacGill's, *My Mother the Judge* (Toronto, 1955), vividly describes some aspects of West End life and especially problems of particular concern to Vancouver women from 1902 to 1947. Several recent articles on aspects of social life deserve mention. Margaret Andrew's two essays on medical history, in *BC Studies* "Epidemic and Public Health: Influenza in Vancouver, 1918-1919," No. 34 (Summer 1977) and "Medical Attendance in Vancouver, 1886-1920," No. 40 (Winter 1978-79), pp. 32-56 open a fascinating part of social history. A related study is Diane L. Matters, "Public Welfare Vancouver Style, 1910-1920," *Journal of Canadian Studies*, Vol. 14 (Spring 1979), pp. 3-15. The reasons for the development or non-development of public parks in the city are outlined in William C. McKee, "The Vancouver Park System, 1886-1929: A Product of Local Businessmen," *Urban History Review*, No. 3-78 (February 1979), pp. 33-49. Finally, in "Union Maids: Organized Women Workers in Vancouver, 1900-1915," *BC Studies*, No. 41 (Spring 1979), pp. 36-55, Star Rosenthal explores a hitherto neglected aspect of social and labour history. The appearance of these articles, all the products of their authors' research as students, bodes well for the historiography of Vancouver.

Index

-751 - Br. domin. V. p 138
p 782